BUTTERWORTHS STUDENT STATUTES

CRIMINAL LAW

BUTTERWORTHS STUDENT STATUTES

Criminal Law

Third edition

GARY SCANLAN, Solicitor

Senior Lecturer in Law

City University

Butterworths
LexisNexis™

Members of the LexisNexis Group worldwide

United Kingdom	LexisNexis Butterworths Tolley, a Division of Reed Elsevier (UK) Ltd, Halsbury House, 35 Chancery Lane, LONDON WC2A 1EL and 4 Hill Street, EDINBURGH EH2 3JZ
Argentina	LexisNexis Argentina, BUENOS AIRES
Australia	LexisNexis Butterworths, CHATSWOOD, New South Wales.
Austria	LexisNexis Verlag ARD Orac GmbH & Co KG, VIENNA
Canada	LexisNexis Butterworths MARKHAM, Ontario
Chile	LexisNexis Chile Ltda, SANTIAGO DE CHILE
Czech Republic	Nakladatelství Orac sro, PRAGUE
France	Editions du Juris-Classeur SA, PARIS
Hong Kong	LexisNexis Butterworths, HONG KONG
Hungary	HVG-Orac, BUDAPEST
India	LexisNexis Butterworths, NEW DELHI
Ireland	Butterworths (Ireland) Ltd, DUBLIN
Italy	Giuffrè Editore, MILAN
Malaysia	Malayan Law Journal Sdn Bhd, KUALA LUMPUR
New Zealand	LexisNexis Butterworths, WELLINGTON
Poland	Wydawnictwo Prawnicze LexisNexis, WARSAW
Singapore	LexisNexis Butterworths, SINGAPORE
South Africa	Butterworths SA, DURBAN
Switzerland	Stämpfli Verlag AG, BERNE
USA	LexisNexis, DAYTON, OHIO

Crown copyright material is reproduced with the permission of the Controller of HMSO and the Queen's Printer for Scotland. Any European material in this work which has been reproduced from EUR-lex, the official European Communities legislation website, is European Communities copyright.

A CIP Catalogue record for this book is available from the British Library.

ISBN 0 406 95944 7

Typeset by Kerrypress Ltd, Luton, Bedfordshire

Printed in England by Clays Ltd, St Ives plc

Visit Butterworths LexisNexis *direct* at www.butterworths.com

Preface

The justification and purpose of the previous editions of this collection of statutory materials has been to provide the student with a readily accessible and user friendly source of the common statutory provisions that form the subject matter of most criminal law courses.

The present edition seeks to maintain that philosophy and purpose. Despite much legislative activity over the two years since the last edition, there have been no major legislative developments which have wrought significant change to 'pure criminal' provisions. The selection of materials has therefore taken this factor into account and has sought to keep the contents both useful and manageable, in this respect consideration has been given to the use of the book as part of accepted materials in an open book examination.

In conclusion I would like to come to the most pleasant part of writing a preface, recording the thanks to persons involved in the process of producing the work. No work is ever the effort of a single individual, despite what may be said on the spine of a book. The editorial staff at Butterworths have been instrumental in producing this edition, and as always have been their highly efficient selves. Conversations with old colleagues, more recently Professor Andrew McGee, Professor Terry Prime, and Margaret Halliwell, Senior Lecturer on the teaching of criminal law and other subjects, have helped in the final selection of materials. Final thanks, as always, must go to Kim Scanlan who, with the prospect of a silver wedding anniversary looming in the very near future, has remained tolerant of my foibles when producing a new edition of a book or an article.

Gary Scanlan
August 2002

Contents

Contents

Vagrancy Act 1824

1824 CHAPTER 83

An Act for the Punishment of idle and disorderly Persons, and Rogues and Vagabonds, in that Part of Great Britain called England

[21st June 1824]

4 Persons committing certain offences shall be deemed rogues and vagabonds and may be imprisoned for three months with hard labour

. . . Every person committing any of the offences herein-before mentioned, after having been convicted as an idle and disorderly person; . . . every person wandering abroad and lodging in any barn or outhouse, or in any deserted or unoccupied building, or in the open air, or under a tent, or in any cart or waggon, . . . and not giving a good account of himself or herself; . . . ; every person wilfully, openly, lewdly, and obscenely exposing his person . . . ,with intent to insult any female; every person wandering abroad, and endeavouring by the exposure of wounds or deformities to obtain or gather alms; every person going about as a gatherer or collector of alms, or endeavouring to procure charitable contributions of any nature or kind, under any false or fraudulent pretence; . . . every person being found in or upon any dwelling house, warehouse, coach-house, stable, or outhouse, or in any inclosed yard, garden, or area, for any unlawful purpose; . . . ; and every person apprehended as an idle and disorderly person, and violently resisting any constable, or other peace officer so apprehending him or her, and being subsequently convicted of the offence for which he or she shall have been so apprehended; shall be deemed a rogue and vagabond, within the true intent and meaning of this Act; and[, subject to section 70 of the Criminal Justice Act 1982,] it shall be lawful for any justice of the peace to commit such offender (being thereof convicted before him by the confession of such offender, or by the evidence on oath of one or more credible witness or witnesses,) to the house of correction . . . for any time not exceeding three calendar months; . . .

NOTES

Words omitted repealed by the Statute Law Revision (No 2) Act 1888; the Criminal Justice Act 1925, ss 42, 49(4), (5), Sch 3, the Vagrancy Act 1935, s 1(2), the National Assistance Act 1948, s 62, Sch 7, Part I, the Criminal Justice Act 1948, s 1(2), the Theft Act 1968, s 33(3), Sch 3, Part I, the Criminal Attempts Act 1981, s 10, Schedule, Part I, the Indecent Displays (Control) Act 1981, s 5(2), Schedule, the Public Order Act 1986, s 40(3), Sch 3 and the Statute Law (Repeals) Act 1989; amendment in square brackets made by the Criminal Justice Act 1982, s 77, Sch 14, para 1.

22 This Act not to extend to Scotland or Ireland, etc

. . . nothing herein contained shall be construed to extend or apply to Scotland or Ireland, . . .

Accessories and Abettors Act 1861

1861 CHAPTER 94

An Act to consolidate and amend the Statute Law of England and Ireland relating to Accessories to and Abettors of indictable Offences

[6th August 1861]

8 Abettors in misdemeanors

Whosoever shall aid, abet, counsel, or procure the commission of [any indictable offence], whether the same be [an offence] at common law or by virtue of any Act passed or to be passed, shall be liable to be tried, indicted, and punished as a principal offender.

10 Act not to extend to Scotland

Nothing in this Act contained shall extend to Scotland . . .

Offences against the Person Act 1861

1861 CHAPTER 100

An Act to consolidate and amend the Statute Law of England and Ireland relating to Offences against the Person

[6th August 1861]

4 Conspiring or soliciting to commit murder

. . . whosoever shall solicit, encourage, persuade, or endeavour to persuade, or shall propose to any person, to murder any other person, whether he be a subject of Her Majesty or not, and whether he be within the Queen's dominions or not, shall be guilty of a misdemeanor, and being convicted thereof shall be liable . . . to [imprisonment for life] . . .

First words omitted repealed by the Criminal Law Act 1977, ss 5(10), 65, Sch 13; other words omitted repealed by the Statute Law Revision Act 1892; amendment in square brackets made by the Criminal Law Act 1977, s 5(10)(b).

Letters threatening to Murder

[16 Threats to kill]

[A person who without lawful excuse makes to another a threat, intending that that other would fear it would be carried out, to kill that other or a third person shall be guilty of an offence and liable on conviction on indictment to imprisonment for a term not exceeding ten years.]

NOTES

Amendment
Substituted by the Criminal Law Act 1977, s 65, Sch 12.

Acts causing or tending to cause Danger to Life or Bodily Harm

18 Shooting or attempting to shoot, or wounding, with intent to do grievous bodily harm, or to resist apprehension

Whosoever shall unlawfully and maliciously by any means whatsoever wound or cause any grievous bodily harm to any person . . . with intent . . . to do some . . . grievous bodily harm to any person, or with intent to resist or prevent the lawful apprehension or detainer of any person, shall be guilty of felony, and being convicted thereof shall be liable, . . . to be kept in penal servitude for life . . .

NOTES
Words omitted repealed by the Statute Law Revision Act 1892, the Statute Law Revision (No 2) Act 1893 and the Criminal Law Act 1967, s 10(2) Sch 3, Part III.

20 Inflicting bodily injury, with or without weapon

Whosoever shall unlawfully and maliciously wound or inflict any grievous bodily harm upon any other person, either with or without any weapon or instrument, shall be guilty of a misdemeanor, and being convicted thereof shall be liable . . . to be kept in penal servitude . . .

NOTES
Words omitted repealed by the Statute Law Revision Act 1892.

23 Maliciously administering poison, etc, so as to endanger life or inflict grievous bodily harm

Whosoever shall unlawfully and maliciously administer to or cause to be administered to or taken by any other person any poison or other destructive or noxious thing, so as thereby to endanger the life of such person, or so as thereby to inflict upon such person any grievous bodily harm, shall be guilty of felony, and being convicted thereof shall be liable . . . to be kept in penal servitude for any term not exceeding ten years . . .

Words omitted repealed by the Statute Law Revision Act 1892.

24 Maliciously administering poison, etc, with intent to injure, aggrieve, or annoy any other person

Whosoever shall unlawfully and maliciously administer to or cause to be administered to or taken by any other person any poison or other destructive or noxious thing, with intent to injure, aggrieve, or annoy such person, shall be guilty of a misdemeanor, and being . . . convicted thereof shall be liable to be kept in penal servitude . . .

Words omitted repealed by the Statute Law Revision Act 1892 and the Statute Law Revision (No 2) Act 1893.

27 Exposing child, whereby life is endangered, or health permanently injured

Whosoever shall unlawfully abandon or expose any child, being under the age of two years, whereby the life of such child shall be endangered, or the health of such child shall have been or shall be likely to be permanently injured, shall be guilty of a misdemeanor, and being convicted thereof shall be liable . . . to be kept in penal servitude . . .

Words omitted repealed by the Statute Law Revision Act 1892 and the Statute Law Revision (No 2) 1893.

28 Causing bodily injury by gunpowder

Whosoever shall unlawfully and maliciously, by the explosion of gunpowder or other explosive substance, burn, maim, disfigure, disable, or do any grievous bodily harm to any person, shall be guilty of felony, and being convicted thereof shall be liable, at the discretion of the court, to be kept in penal servitude for life . . . or to be imprisoned . . .

Words omitted repealed by the Statute Law Revision Act 1892, the Statute Law Revision (No 2) Act 1893, and the Criminal Justice Act 1948, s 83(3), Sch 10, Part I.

29 Causing gunpowder to explode, or sending to any person an explosive substance, or throwing corrosive fluid on a person, with intent to do grievous bodily harm

Whosoever shall unlawfully and maliciously cause any gunpowder or other explosive substance to explode, or send or deliver to or cause to be taken or received by any person any explosive substance or any other dangerous or noxious thing, or put or lay at any place, or cast or throw at or upon or otherwise apply to any person, any corrosive fluid or any destructive or explosive substance, with intent in any of the cases aforesaid to burn, maim, disfigure, or disable any person, or to do some grievous bodily harm to any person, shall, whether any bodily injury be effected or not, be guilty of felony, and being convicted thereof shall be liable at the discretion of the court, to be kept in penal servitude for life . . . or to be imprisoned . . .

NOTES

Words omitted repealed by the Statute Law Revision Act 1893, the Statute Law Revision (No 2) Act 1893, and the Criminal Justice Act 1948, s 83(3), Sch 10, Part I.

30 Placing gunpowder near a building, etc, with intent to do bodily injury to any person

Whosoever shall unlawfully and maliciously place or throw in, into, upon, against, or near any building, ship, or vessel any gunpowder or other explosive substance, with intent to do any bodily injury to any person, shall, whether or not any explosion take place, and whether or not any bodily injury be effected, be guilty of felony, and being convicted thereof shall be liable, at the discretion of the court, to be kept in penal servitude for any term not exceeding fourteen years . . . or to be imprisoned . . .

NOTES

Words omitted repealed by the Statute Law Revision Act 1892, the Statute Law Revision Act 1893, the Statute Law Revision (No 2) Act 1893, and the Criminal Justice Act 1948, s 83(3), Sch 10, Part I.

Assaults

44 If the magistrates shall dismiss any complaint of assault or battery, they shall make out a certificate to that effect

If the justices, upon the hearing of any *such* case of assault or battery upon the merits, where the complaint was preferred by or on behalf of the party aggrieved, *under either of the last two preceding sections,* shall deem the offence not to be proved, or shall find the assault or battery to have been justified, or so trifling as not to merit any punishment, and shall accordingly dismiss the complaint, they shall forthwith make out a certificate under their hands stating the fact of such dismissal, and shall deliver such certificate to the party against whom the complaint was preferred.

NOTES

Words in italics repealed except in relation to Northern Ireland by the Criminal Justice Act 1988, s 170(1), (2), (11), Sch 15, paras 2, 3, Sch 16, Note 1.

45 Certificate or conviction shall be a bar to any other proceedings

If any person against whom any such complaint as [is mentioned in section 44 of this Act] shall have been preferred by or on the behalf of the party aggrieved shall have obtained such certificate, or, having been convicted, shall have paid the whole amount adjudged to be paid, or shall have suffered the imprisonment . . . awarded, in every such case he shall be released from all further or other proceedings, civil or criminal, for the same cause.

NOTES

Words in square brackets substituted except in relation to Northern Ireland by the Criminal Justice Act 1988, s 170(1), (11), Sch 15, paras 2, 4; words omitted repealed by the Criminal Justice Act 1948, s 1(2).

47 Assault occasioning bodily harm—Common assault

Whosoever shall be convicted upon an indictment of any assault occasioning actual bodily harm shall be liable . . . to be kept in penal servitude . . . ; . . .

NOTES

Words omitted repealed by the Statute Law Revision Act 1892, the Criminal Justice Act 1948, s 1(2) and the Criminal Justice Act 1988, s 170(2), Sch 16, Note 1.

Bigamy

57 Bigamy

Whosoever, being married, shall marry any other person during the life of the former husband or wife, whether the second marriage shall have taken place in England or Ireland or elsewhere, shall be guilty of felony, and being convicted thereof shall be liable to be kept in penal servitude for any term not exceeding seven years . . . : Provided, that nothing in this section contained shall extend to any second marriage contracted elsewhere than in England and Ireland by any other than a subject of Her Majesty, or to any person marrying a second time whose husband or wife shall have been continually absent from such person for the space of seven years then last past, and shall not have been known by such person to be living within that time, or shall extend to any person who, at the time of such second marriage, shall have been divorced from the bond of the first marriage, or to any person whose former marriage shall have been declared void by the sentence of any court of competent jurisdiction.

NOTES

Words omitted repealed by the Criminal Justice Act 1925, s 49, Sch 3, and the Criminal Law Act 1967, s 10(2), Sch 3, Part III.

Attempts to procure Abortion

58 Administering drugs or using instruments to procure abortion

Every woman, being with child, who, with intent to procure her own miscarriage, shall unlawfully administer to herself any poison or other noxious thing, or shall unlawfully use any instrument or other means whatsoever with the like intent, and whosoever, with intent to procure the miscarriage of any woman, whether she be or be not with child, shall unlawfully administer to her or cause to be taken by her any poison or other noxious thing, or shall unlawfully use any instrument or other means whatsoever with the like intent, shall be guilty of felony, and being convicted thereof shall be liable . . . to be kept in penal servitude for life . . .

NOTES

Words omitted repealed by the Statute Law Revision Act 1892 and the Statute Law Revision (No 2) Act 1893.

59 Procuring drugs, etc, to cause abortion

Whosoever shall unlawfully supply or procure any poison or other noxious thing, or any instrument or thing whatsoever, knowing that the same is intended to be unlawfully used or employed with intent to procure the miscarriage of any woman, whether she be or be not with child, shall be guilty of a misdemeanor, and being convicted thereof shall be liable . . . to be kept in penal servitude . . .

NOTES

Words omitted repealed by the Statute Law Revision Act 1892.

Concealing the birth of a child

60 Concealing the Birth of a Child

If any woman shall be delivered of a child, every person who shall, by any secret disposition of the dead body of the said child, whether such child died before, at, or after its birth, endeavour to conceal the birth thereof, shall be guilty of a misdemeanor, and being convicted thereof shall be liable, at the discretion of the court, to be imprisoned for any term not exceeding two years, . . .

NOTES

Words omitted repealed by the Criminal Justice Act 1948, s 1(2), and the Criminal Law Act 1967, s 10, Sch 2, para 13(1), Sch 3, Part III.

78 Extent of Act

Nothing in this Act contained shall extend to Scotland, except as herein-before otherwise expressly provided.

Licensing Act 1872

1872 CHAPTER 94

An Act for Regulating the Sale of Intoxicating Liquors

[10th August 1872]

Preliminary

1 Short title

This Act may be cited as "The Licensing Act 1872."

NOTES

Amendment

Repealed, in relation to Northern Ireland, by the Criminal Justice (Northern Ireland) Order 1980, SI 1980 No 704, art 13, Sch 2.

2 Extent

This Act shall not extend to Scotland.

NOTES

Repealed, in relation to Northern Ireland, by the Criminal Justice (Northern Ireland) Order 1980, SI 1980/704, art 13, Sch 2.

Offences against Public Order

12 Penalty on persons found drunk

Every person found drunk in any highway or other public place, whether a building or not, or on any licensed premises, shall be liable to a penalty not exceeding [level 1 on the standard scale].

Every person < . . . > who is drunk while in charge on any highway or other public place of any carriage, horse, cattle, or steam engine, or who is drunk when in possession of any loaded firearms, may be apprehended, and shall be liable to a penalty not exceeding [level 1 on the standard scale] or in the discretion of the court to imprisonment < . . . > for any term not exceeding one month.

< . . . >

NOTES

First words omitted repealed by the Criminal Justice Act 1967, ss 103(2), 106(5), Sch 7, Part I; first-mentioned maximum pecuniary penalty increased by the Criminal Law Act 1977, s 31, Sch 6, and converted to a level on the standard scale by the Criminal Justice Act 1982, ss 37, 46; second-mentioned maximum pecuniary penalty increased by virtue of the Penalties for Drunkenness Act 1962, s 1, and converted to a level on the standard scale by the Criminal Justice Act 1982, ss 37, 38, 46; second and third words omitted repealed by the Statute Law

Revision Act 1953.

Repealed, in relation to Northern Ireland, by the Criminal Justice (Northern Ireland) Order 1980, SI 1980/704, art 13, Sch 2.

Trial of Lunatics Act 1883

1883 CHAPTER 38

An Act to amend the Law respecting the Trial and Custody of Insane Persons charged with offences

[25th August 1883]

1 Short title

This Act may be cited as the Trial of Lunatics Act 1883.

2 Special verdict where accused found guilty, but insane at date of act or omission charged, and orders thereupon

(1)   Where in any indictment or information any act or omission is charged against any person as an offence, and it is given in evidence on the trial of such person for that offence that he was insane, so as not to be responsible, according to law, for his actions at the time when the act was done or omission made, then, if it appears to the jury before whom such person is tried that he did the act or made the omission charged, but was insane as aforesaid at the time when he did or made the same, the jury shall return [a special verdict that the accused is not guilty by reason of insanity].

(2)–(4)   . . .

NOTESt

Sub-s (1): words in square brackets substituted by the Criminal Procedure (Insanity) Act 1964, s 1.

Sub-ss (2), (4): repealed by the Criminal Procedure (Insanity) Act 1964, s 8(5)(a).

Sub-s (3): repealed by the Criminal Lunatics Act 1884, s 17, Sch 2.

3 Extent of Act

(1)   . . .

(2)   This Act shall not extend to Scotland.

NOTES

Sub-s (1): repealed by the Mental Health Act (Northern Ireland) 1961, s 116, Sch 7.

Licensing Act 1902

1902 CHAPTER 28

An Act to amend the Law relating to the Sale of Intoxicating Liquors and to Drunkenness . . .

[8th August 1902]

NOTES

Words omitted repealed by the Statute Law Revision Act 1927.

PART I
AMENDMENT OF LAW AS TO DRUNKENNESS

8 Interpretation of "public place"

For the purposes of section twelve of the Licensing Act 1872 and of sections one and two of this Act, the expression "public place" shall include any place to which the public have access, whether on payment or otherwise.

PART IV
SUPPLEMENTAL

34 Short title, construction and extent

(1) This Act may be cited as the Licensing Act 1902 and may be cited, and shall be construed, as one with the Licensing Acts 1828 to 1886.

(2) This Act shall not extend to Scotland or Ireland.

(3) . . .

NOTES

Sub-s (3): repealed by the Statute Law Revision Act 1927.

Perjury Act 1911

1911 CHAPTER 6

An Act to consolidate and simplify the Law relating to Perjury and kindred offences
[29th June 1911]

1 Perjury

(1) If any person lawfully sworn as a witness or as an interpreter in a judicial proceeding wilfully makes a statement material in that proceeding, which he knows

to be false or does not believe to be true, he shall be guilty of perjury, and shall, on conviction thereof on indictment, be liable to penal servitude for a term not exceeding seven years, or to imprisonment . . . for a term not exceeding two years, or to a fine or to both such penal servitude or imprisonment and fine.

(2)   The expression "judicial proceeding" includes a proceeding before any court, tribunal, or person having by law power to hear, receive, and examine evidence on oath.

(3)   Where a statement made for the purposes of a judicial proceeding is not made before the tribunal itself, but is made on oath before a person authorised by law to administer an oath to the person who makes the statement, and to record or authenticate the statement, it shall, for the purposes of this section, be treated as having been made in a judicial proceeding.

(4)   A statement made by a person lawfully sworn in England for the purposes of a judicial proceeding—
   (a)   in another part of His Majesty's dominions; or
   (b)   in a British tribunal lawfully constituted in any place by sea or land outside His Majesty's dominions; or
   (c)   in a tribunal of any foreign state,

shall, for the purposes of this section, be treated as a statement made in a judicial proceeding in England.

(5)   Where, for the purposes of a judicial proceeding in England, a person is lawfully sworn under the authority of an Act of Parliament—
   (a)   in any other part of His Majesty's dominions; or
   (b)   before a British tribunal or a British officer in a foreign country, or within the jurisdiction of the Admiralty of England;

a statement made by such person so sworn as aforesaid (unless the Act of Parliament under which it was made otherwise specifically provides) shall be treated for the purposes of this section as having been made in the judicial proceeding in England for the purposes whereof it was made.

(6)   The question whether a statement on which perjury is assigned was material is a question of law to be determined by the court of trial.

NOTES

Words omitted repealed by the Criminal Justice Act 1948, s 1(2).

[1A   False unsworn statement under Evidence (Proceedings in Other Jurisdictions) Act 1975

If any person, in giving any testimony (either orally or in writing) otherwise than on oath, where required to do so by an order under section 2 of the Evidence (Proceedings in Other Jurisdictions) Act 1975, makes a statement—
   (a)   which he knows to be false in a material particular, or
   (b)   which is false in a material particular and which he does not believe to be true,

he shall be guilty of an offence and shall be liable on conviction on indictment to imprisonment for a term not exceeding two years or a fine or both.]

NOTES

Inserted by the Evidence (Proceedings in Other Jurisdictions) Act 1975, s 8(1), Sch 1.

2 False statements on oath made otherwise than in a judicial proceeding

If any person—

(1) being required or authorised by law to make any statement on oath for any purpose, and being lawfully sworn (otherwise than in a judicial proceeding) wilfully makes a statement which is material for that purpose and which he knows to be false or does not believe to be true; or

(2) wilfully uses any false affidavit for the purposes of the Bills of Sale Act 1878, as amended by any subsequent enactment,

he shall be guilty of a misdemeanour, and, on conviction thereof on indictment, shall be liable to penal servitude for a term not exceeding seven years or to imprisonment . . . for a term not exceeding two years, or to a fine or to both such penal servitude or imprisonment and fine.

NOTES

Words omitted repealed by the Criminal Justice Act 1948, s 1(2).

7 Aiders, abettors, suborners, etc

(1) Every person who aids, abets, counsels, procures, or suborns another person to commit an offence against this Act shall be liable to be proceeded against, indicted, tried and punished as if he were a principal offender.

(2) Every person who incites . . . another person to commit an offence against this Act shall be guilty of a misdemeanour, and, on conviction thereof on indictment, shall be liable to imprisonment, or to a fine, or to both such imprisonment and fine.

NOTES

Words omitted repealed by the Criminal Attempts Act 1981, s 10, Schedule, Part I.

15 Interpretation, etc

(1) For the purposes of this Act, the forms and ceremonies used in administering an oath are immaterial, if the court or person before whom the oath is taken has power to administer an oath for the purpose of verifying the statement in question, and if the oath has been administered in a form and with ceremonies which the person taking the oath has accepted without objection, or has declared to be binding on him.

(2) In this Act—

The expression "oath" . . . includes "affirmation" and "declaration," and the expression "swear" . . . includes "affirm" and "declare"; and

The expression "statutory declaration" means a declaration made by virtue of the

Statutory Declarations Act 1835, or of any Act, Order in Council, rule or regulation applying or extending the provisions thereof; and . . .

NOTES

First and second words omitted repealed by the Administration of Justice Act 1977, ss 8(3), 32(4), Sch 5, Part III; final words omitted repealed by the Criminal Law Act 1967, s 10(2), Sch 3, Part III.

18 Extent

This Act shall not extend to Scotland or Ireland.

19 Short title . . .

This Act may be cited as the Perjury Act 1911 . . .

NOTES

Words omitted repealed by the Statute Law Revision Act 1927.

Criminal Justice Act 1925

1925 CHAPTER 86

An Act to amend the law with respect to the administration of criminal justice in England, and otherwise to amend the criminal law

[22nd December 1925]

PART IV
MISCELLANEOUS AND GENERAL

47 Abolition of presumption of coercion of married woman by husband

Any presumption of law that an offence committed by a wife in the presence of her husband is committed under the coercion of the husband is hereby abolished, but on a charge against a wife for any offence other than treason or murder it shall be a good defence to prove that the offence was committed in the presence of, and under the coercion of, the husband.

49 Short title, interpretation, extent, repeal and commencement

(1) This Act may be cited as the Criminal Justice Act 1925.

(2) In this Act, unless the context otherwise requires—
The expression "examining justices" means the justices before whom a charge is made against any person for an indictable offence, and references to examining justices include a reference to a single examining justice:
. . .

(3) This Act shall not extend to Scotland or Northern Ireland, and references therein to warrants issued shall not be construed as including warrants issued elsewhere than in England or Wales.

(4), (5)   . . .

NOTES

Sub-s (2): words omitted repealed by the Courts Act 1971, s 56(4), Sch 11, Pt IV.
Sub-ss (4), (5): repealed by the Statute Law Revision Act 1950.

Infant Life (Preservation) Act 1929

1929 CHAPTER 34

An Act to amend the law with regard to the destruction of children at or before birth
[10th May 1929]

1 Punishment for child destruction

(1) Subject as hereinafter in this subsection provided, any person who, with intent to destroy the life of a child capable of being born alive, by any wilful act causes a child to die before it has an existence independent of its mother, shall be guilty of felony, to wit, of child destruction, and shall be liable on conviction thereof on indictment to penal servitude for life:

Provided that no person shall be found guilty of an offence under this section unless it is proved that the act which caused the death of the child was not done in good faith for the purpose only of preserving the life of the mother.

(2) For the purposes of this Act, evidence that a woman had at any material time been pregnant for a period of twenty-eight weeks or more shall be prima facie proof that she was at that time pregnant of a child capable of being born alive.

2 Prosecution of offences

(1)   . . .

(2) Where upon the trial of any person for the murder or manslaughter of any child, or for infanticide, or for an offence under section fifty-eight of the Offences against the Person Act 1861 (which relates to administering drugs or using instruments to procure abortion), the jury are of opinion that the person charged is not guilty of murder, manslaughter or infanticide, or of an offence under the said section fifty-eight, as the case may be, but that he is shown by the evidence to be guilty of the felony of child destruction, the jury may find him guilty of that felony, and thereupon the person convicted shall be liable to be punished as if he had been convicted upon an indictment for child destruction.

(3) Where upon the trial of any person for the felony of child destruction the jury are of opinion that the person charged is not guilty of that felony, but that he is

shown by the evidence to be guilty of an offence under the said section fifty-eight of the Offences against the Person Act 1861, the jury may find him guilty of that offence, and thereupon the person convicted shall be liable to be punished as if he had been convicted upon an indictment under that section.

(4), (5)　　. . .

Sub-ss (1), (4): repealed by the Criminal Law Act 1967, s 10(2), Sch 3, Part II.
Sub-s (5): repealed by the Police and Criminal Evidence Act 1984, s 119, Sch 7, Part V.

3 Short title and extent

(1)　This Act may be cited as the Infant Life (Preservation) Act 1929.

(2)　This Act shall not extend to Scotland or Northern Ireland.

Children and Young Persons Act 1933

1933 CHAPTER 12

An Act to consolidate certain enactments relating to persons under the age of eighteen years

[13th April 1933]

PART I
PREVENTION OF CRUELTY AND EXPOSURE TO MORAL AND PHYSICAL DANGER

Offences

1 Cruelty to persons under sixteen

(1)　If any person who has attained the age of sixteen years and [has responsibility for] any child or young person under that age, wilfully assaults, ill-treats, neglects, abandons, or exposes him, or causes or procures him to be assaulted, ill-treated, neglected, abandoned, or exposed, in a manner likely to cause him unnecessary suffering or injury to health (including injury to or loss of sight, or hearing, or limb, or organ of the body, and any mental derangement), that person shall be guilty of a misdemeanour, and shall be liable—
  - (a)　on conviction on indictment, to a fine . . . , or alternatively, . . . or in addition thereto, to imprisonment for any term not exceeding [ten] years;
  - (b)　on summary conviction, to a fine not exceeding [the prescribed sum] or alternatively, . . . or in addition thereto, to imprisonment for any term not exceeding six months.

(2)   For the purposes of this section—

(a)   a parent or other person legally liable to maintain a child or young person [, or the legal guardian of a child or young person,] shall be deemed to have neglected him in a manner likely to cause injury to his health if he has failed to provide adequate food, clothing, medical aid or lodging for him, or if, having been unable otherwise to provide such food, clothing, medical aid or lodging, he has failed to take steps to procure it to be provided under [the enactments applicable in that behalf];

(b)   where it is proved that the death of an infant under three years of age was caused by suffocation (not being suffocation caused by disease or the presence of any foreign body in the throat or air passages of the infant) while the infant was in bed with some other person who has attained the age of sixteen years, that other person shall, if he was, when he went to bed, under the influence of drink, be deemed to have neglected the infant in a manner likely to cause injury to its health.

(3)   A person may be convicted of an offence under this section—

(a)   notwithstanding that actual suffering or injury to health, or the likelihood of actual suffering or injury to health, was obviated by the action of another person;

(b)   notwithstanding the death of the child or young person in question.

(4)–(6)   . . .

(7)   Nothing in this section shall be construed as affecting the right of any parent, [or (subject to section 548 of the Education Act 1996) any other person,] having the lawful control or charge of a child or young person to administer punishment to him.

NOTES

Sub-s (1): first words in square brackets substituted by the Children Act 1989, s 108(5), Sch 13, para 2; first words omitted repealed by the Children Act 1975, s 108(1)(b), Sch 4, Part III; second and third words omitted repealed by the Children and Young Persons Act 1963, s 64(1), (3), Sch 3, para 1, Sch 5; second word in square brackets substituted, in relation to the punishment for an offence committed on or after 29 September 1988, by the Criminal Justice Act 1988, s 45; final words in square brackets substituted by virtue of by the Magistrates' Courts Act 1980, s 32(2).

Sub-s (2): first words in square brackets inserted by the Children Act 1989, s 108(4), Sch 12, para 2; second words in square brackets substituted by the National Assistance (Adaptation of Enactments) Regulations 1950, SI 1951/174.

Sub-s (4): repealed by the Criminal Law Act 1967, s 10, Sch 2, para 13(1), Sch 3, Part III.

Sub-ss (5), (6): repealed by the Criminal Justice Act 1988, s 170(2), Sch 16.

Sub-s (7): words "or (subject to section 548 of the Education Act 1996) any other person," in square brackets substituted by the School Standards and Framework Act 1998, s 140(1), Sch 30, para 1.

Date in force: 1 September 1999: see SI 1999/2323, art 2(1), Sch 1.

PART III
PROTECTION OF CHILDREN AND YOUNG PERSONS IN RELATION TO CRIMINAL AND SUMMARY PROCEEDINGS

Juvenile Offenders

50 Age of criminal responsibility

It shall be conclusively presumed that no child under the age of [ten] years can be guilty of any offence.

NOTES

Word in square brackets substituted by the Children and Young Persons Act 1963, s 16(1).

PART VI
SUPPLEMENTAL

General

109 Short title, commencement, extent and repeals

(1)   This Act may be cited as the Children and Young Persons Act 1933.

(2)   . . .

(3)   Save as therein otherwise expressly provided, this Act shall not extend to Scotland or Northern Ireland.

(4)   . . .

NOTES

Sub-ss (2), (4): repealed by the Statute Law Revision Act 1950.

Infanticide Act 1938

1938 CHAPTER 36

An Act to repeal and re-enact with modifications the provisions of the Infanticide Act 1922

[23rd June 1938]

1 Offence of infanticide

(1)   Where a woman by any wilful act or omission causes the death of her child being a child under the age of twelve months, but at the time of the act or omission the balance of her mind was disturbed by reason of her not having fully recovered from the effect of giving birth to the child or by reason of the effect of lactation consequent upon the birth of the child, then, notwithstanding that the circumstances

were such that but for this Act the offence would have amounted to murder, she shall be guilty of felony, to wit of infanticide, and may for such offence be dealt with and punished as if she had been guilty of the offence of manslaughter of the child.

(2)   Where upon the trial of a woman for the murder of her child, being a child under the age of twelve months, the jury are of opinion that she by any wilful act or omission caused its death, but that at the time of the act or omission the balance of her mind was disturbed by reason of her not having fully recovered from the effect of giving birth to the child or by reason of the effect of lactation consequent upon the birth of the child, then the jury may, notwithstanding that the circumstances were such that but for the provisions of this Act they might have returned a verdict of murder, return in lieu thereof a verdict of infanticide.

(3)   Nothing in this Act shall affect the power of the jury upon an indictment for the murder of a child to return a verdict of manslaughter, or a verdict of guilty but insane . . .

(4)   . . .

NOTES

Words omitted repealed by the Criminal Law Act 1967, s 10(2), Sch 3, Part III.

2 Short title, extent and repeal

(1)   This Act may be cited as the Infanticide Act 1938.

(2)   This Act shall not extend to Scotland or Northern Ireland.

(3)   . . .

NOTES

Sub-s (3): repealed by the Statute Law Revision Act 1950.

Prison Act 1952

1952 CHAPTER 52

An Act to consolidate certain enactments relating to prisons and other institutions for offenders and related matters with corrections and improvements made under the Consolidation of Enactments (Procedure) Act 1949

[1st August 1952]

Offences

39 Assisting prisoner to escape

Any person who aids any prisoner in escaping or attempting to escape from a prison or who, with intent to facilitate the escape of any prisoner, conveys any thing into a prison or to a prisoner [sends any thing (by post or otherwise) into a prison or to a prisoner] or places any thing anywhere outside a prison with a view to its coming into the possession of a prisoner, shall be guilty of felony and liable to imprisonment for a term not exceeding [ten years].

NOTES

First words in square brackets inserted and second words in square brackets substituted, by the Prison Security Act 1992, s 2(1), (4).

Supplemental

55 Short title, commencement and extent

(1)   This Act may be cited as the Prison Act 1952.

(2)   This Act shall come into operation on the first day of October, nineteen hundred and fifty-two.

(3)   . . .

(4)   Except as provided in . . . [the Criminal Justice Act 1961], this Act shall not extend to Scotland.

[(4A)   Subsections (2) to (5) of section 5A, as applied by subsection (5A) of that section, extend to Scotland.]

(5)   This Act shall not extend to Northern Ireland.

NOTES

Sub-s (3): repealed by the Statute Law (Repeals) Act 1993.
Sub-s (4): words omitted repealed by the Statute Law (Repeals) Act 1993; words in square brackets substituted by the Criminal Justice Act 1961, s 41, Sch 4.
Sub-s (4A): inserted by the Immigration and Asylum Act 1999, s 169(1), Sch 14, para 33.
Date in force: to be appointed: see the Immigration and Asylum Act 1999, s 170(4).

Prevention of Crime Act 1953

1953 CHAPTER 14

An Act to prohibit the carrying of offensive weapons in public places without lawful authority or reasonable excuse

[6th May 1953]

1 Prohibition of the carrying of offensive weapons without lawful authority or reasonable excuse

(1)   Any person who without lawful authority or reasonable excuse, the proof whereof shall lie on him, has with him in any public place any offensive weapon shall be guilty of an offence, and shall be liable—

(a) on summary conviction, to imprisonment for a term not exceeding [six months] or a fine not exceeding [the prescribed sum] or both;

(b) on conviction on indictment, to imprisonment for a term not exceeding [four] years or a fine < . . . > or both.

(2) Where any person is convicted of an offence under subsection (1) of this section the court may make an order for the forfeiture or disposal of any weapon in respect of which the offence was committed.

(3)   < . . . >

(4) In this section "public place" includes any highway and any other premises or place to which at the material time the public have or are permitted to have access, whether on payment or otherwise; and "offensive weapon" means any article made or adapted for use for causing injury to the person, or intended by the person having it with him for such use by him [or by some other person].

NOTES

Repealed, in relation to Scotland only, by the Criminal Procedure (Consequential Provisions) (Scotland) Act 1995, s 6, Sch 5.

Sub-s (1): in para (a) first words in square brackets substituted by the Criminal Justice Act 1988, s 46(1), (3), reference to "the prescribed sum" in square brackets substituted by virtue of the Magistrates's Courts Act 1980, s 32(2); word in square brackets in para (b) substituted by the Offensive Weapons Act 1996, s 2(1), (4), words omitted repealed by the Criminal Law Act 1977, s 32(1).

Sub-s (3): repealed by the Police and Criminal Evidence Act 1984, s 119, Sch 7, Part I.

Sub-s (4): words in square brackets inserted by the Public Order Act 1986, s 40(2), Sch 2, para 2.

2 Short title, commencement and extent

(1)   This Act may be cited as the Prevention of Crime Act 1953.

(2)   This Act shall come into operation on the expiration of one month from the passing thereof.

(3)   This Act shall not extend to Northern Ireland.

Children and Young Persons (Harmful Publications) Act 1955

1955 CHAPTER 28

An Act to prevent the dissemination of certain pictorial publications harmful to children and young persons

[6th May 1955]

1 Works to which this Act applies

This Act applies to any book, magazine or other like work which is of a kind likely to fall into the hands of children or young persons and consists wholly or mainly of stories told in pictures (with or without the addition of written matter), being stories portraying—

    (a)   the commission of crimes; or

    (b)   acts of violence or cruelty; or

    (c)   incidents of a repulsive or horrible nature;

in such a way that the work as a whole would tend to corrupt a child or young person into whose hands it might fall.

2 Penalty for printing, publishing, selling, &c, works to which this Act applies

(1)   A person who prints, publishes, sells or lets on hire a work to which this Act applies, or has any such work in his possession for the purpose of selling it or letting it on hire, shall be guilty of an offence and liable, on summary conviction, to imprisonment for a term not exceeding four months or to a fine not exceeding [level 3 on the standard scale] or to both:

    Provided that, in any proceedings taken under this subsection against a person in respect of selling or letting on hire a work or of having it in his possession for the purpose of selling it or letting it on hire, it shall be a defence for him to prove that he had not examined the contents of the work and had no reasonable cause to suspect that it was one to which this Act applies.

(2)   A prosecution for an offence under this section shall not, in England or Wales, be instituted except by, or with the consent of, the Attorney General.

NOTES

    Sub-s (1): maximum fine increased and converted to a level on the standard scale by the Criminal Justice Act 1982, ss 37, 38, 46.

4 Prohibition of importation of works to which this Act applies and articles for printing them

The importation of—
  (a) any work to which this Act applies; and
  (b) any plate prepared for the purpose of printing copies of any such work and any photographic film prepared for that purpose;

is hereby prohibited.

5 Short title, interpretation, extent, commencement and duration

(1) This Act may be cited as the Children and Young Persons (Harmful Publications) Act 1955.

(2) In this Act the expressions "child" and "young person" have the meanings assigned to them respectively by section one hundred and seven of the Children and Young Persons Act 1933 or, in Scotland, by section one hundred and ten of the Children and Young Persons (Scotland) Act 1937 the expression "plate" (except where it occurs in the expression "photographic plate") includes block, mould, matrix and stencil and the expression "photographic film" includes photographic plate.

(3) No provision of this Act, other than the provisions of the last foregoing section, shall extend to Northern Ireland.

(4) This Act shall come into operation at the expiration of one month beginning with the date of its passing.

(5) This Act shall continue in force until the thirty-first day of December, nineteen hundred and sixty-five, and shall then expire, unless Parliament otherwise determines, and upon the expiration of this Act, subsection (2) of section thirty-eight of the Interpretation Act 1889 shall apply as if this Act had then been repealed by another Act.

Sexual Offences Act 1956

1956 CHAPTER 69

An Act to consolidate (with corrections and improvements made under the Consolidation of Enactments (Procedure) Act 1949) the statute law of England and Wales relating to sexual crimes, to the abduction, procuration and prostitution of women and to kindred offences, and to make such adaptations of statutes extending beyond England and Wales as are needed in consequence of that consolidation

[2nd August 1956]

PART I
OFFENCES, AND THE PROSECUTION AND PUNISHMENT OF OFFENCES

Intercourse by force, intimidation, etc

[1 Rape of woman or man]

[(1)   It is an offence for a man to rape a woman or another man.

(2)   A man commits rape if—
  (a)   he has sexual intercourse with a person (whether vaginal or anal) who at the time of the intercourse does not consent to it; and
  (b)   at the time he knows that the person does not consent to the intercourse or is reckless as to whether that person consents to it.

(3)   A man also commits rape if he induces a married woman to have sexual intercourse with him by impersonating her husband.

(4)   Subsection (2) applies for the purpose of any enactment.]

NOTES

Substituted by the Criminal Justice and Public Order Act 1994, s 142.

Abduction

20 Abduction of unmarried girl under sixteen from parent or guardian

(1)   It is an offence for a person acting without lawful authority or excuse to take an unmarried girl under the age of sixteen out of the possession of her parent or guardian against his will.

(2)   In the foregoing subsection "guardian" means any person having [parental responsibility for or care of] the girl.

Sub-s (2): words in square brackets substituted by the Children Act 1989, s 108(4), (6), Sch 12, para 12, Sch 14, para 1.

PART II
SUPPLEMENTARY

Consequential ammendments

54 Extent

(1)   This Act shall not extend to Scotland, . . .

(2)   This Act shall not extend to Northern Ireland, except section fifty . . .

Words omitted repealed by the Statute Law (Repeals) Act 1993.

55 Short title

This Act may be cited as the Sexual Offences Act 1956.

Homicide Act 1957

1957 CHAPTER 11

An Act to make for England and Wales (and for courts-martial wherever sitting) amendments of law relating to homicide and the trial and punishment of murder, and for Scotland amendments of the law relating to the trial and punishment of murder and attempts to murder

[21st March 1957]

PART I
AMENDMENTS OF LAW OF ENGLAND AND WALES AS TO FACT OF MURDER

1 Abolition of "constructive malice"

(1)   Where a person kills another in the course or furtherance of some other offence, the killing shall not amount to murder unless done with the same malice aforethought (express or implied) as is required for a killing to amount to murder when not done in the course or furtherance of another offence.

(2)   For the purposes of the foregoing subsection, a killing done in the course or for the purpose of resisting an officer of justice, or of resisting or avoiding or preventing a lawful arrest, or of effecting or assisting an escape or rescue from legal custody, shall be treated as a killing in the course or furtherance of an offence.

2 Persons suffering from diminished responsibility

(1)   Where a person kills or is a party to the killing of another, he shall not be convicted of murder if he was suffering from such abnormality of mind (whether arising from a condition of arrested or retarded development of mind or any inherent causes or induced by disease or injury) as substantially impaired his mental responsibility for his acts and omissions in doing or being a party to the killing.

(2)   On a charge of murder, it shall be for the defence to prove that the person charged is by virtue of this section not liable to be convicted of murder.

(3)   A person who but for this section would be liable, whether as principal or as accessory, to be convicted of murder shall be liable instead to be convicted of manslaughter.

(4)   The fact that one party to a killing is by virtue of this section not liable to be convicted of murder shall not affect the question whether the killing amounted to murder in the case of any party to it.

3 Provocation

Where on a charge of murder there is evidence on which the jury can find that the person charged was provoked (whether by things done or by things said or by both together) to lose his self-control, the question whether the provocation was enough to make a reasonable man do as he did shall be left to be determined by the jury; and in determining that question the jury shall take into account everything both done and said according to the effect which in their opinion, it would have on a reasonable man.

4 Suicide pacts

(1)   It shall be manslaughter, and shall not be murder, for a person acting in pursuance of a suicide pact between him and another to kill the other or be a party to the other . . . being killed by a third person.

(2)   Where it is shown that a person charged with the murder of another killed the other or was a party to his . . . being killed, it shall be for the defence to prove that the person charged was acting in pursuance of a suicide pact between him and the other.

(3)   For the purposes of this section "suicide pact" means a common agreement between two or more persons having for its object the death of all of them, whether or not each is to take his own life, but nothing done by a person who enters into a suicide pact shall be treated as done by him in pursuance of the pact unless it is done while he has the settled intention of dying in pursuance of the pact.

NOTES

Words omitted repealed by the Suicide Act 1961, s 3(2), Sch 2.

PART V
COMMENCEMENT, ETC

17 Short title, repeal and extent

(1) This Act may be cited as the Homicide Act 1957.

(2) . . .

(3) This Act, except as regards courts-martial, shall not extend to Northern Ireland.

NOTES

Words omitted repealed by the Statute Law (Repeals) Act 1974.

Restriction of Offensive Weapons Act 1959

1959 CHAPTER 37

An Act to amend the law in relation to the making and disposing and importation of flick knives and other dangerous weapons

[14th May 1959]

1 Penalties for offences in connection with dangerous weapons

(1) Any person who manufactures, sells or hires or offers for sale or hire [or exposes or has in his possession for the purpose of sale or hire], or lends or gives to any other person—
  (a) any knife which has a blade which opens automatically by hand pressure applied to a button, spring or other device in or attached to the handle of the knife, sometimes known as a "flick knife" or "flick gun"; or
  (b) any knife which has a blade which is released from the handle or sheath thereof by the force of gravity or the application of centrifugal force and which, when released, is locked in place by means of a button, spring, lever, or other device, sometimes known as a "gravity knife",

shall be guilty of an offence and shall be liable on summary conviction [to imprisonment for a term not exceeding six months or to a fine not exceeding level [5] on the standard scale or to both such imprisonment and fine].

(2) The importation of any such knife as is described in the foregoing subsection is hereby prohibited.

NOTES

Sub-s (1): first amendment made by the Restriction of Offensive Weapons Act 1961, s 1; enhanced penalty on a subsequent conviction abolished, maximum fine on any conviction increased and converted to a level on the standard scale by the Criminal Justice Act 1982, ss

35, 37, 38, 46, level on the standard scale raised by the Criminal Justice Act 1988, s 46(2), (3), in relation to anything done on or after 29 September 1988.

2 Short title, commencement and extent

(1)   This Act may be cited as the Restriction of Offensive Weapons Act 1959.

(2)   This Act shall come into operation at the expiration of the period of one month beginning with the day on which it is passed.

(3)   This Act shall not extend to Northern Ireland.

Street Offences Act 1959

1959 CHAPTER 57

An Act to make, as respects England and Wales, further provision against loitering or soliciting in public places for the purpose of prostitution and for the punishment of those guilty of certain offences in connection with refreshment houses and those who live on the earnings of or control prostitutes

[16th July 1959]

1 Loitering or soliciting for purposes of prostitution

(1)   It shall be an offence for a common prostitute to loiter or solicit in a street or public place for the purpose of prostitution.

[(2)   A person guilty of an offence under this section shall be liable on summary conviction to a fine of an amount not exceeding level 2 on the standard scale, . . . or, for an offence committed after a previous conviction, to a fine of an amount not exceeding level 3 on that scale.]

(3)   A constable may arrest without warrant anyone he finds in a street or public place and suspects, with reasonable cause, to be committing an offence under this section.

(4)   For the purposes of this section "street" includes any bridge, road, lane, footway, subway, square, court, alley or passage, whether a thoroughfare or not, which is for the time being open to the public; and the doorways and entrances of premises abutting on a street (as hereinbefore defined), and any ground adjoining and open to a street, shall be treated as forming part of the street.

(5)   . . .

NOTES

Sub-s (2): substituted by the Criminal Justice Act 1982, s 71; words omitted repealed by the Statute Law (Repeals) Act 1993.

Sub-s (5): repealed by the Statute Law (Repeals) Act 1989.

5 Short title, repeal, extent and commencement

(1) This Act may be cited as the Street Offences Act 1959.

(2) . . .

(3) This Act shall not extend to Scotland or Northern Ireland.

(4) This Act shall come into force at the expiration of one month beginning with the date on which it is passed.

NOTES

Words omitted repealed by the Statute Law (Repeals) Act 1974.

Obscene Publications Act 1959

1959 CHAPTER 66

An Act to amend the law relating to the publication of obscene matter; to provide for the protection of literature; and to strengthen the law concerning pornography

[29th July 1959]

1 Test of obscenity

(1) For the purposes of this Act an article shall be deemed to be obscene if its effect or (where the article comprises two or more distinct items) the effect of any one of its items is, if taken as a whole, such as to tend to deprave and corrupt persons who are likely, having regard to all relevant circumstances, to read, see or hear the matter contained or embodied in it.

(2) In this Act "article" means any description of article containing or embodying matter to be read or looked at or both, any sound record, and any film or other record of a picture or pictures.

(3) For the purposes of this Act a person publishes an article who—
  (a) distributes, circulates, sells, lets on hire, gives, or lends it, or who offers it for sale or for letting on hire; or
  (b) in the case of an article containing or embodying matter to be looked at or a record, shows, plays or projects it[, or, where the matter is data stored electronically, transmits that data.]:

. . . .

[(4) For the purposes of this Act a person also publishes an article to the extent that any matter recorded on it is included by him in a programme included in a programme service.

(5) Where the inclusion of any matter in a programme so included would, if that matter were recorded matter, constitute the publication of an obscene article for the

purposes of this Act by virtue of subsection (4) above, this Act shall have effect in relation to the inclusion of that matter in that programme as if it were recorded matter.

(6)   In this section "programme" and "programme service" have the same meaning as in the Broadcasting Act 1990.]

NOTES

Sub-s (3): words in square brackets in para (b) inserted by the Criminal Justice and Public Order Act 1994, s 168(1), Sch 9, para 3; words omitted repealed by the Broadcasting Act 1990, ss 162(1), 203(3), Sch 21.

Sub-ss (4)–(6): inserted by the Broadcasting Act 1990, s 162(1).

2 Prohibition of publication of obscene matter

(1)   Subject as hereinafter provided, any person who, whether for gain or not publishes an obscene article [or who has an obscene article for publication for gain (whether gain to himself or gain to another)] shall be liable—

(a)   on summary conviction to a fine not exceeding [the prescribed sum] or to imprisonment for a term not exceeding six months;

(b)   on conviction on indictment to a fine or to imprisonment for a term not exceeding three years or both.

(2)   . . .

(3)   A prosecution . . . for an offence against this section shall not be commenced more than two years after the commission of the offence.

[(3A)   Proceedings for an offence under this section shall not be instituted except by or with the consent of the Director of Public Prosecutions in any case where the article in question is a moving picture film of a width of not less than sixteen millimetres and the relevant publication or the only other publication which followed or could reasonably have been expected to follow from the relevant publication took place or (as the case may be) was to take place in the course of a [film exhibition]; and in this subsection "the relevant publication" means—

(a)   in the case of any proceedings under this section for publishing an obscene article, the publication in respect of which the defendant would be charged if the proceedings were brought; and

(b)   in the case of any proceedings under this section for having an obscene article for publication for gain, the publication which, if the proceedings were brought, the defendant would be alleged to have had in contemplation.]

(4)   A person publishing an article shall not be proceeded against for an offence at common law consisting of the publication of any matter contained or embodied in the article where it is of the essence of the offence that the matter is obscene.

[(4A)   Without prejudice to subsection (4) above, a person shall not be proceeded against for an offence at common law—

(a)   in respect of a [film exhibition] or anything said or done in the course of a [film exhibition], where it is of the essence of the common law offence that the exhibition or, as the case may be, what was said or done was obscene, indecent, offensive, disgusting or injurious to morality; or

(b) in respect of an agreement to give a [film exhibition] or to cause anything to be said or done in the course of such an exhibition where the common law offence consists of conspiring to corrupt public morals or to do any act contrary to public morals or decency.]

(5) A person shall not be convicted of an offence against this section if he proves that he had not examined the article in respect of which he is charged and had no reasonable cause to suspect that it was such that his publication of it would make him liable to be convicted of an offence against this section.

(6) In any proceedings against a person under this section the question whether an article is obscene shall be determined without regard to any publication by another person unless it could reasonably have been expected that the publication by the other person would follow from publication by the person charged.

[(7) In this section "film exhibition" has the same meaning as in the Cinemas Act 1985.]

NOTES

Sub-s (1): first words in square brackets inserted by the Obscene Publications Act 1964, s 1(1); reference to "the prescribed sum" substituted by virtue of the Magistrates' Courts Act 1980, s 32(2).

Sub-s (2): repealed by the Criminal Law Act 1977, s 65, Sch 13.

Sub-s (3): words omitted repealed by the Criminal Law Act 1977, s 65, Sch 13.

Sub-ss (3A), (4A): inserted by the Criminal Law Act 1977, s 53; words in square brackets substituted by the Cinemas Act 1985, s 24(1), Sch 2, para 6.

Sub-s (7): inserted by the Criminal Law Act 1977, s 53; substituted by the Cinemas Act 1985, s 24(1), Sch 2, para 6.

4 Defence of public good

(1) [Subject to subsection (1A) of this section] a person shall not be convicted of an offence against section two of this Act, and an order for forfeiture shall not be made under the foregoing section, if it is proved that publication of the article in question is justified as being for the public good on the ground that it is in the interests of science, literature, art or learning, or of other objects of general concern.

[(1A) Subsection (1) of this section shall not apply where the article in question is a moving picture film or soundtrack, but—
(a) a person shall not be convicted of an offence against section 2 of this Act in relation to any such film or soundtrack, and
(b) an order for forfeiture of any such film or soundtrack shall not be made under section 3 of this Act,

if it is proved that publication of the film or soundtrack is justified as being for the public good on the ground that it is in the interests of drama, opera, ballet or any other art, or of literature or learning.]

(2) It is hereby declared that the opinion of experts as to the literary, artistic, scientific or other merits of an article may be admitted in any proceedings under this Act either to establish or to negative the said ground.

[(3)   In this section "moving picture soundtrack" means any sound record designed for playing with a moving picture film, whether incorporated with the film or not.]

NOTES

Sub-s (1): words in square brackets inserted by the Criminal Law Act 1977, s 53(6).
Sub-ss (1A), (3): inserted by the Criminal Law Act 1977, s 53(6), (7).

5 Citation, commencement and extent

(1)   This Act may be cited as the Obscene Publications Act 1959.

(2)   This Act shall come into operation on the expiration of one month beginning with the date of the passing thereof.

(3)   This Act shall not extend to Scotland or to Northern Ireland.

Indecency with Children Act 1960

1960 CHAPTER 33

An Act to make further provision for the punishment of indecent conduct towards young children, and to increase the maximum sentence of imprisonment under the Sexual Offences Act 1956, for certain existing offences against young girls
[2nd June 1960]

1 Indecent conduct towards young child

(1)   Any person who commits an act of gross indecency with or towards a child under the age of [sixteen], or who incites a child under that age to such an act with him or another, shall be liable on conviction on indictment to imprisonment for a term not exceeding [ten years], or on summary conviction to imprisonment for a term not exceeding six months, to a fine not exceeding [the prescribed sum], or to both.

(2)   . . .

(3)   References in the Children and Young Persons Act 1933 . . . to the offences mentioned in the First Schedule to that Act shall include offences under this section.

(4)   Offences under this section shall be deemed to be offences against the person for the purpose of section three of the Visiting Forces Act 1952 (which restricts the trial by the United Kingdom courts of offenders connected with visiting forces).

NOTES

Sub-s (1): word "sixteen" in square brackets substituted by the Criminal Justice and Court Services Act 2000, s 39.

Date in force: 11 January 2001: see SI 2000/3302, art 2(a).

Sub-s (1): words "ten years" in square brackets substituted by the Crime (Sentences) Act 1997, s 52.

Sub-s (1): words "the prescribed sum" in square brackets substituted by the Magistrates'

Courts Act 1980, s 32(2).

Sub-s (2): repealed by the Police and Criminal Evidence Act 1984, s 119, Sch 7, Part V.

Sub-s (3): words omitted repealed by the Police and Criminal Evidence Act 1984, s 119, Sch 7, Part V.

3 Short title, extent and commencement

(1) This Act may be cited as the Indecency with Children Act 1960.

(2) This Act shall not extend to Scotland or Northern Ireland.

(3) This Act shall come into force at the expiration of one month beginning with the date it is passed.

Suicide Act 1961

1961 CHAPTER 60

An Act to amend the law of England and Wales relating to suicide, and for purposes connected therewith

[3rd August 1961]

1 Suicide to cease to be a crime

The rule of law whereby it is a crime for a person to commit suicide is hereby abrogated.

2 Criminal liability for complicity in another's suicide

(1) A person who aids, abets, counsels or procures the suicide of another, or an attempt by another to commit suicide, shall be liable on conviction on indictment to imprisonment for a term not exceeding fourteen years.

(2) If on the trial of an indictment for murder or manslaughter it is proved that the accused aided, abetted, counselled or procured the suicide of the person in question, the jury may find him guilty of that offence.

(3) The enactments mentioned in the first column of the First Schedule to this Act shall have effect subject to the amendments provided for in the second column (which preserve in relation to offences under this section the previous operation of those enactments in relation to murder or manslaughter).

(4) . . . no proceedings shall be instituted for an offence under this section except by or with the consent of the Director of Public Prosecutions.

NOTES

Words omitted repealed by the Criminal Law Act 1967, s 10(2), Sch 3, Part II and the Criminal Jurisdiction Act 1975, s 14(5), Sch 6, Part I.

3 Short title, repeal and extent

(1) This Act may be cited as the Suicide Act 1961.

(2) . . .

(3) This Act shall extend to England and Wales only, except as regards the amendments made by Part II of the First Schedule and except that the Interments (felo de se) Act 1882, shall be repealed also for the Channel Islands.

NOTES

Words omitted repealed by the Statute Law (Repeals) Act 1974.

Licensing Act 1964

1964 CHAPTER 26

An Act to consolidate certain enactments relating to the sale and supply of intoxicating liquor in England and Wales and to matters connected therewith; with corrections and improvements made under the Consolidation of Enactments (Procedure) Act 1949

[25th March 1964]

PART III
PERMITTED HOURS

Prohibition of sale, etc of intoxicating liquor outside permitted hours

59 Prohibition of sale, etc of intoxicating liquor outside permitted hours

(1) Subject to the provisions of this Act, no person shall, except during the permitted hours—
  (a) himself or by his servant or agent sell or supply to any person in licensed premises or in premises in respect of which a club is registered any intoxicating liquor, whether to be consumed on or off the premises; or
  (b) consume in or take from such premises any intoxicating liquor.

(2) If any person contravenes this section he shall be liable to a fine not exceeding [level 3 on the standard scale].

(3) This section does not apply in relation to intoxicating liquor sold under an occasional licence.

NOTES

Sub-s (2): maximum fine increased and converted to a level on the standard scale by the Criminal Justice Act 1982, ss 37, 38, 46.

PART XI

GENERAL PROVISIONS REGULATING SALE, ETC, POSSESSION AND DELIVERY
OF INTOXICATING LIQUOR

160 Selling liquor without licence

(1) Subject to the provisions of this Act, if any person—

  (a) sells or exposes for sale by retail any intoxicating liquor without holding a justices' licence or canteen licence [or occasional permission] authorising . . . the sale of that liquor, or

  (b) holding a justices' licence [an occasional licence] or a canteen licence [or occasional permission] sells or exposes for sale by retail any intoxicating liquor except at the place for which that licence [or permission] authorises . . . the sale of that liquor,

he shall be guilty of an offence under this section.

(2) Where intoxicating liquor is sold in contravention of this section on any premises, every occupier of the premises who is proved to have been privy or consenting to the sale shall be guilty of an offence under this section.

(3) A person guilty of an offence under this section shall be liable to imprisonment for a term not exceeding six months or to a fine not exceeding [level 4 on the standard scale], or to both.

(4) The holder of a justices' licence or a canteen licence shall, on his second or subsequent conviction of an offence under this section, forfeit the licence.

(5) The court by or before which a person is convicted of an offence under this section committed after a previous conviction of such an offence may order him to be disqualified for holding a justices' licence—

  (a) on a second conviction, for a period not exceeding five years;

  (b) on a third or subsequent conviction, for any term of years or for life.

(6) The court by or before which the holder of a justices' licence [an occasional licence] or a canteen licence is convicted of an offence under this section may declare all intoxicating liquor found in his possession, and the vessels containing it, to be forfeited.

[(7) In subsection (1) of this section "occasional permission" means a permission granted under the Licensing (Occasional Permissions) Act 1983.]

NOTES

Sub-s (1): words omitted repealed, and second words in square brackets inserted, by the Finance Act 1967, ss 5(1), 45(8), Sch 7, para 12, Sch 16, Part I; other words in square brackets inserted by the Licensing (Occasional Permissions) Act 1983, s 4.

Sub-s (3): maximum fine increased and converted to a level on the standard scale by the Criminal Justice Act 1982, ss 37, 38, 46.

Sub-s (6): words in square brackets inserted by the Finance Act 1967, s 5(1), Sch 7, para 12.

Sub-s (7): inserted by the Licensing (Occasional Permissions) Act 1983, s 4.

PART XII
PROTECTION OF PERSONS UNDER EIGHTEEN AND OTHER PROVISIONS AS TO CONDUCT OF LICENSED PREMISES AND LICENSED CANTEENS

Persons under eighteen

168 Children prohibited from bars

(1)   The holder of a justices' licence shall not allow a person under fourteen to be in the bar of the licensed premises during the permitted hours.

(2)   No person shall cause or procure, or attempt to cause or procure, any person under fourteen to be in the bar of licensed premises during the permitted hours.

(3)   Where it is shown that a person under fourteen was in the bar of any licensed premises during the permitted hours, the holder of the justices' licence shall be guilty of an offence under this section unless he proves either—
  (a)   that he [exercised all] due diligence to prevent the person under fourteen from being admitted to the bar, or
  (b)   that the person under fourteen had apparently attained that age.

[(3A)   No offence shall be committed under subsection (1) of this section if—
  (a)   the person under fourteen is in the bar in the company of a person who is eighteen or over,
  (b)   there is in force a certificate under section 168A(1) of this Act relating to the bar, and
  (c)   the certificate is operational or subsection (3B) of this section applies.

(3B)   This subsection applies where—
  (a)   the person under fourteen, or a person in whose company he is, is consuming a meal purchased before the certificate ceased to be operational, and
  (b)   no more than thirty minutes have elapsed since the certificate ceased to be operational.

(3C)   No offence shall be committed under subsection (2) of this section if the person causes or procures, or attempts to cause or procure, the person under fourteen to be in the bar in the circumstances mentioned in paragraphs (a) to (c) of subsection (3A) of this section.]

(4)   No offence shall be committed under this section if the person under fourteen—
  (a)   is the licence-holder's child, or
  (b)   resides in the premises, but is not employed there, or
  (c)   is in the bar solely for the purpose of passing to or from some part of the premises which is not a bar and to or from which there is no other convenient means of access or egress.

(5)   No offence shall be committed under this section if the bar is in any railway refreshment-rooms or other premises constructed, fitted and intended to be used bona fide for any purpose to which the holding of a justices' licence is merely ancillary.

(6) If any person contravenes this section he shall be liable [to a fine not exceeding level 1 on the standard scale].

(7) A local education authority may institute proceedings for an offence under this section.

(8) Where in any proceedings under this section it is alleged that a person was at any time under fourteen, and he appears to the court to have then been under that age, he shall be deemed for the purposes of the proceedings to have then been under that age, unless the contrary is shown.

NOTES

Sub-s (3): words in square brackets substituted by the Licensing Act 1988, s 19, Sch 3, para 16.

Sub-ss (3A)–(3C): inserted by the Deregulation and Contracting Out Act 1994, s 19(1).

Sub-s (6): maximum fines on first or subsequent convictions increased to the same amount by the Criminal Law Act 1977, s 31(6), (9), and converted to level 1 on the standard scale by the Criminal Justice Act 1982, ss 37, 46.

[168A Children's certificates]

[(1) The holder of a justices' licence may apply to the licensing justices for the grant of a certificate in relation to any area of the premises for which the licence is in force which consists of or includes a bar.

(2) Licensing justices may grant an application for a certificate under subsection (1) of this section ("a children's certificate") if it appears to them to be appropriate to do so, but shall not do so unless they are satisfied—
  (a) that the area to which the application relates constitutes an environment in which it is suitable for persons under fourteen to be present, and
  (b) that meals and beverages other than intoxicating liquor will be available for sale for consumption in that area.

(3) Where a children's certificate is in force, the holder of the justices' licence for the licensed premises to which the certificate relates shall keep posted in some conspicuous place in the area to which the certificate relates a notice which—
  (a) states that a children's certificate is in force in relation to the area, and
  (b) explains the effect of the certificate and of any conditions attached to it.

(4) A person who fails to perform the duty imposed on him by subsection (3) of this section shall be guilty of an offence and liable on summary conviction to a fine of an amount not exceeding level 1 on the standard scale.

(5) In any proceedings for an offence under subsection (4) of this section, it shall be a defence for the accused to prove that he took all reasonable precautions, and exercised all due diligence, to avoid the commission of the offence.

(6) Schedule 12A to this Act (supplementary provisions) shall have effect.

(7) Subsection (1) of this section shall apply to an applicant for a justices' licence as it applies to the holder of a justices' licence, and, in its application by virtue of this subsection, shall have effect as if the reference to the premises for which the

licence is in force were to the premises which are the subject of the application for a justices' licence.]

NOTES

Inserted by the Deregulation and Contracting Out Act 1994, s 19(2).

[169A Sale of intoxicating liquor to a person under 18]

[(1)   A person shall be guilty of an offence if, in licensed premises, he sells intoxicating liquor to a person under eighteen.

(2)   It is a defence for a person charged with an offence under subsection (1) of this section, where he is charged by reason of his own act, [to prove—
   (a)   that he believed that the person was not under eighteen; and
   (b)   either that he had taken all reasonable steps to establish the person's age or that nobody could reasonably have suspected from his appearance that the person was under eighteen.

(2A)   For the purposes of subsection (2) of this section a person shall be treated as having taken all reasonable steps to establish another person's age if he asks the other person for evidence of his age unless it is shown that the evidence was such that no reasonable person would have been convinced by it].

(3)   It is a defence for a person charged with an offence under subsection (1) of this section, where he is charged by reason of the act or default of some other person, to prove that he exercised all due diligence to avoid the commission of an offence under that subsection.

(4)   Subsection (1) of this section has effect subject to section 169D of this Act.]

NOTES

Substituted, together with ss 169B–169H, for s 169 as originally enacted, by the Licensing (Young Persons) Act 2000, s 1.
   Date in force: 23 January 2001: see the Licensing (Young Persons) Act 2000, s 3(2).
   Sub-ss (2), (2A): words from "to prove—" to "convinced by it" in square brackets substituted by the Criminal Justice and Police Act 2001, s 30(1).
   Date in force: 1 December 2001 (except in relation to any sale of intoxicating liquor made before that date): see the Criminal Justice and Police Act 2001, s 30(2) and SI 2001/3736, art 2(b).

[169B Allowing the sale of intoxicating liquor to a person under 18]

[(1)   A person to whom this subsection applies shall be guilty of an offence if, in licensed premises, he knowingly allows any person to sell intoxicating liquor to a person under eighteen.

(2)   Subsection (1) of this section applies to a person who works in the licensed premises in a capacity, whether paid or unpaid, which gives him authority to prevent the sale.

(3)   Subsection (1) of this section has effect subject to section 169D of this Act.]

NOTES
Substituted, together with ss 169A, 169C–169H, for s 169 as originally enacted, by the
Licensing (Young Persons) Act 2000, s 1.
Date in force: 23 January 2001: see the Licensing (Young Persons) Act 2000, s 3(2).

[169C Purchase of intoxicating liquor by or for a person under 18]

[(1)   A person under eighteen shall be guilty of an offence if, in licensed premises,
he buys or attempts to buy intoxicating liquor.

[(1A)   Subsection (1) of this section does not apply where the person under
eighteen buys or attempts to buy the intoxicating liquor at the request of—
  (a)   a constable, or
  (b)   an inspector of weights and measures appointed under section 72(1) of the
        Weights and Measures Act 1985 (c 72),

who is acting in the course of his duty.]

(2)   A person shall be guilty of an offence if, in licensed premises, he buys or
attempts to buy intoxicating liquor on behalf of a person under eighteen.

(3)   A person shall be guilty of an offence if he buys or attempts to buy
intoxicating liquor for consumption in a bar in licensed premises by a person under
eighteen.

(4)   It is a defence for a person charged with an offence under subsection (2) or (3)
of this section to prove that he had no reason to suspect that the person was under
eighteen.

(5)   Subsections (1) and (2) of this section have effect subject to section 169D of
this Act.]

NOTES
Substituted, together with ss 169A, 169B, 169D–169H, for s 169 as originally enacted, by
the Licensing (Young Persons) Act 2000, s 1.
Date in force: 23 January 2001: see the Licensing (Young Persons) Act 2000, s 3(2).
Sub-s (1A): inserted by the Criminal Justice and Police Act 2001, s 31(1).
Date in force: 1 December 2001: see SI 2001/3736, art 2(b).

[169D Exception to the section 169A–C offences]

[Sections 169A(1), 169B(1), and 169C(1) and (2) of this Act do not apply where—
  (a)   the person under eighteen has attained the age of sixteen,
  (b)   the intoxicating liquor in question is beer, porter or cider, and
  (c)   its sale or purchase is for consumption at a meal in a part of the licensed
        premises which is not a bar and is usually set apart for the service of meals.]

NOTES
Substituted, together with ss 169A–169C, 169E–169H, for s 169 as originally enacted, by
the Licensing (Young Persons) Act 2000, s 1.
Date in force: 23 January 2001: see the Licensing (Young Persons) Act 2000, s 3(2).

[169E Consumption of intoxicating liquor by a person under 18]

[(1) A person under eighteen shall be guilty of an offence if, in a bar in licensed premises, he consumes intoxicating liquor.

(2) A person to whom this subsection applies shall be guilty of an offence if, in licensed premises, he knowingly allows a person under eighteen to consume intoxicating liquor in a bar.

(3) Subsection (2) of this section applies to a person who works in the licensed premises in a capacity, whether paid or unpaid, which gives him authority to prevent the consumption.]

NOTES

Substituted, together with ss 169A–169D, 169F–169H, for s 169 as originally enacted, by the Licensing (Young Persons) Act 2000, s 1.

Date in force: 23 January 2001: see the Licensing (Young Persons) Act 2000, s 3(2).

[169F Delivery of intoxicating liquor to a person under 18]

[(1) A person who works in licensed premises, whether paid or unpaid, shall be guilty of an offence if he knowingly delivers to a person under eighteen intoxicating liquor sold in those premises for consumption off the premises.

(2) A person to whom this subsection applies shall be guilty of an offence if he knowingly allows any person to deliver to a person under eighteen intoxicating liquor sold in licensed premises for consumption off the premises.

(3) Subsection (2) of this section applies to a person who works in the licensed premises in a capacity, whether paid or unpaid, which gives him authority to prevent the delivery.

(4) Subsections (1) and (2) of this section do not apply where—
    (a) the delivery is made at the residence or working place of the purchaser, or
    (b) the person under eighteen works in the licensed premises in a capacity, whether paid or unpaid, which includes the delivery of intoxicating liquor.]

NOTES

Substituted, together with ss 169A–169E, 169G, 169H, for s 169 as originally enacted, by the Licensing (Young Persons) Act 2000, s 1.

Date in force: 23 January 2001: see the Licensing (Young Persons) Act 2000, s 3(2).

[169G Sending a person under 18 to obtain intoxicating liquor]

[(1) A person shall be guilty of an offence if he knowingly sends a person under eighteen for the purpose of obtaining intoxicating liquor sold or to be sold in licensed premises for consumption off the premises.

(2) Subsection (1) of this section applies regardless of whether the liquor is to be obtained from the licensed premises or from other premises from which it is delivered in pursuance of the sale.

(3) Subsection (1) of this section does not apply where the person under eighteen works in the licensed premises where the sale has been or is to be made, in a capacity, whether paid or unpaid, which includes the delivery of intoxicating liquor.

[(4) Subsection (1) of this section does not apply where the person under eighteen is sent by—

(a) a constable, or

(b) an inspector of weights and measures appointed under section 72(1) of the Weights and Measures Act 1985 (c 72),

who is acting in the course of his duty.]]

[169H Penalty for offences]

[(1) A person guilty of an offence under section 169A, 169B, 169C, 169E, 169F, or 169G of this Act shall be liable to a fine not exceeding level 3 on the standard scale.

(2) Where the holder of a justices' licence is convicted of any of the offences referred to in subsection (1) and the licence is held in respect of the licensed premises in relation to which the offence was committed, the court may order that he shall forfeit the licence if—

(a) he already has one or more convictions of that or any other offence referred to in subsection (1) of this section, or

(b) he already has one or more convictions of an offence under section 169 of this Act.]

[169I Enforcement role for weights and measures authorities in relation to certain offences]

[(1) It is the duty of every local weights and measures authority in England and Wales to enforce within their area the provisions of sections 169A and 169B of this Act.

(2) A local weights and measures authority shall have power to make, or to authorise any person to make on their behalf, such purchases of goods as may appear expedient for the purpose of determining whether or not the provisions of section 169A or 169B of this Act are being complied with.

(3)   In this section "local weights and measures authority" has the meaning given by section 69 of the Weights and Measures Act 1985 (local weights and measures authorities).]

NOTES

Inserted by the Criminal Justice and Police Act 2001, s 31(3).
Date in force: 1 December 2001: see SI 2001/3736, art 2(b).

Preservation of order

172 Licence holder not to permit drunkenness, etc

(1)   The holder of a justices' licence shall not permit drunkenness or any violent, quarrelsome or riotous conduct to take place in the licensed premises.

(2)   If the holder of a justices' licence is charged under subsection (1) of this section with permitting drunkenness, and it is proved that any person was drunk in the licensed premises, the burden of proving that the licence holder and the persons employed by him took all reasonable steps for preventing drunkenness in the premises shall lie upon him.

(3)   The holder of a justices' licence shall not sell intoxicating liquor to a drunken person.

(4)   If any person contravenes this section he shall be liable [to a fine not exceeding [level 3] on the standard scale].

NOTES

Sub-s (4): enhanced penalty on a subsequent conviction abolished and penalty on any conviction now a fine not exceeding level 2 on the standard scale by virtue of the Criminal Law Act 1977, s 31(6), (9), and the Criminal Justice Act 1982, ss 35, 37, 46.

Sub-s (4): words "level 3" in square brackets substituted by the Criminal Justice and Police Act 2001, s 32(1).

Date in force: 1 December 2001 (except in relation to any offence committed before that date): see the Criminal Justice and Police Act 2001, s 32(7) and SI 2001/3736, art 2(b).

175 Prostitutes not to be allowed to assemble on licensed premises

(1)   The holder of a justices' licence shall not knowingly allow the licensed premises to be the habitual resort or place of meeting of reputed prostitutes, whether the object of their so resorting or meeting is or is not prostitution; but this section does not prohibit his allowing any such persons to remain in the premises for the purpose of obtaining reasonable refreshment for such time as is necessary for that purpose.

(2)   If the holder of a justices' licence contravenes this section he shall be liable [to a fine not exceeding level 2 on the standard scale].

NOTES

Sub-s (2): enhanced penalty on a subsequent conviction abolished and penalty on any conviction now a fine not exceeding level 2 on the standard scale by virtue of the Criminal Law Act 1977, s 31(6), (9), and the Criminal Justice Act 1982, ss 35, 37, 46.

Offences in relation to constables

178 Offences in relation to constables

If the holder of a justices' licence—
    (a) knowingly suffers to remain on the licensed premises any constable during any part of the time appointed for the constable's being on duty, except for the purpose of the execution of the constable's duty, or
    (b) supplies any liquor or refreshment, whether by way of gift or sale, to any constable on duty except by authority of a superior officer of the constable, or
    (c) bribes or attempts to bribe any constable,

he shall be liable [to a fine not exceeding level 2 on the standard scale].

NOTES

Enhanced penalty on a subsequent conviction abolished and penalty on any conviction now a fine not exceeding level 2 on the standard scale by virtue of the Criminal Law Act 1977, s 31(6), (9), and the Criminal Justice Act 1982, ss 35, 37, 46.

PART XIV
SUPPLEMENTAL

204 Short title, commencement and extent

(1)   This Act may be cited as the Licensing Act 1964.

(2)   This Act shall come into force on 1st January 1965.

(3)   This Act does not extend to Scotland or Northern Ireland.

Criminal Procedure (Insanity) Act 1964

1964 CHAPTER 84

An Act to amend the form of the special verdict required by section 2 of the Trial of Lunatics Act 1883 and the procedure for determining whether an accused person is under a disability such as to constitute a bar to his being tried; to provide for an appeal against such a special verdict or a finding that the accused is under such a disability; to confer on the court of trial and the Court of Criminal Appeal further powers of making orders for admission to hospital; to empower the prosecution to put forward evidence of insanity or diminished responsibility; and for purposes connected with the matters aforesaid

[31st July 1964]

[4 Finding of unfitness to plead]

[(1)   This section applies where on the trial of a person the question arises (at the instance of the defence or otherwise) whether the accused is under a disability, that is to say, under any disability such that apart from this Act it would constitute a bar to his being tried.

(2)   If, having regard to the nature of the supposed disability, the court are of opinion that it is expedient to do so and in the interests of the accused, they may postpone consideration of the question of fitness to be tried until any time up to the opening of the case for the defence.

(3)   If, before the question of fitness to be tried falls to be determined, the jury return a verdict of acquittal on the count or each of the counts on which the accused is being tried, that question shall not be determined.

(4)   Subject to subsections (2) and (3) above, the question of fitness to be tried shall be determined as soon as it arises.

(5)   The question of fitness to be tried shall be determined by a jury and—
   (a)   where it falls to be determined on the arraignment of the accused and the trial proceeds, the accused shall be tried by a jury other than that which determined that question;
   (b)   where it falls to be determined at any later time, it shall be determined by a separate jury or by the jury by whom the accused is being tried, as the court may direct.

(6)   A jury shall not make a determination under subsection (5) above except on the written or oral evidence of two or more registered medical practitioners at least one of whom is duly approved.]

NOTES
   Substituted, together with s 4A, for s 4 as originally enacted, by the Criminal Procedure (Insanity and Unfitness to Plead) Act 1991, s 2.

[4A Finding that the accused did the act or made the omission charged against him]

[(1)   This section applies where in accordance with section 4(5) above it is determined by a jury that the accused is under a disability.

(2)   The trial shall not proceed or further proceed but it shall be determined by a jury—
   (a)   on the evidence (if any) already given in the trial; and
   (b)   on such evidence as may be adduced or further adduced by the prosecution, or adduced by a person appointed by the court under this section to put the case for the defence,

whether they are satisfied, as respects the count or each of the counts on which the accused was to be or was being tried, that he did the act or made the omission charged against him as the offence.

(3)   If as respects that count or any of those counts the jury are satisfied as mentioned in subsection (2) above, they shall make a finding that the accused did the act or made the omission charged against him.

(4)   If as respects that count or any of those counts the jury are not so satisfied, they shall return a verdict of acquittal as if on the count in question the trial had proceeded to a conclusion.

(5)   A determination under subsection (2) above shall be made—
- (a)   where the question of disability was determined on the arraignment of the accused, by a jury other than that which determined that question; and
- (b)   where that question was determined at any later time, by the jury by whom the accused was being tried.]

NOTES

Substituted, together with s 4, for s 4 as originally enacted, by the Criminal Procedure (Insanity and Unfitness to Plead) Act 1991, s 2.

[5 Powers to deal with persons not guilty by reason of insanity or unfit to plead etc]

[(1)   This section applies where—
- (a)   a special verdict is returned that the accused is not guilty by reason of insanity; or
- (b)   findings are recorded that the accused is under a disability and that he did the act or made the omission charged against him.

(2)   Subject to subsection (3) below, the court shall either—
- (a)   make an order that the accused be admitted, in accordance with the provisions of Schedule 1 to the Criminal Procedure (Insanity and Unfitness to Plead) Act 1991, to such hospital as may be specified by the Secretary of State; or
- (b)   where they have the power to do so by virtue of section 5 of that Act, make in respect of the accused such one of the following orders as they think most suitable in all the circumstances of the case, namely—
  - (i)   a guardianship order within the meaning of the Mental Health Act 1983;
  - (ii)   a supervision and treatment order within the meaning of Schedule 2 to the said Act of 1991; and
  - (iii) an order for his absolute discharge.

(3)   Paragraph (b) of subsection (2) above shall not apply where the offence to which the special verdict or findings relate is an offence the sentence for which is fixed by law.]

NOTES

Substituted by the Criminal Procedure (Insanity and Unfitness to Plead) Act 1991, s 3.

6 Evidence by prosecution of insanity or diminished responsibility

Where on a trial for murder the accused contends—
- (a)   that at the time of the alleged offence he was insane so as not to be responsible according to law for his actions; or
- (b)   that at that time he was suffering from such abnormality of mind as is specified in subsection (1) of section 2 of the Homicide Act 1957 (diminished responsibility),

the court shall allow the prosecution to adduce or elicit evidence tending to prove the other of those contentions, and may give directions as to the stage of the proceedings at which the prosecution may adduce such evidence.

8 Short title, interpretation, commencement, extent and repeals

(1)   This Act may be cited as the Criminal Procedure (Insanity) Act 1964.

(2)   In this Act—

["duly approved" in relation to a registered medical practitioner, means approved for the purposes of section 12 of the Mental Health Act 1983 by the Secretary of State as having special experience in the diagnosis or treatment of mental disorder;

"registered medical practitioner" means a fully registered person within the meaning of the Medical Act 1983;]

"special verdict" has the meaning assigned by section 1 of this Act,

"under disability" has the meaning assigned by section 4 of this Act,

"verdict of acquittal" does not include a special verdict, and any reference to acquittal shall be construed accordingly,

and other expressions used in this Act and in [the Mental Health Act 1983] have the same meanings in this Act as in [Part III] of that Act; . . .

[(2A)   Subsections (2) and (3) of section 54 of the Mental Health Act 1983 shall have effect with respect to proof of the accused's mental condition for the purposes of section 4 of this Act as they have effect with respect to proof of an offender's mental condition for the purposes of section 37(2)(a) of that Act.]

(3)   This Act shall come into operation at the time of expiration of a period of one month beginning with the day on which it was passed:

Provided that—

(a)   sections 1, 4(1) to (5), 5(1)(a) and (c) and 6 shall not apply where the accused was arraigned before the said time;

(b)   . . .

(c)   section 7 shall apply in relation to courts-martial whenever commenced, except that it shall not have effect in relation to any finding come to by a court-martial before the said time or affect the procedure in a court-martial commenced before that time for determining the question whether the accused is unfit to stand his trial.

(4)   This Act, except as respects courts-martial and matters arising out of proceedings in courts-martial, shall extend to England and Wales only,

(5)   . . .

NOTES

Sub-s (2): definitions "duly approved", "registered medical practitioner" inserted, and words omitted repealed, by the Criminal Procedure (Insanity and Unfitness to Plead) Act 1991, ss 7, 8(1)(c), (3), Sch 3, para 1, Sch 4; words "the Mental Health Act 1983" and "Part III" in square brackets substituted by the Mental Health Act 1983, s 148(1), (2), Sch 4, para 18(b).

Sub-s (2A): inserted by the Criminal Procedure (Insanity and Unfitness to Plead) Act 1991, s 7, Sch 3, para 1.

Sub-s (3): para (b) spent.
Sub-s (5): repealed by the Statute Law (Repeals) Act 1974.

Criminal Law Act 1967

1967 CHAPTER 58

An Act to amend the law of England and Wales by abolishing the division of crimes into felonies and misdemeanours and to amend and simplify the law in respect of matters arising from or related to that division or the abolition of it; to do away (within or without England and Wales) with certain obsolete crimes together with the torts of maintenance and champerty; and for purposes connected therewith
[21st July 1967]

PART I
FELONY AND MISDEMEANOUR

1 Abolition of distinction between felony and misdemeanour

(1)   All distinctions between felony and misdemeanour are hereby abolished.

(2)   Subject to the provisions of this Act, on all matters on which a distinction has previously been made between felony and misdemeanour, including mode of trial, the law and practice in relation to all offences cognisable under the law of England and Wales (including piracy) shall be the law and practice applicable at the commencement of this Act in relation to misdemeanour.

3 Use of force in making arrest, etc

(1)   A person may use such force as is reasonable in the circumstances in the prevention of crime, or in effecting or assisting in the lawful arrest of offenders or suspected offenders or of persons unlawfully at large.

(2)   Subsection (1) above shall replace the rules of the common law on the question when force used for a purpose mentioned in the subsection is justified by that purpose.

4 Penalties for assisting offenders

(1)   Where a person has committed an arrestable offence, any other person who, knowing or believing him to be guilty of the offence or of some other arrestable offence, does without lawful authority or reasonable excuse any act with intent to impede his apprehension or prosecution shall be guilty of an offence.

[(1A)   In this section and section 5 below "arrestable offence" has the meaning assigned to it by section 24 of the Police and Criminal Evidence Act 1984.]

(2)   If on the trial of an indictment for an arrestable offence the jury are satisfied that the offence charged (or some other offence of which the accused might on that

charge be found guilty) was committed, but find the accused not guilty of it, they may find him guilty of any offence under subsection (1) above of which they are satisfied that he is guilty in relation to the offence charged (or that other offence).

(3)   A person committing an offence under subsection (1) above with intent to impede another person's apprehension or prosecution shall on conviction on indictment be liable to imprisonment according to the gravity of the other person's offence, as follows:—

(a)   if that offence is one for which the sentence is fixed by law, he shall be liable to imprisonment for not more than ten years;

(b)   if it is one for which a person (not previously convicted) may be sentenced to imprisonment for a term of fourteen years, he shall be liable to imprisonment for not more than seven years;

(c)   if it is not one included above but is one for which a person (not previously convicted) may be sentenced to imprisonment for a term of ten years, he shall be liable to imprisonment for not more than five years;

(d)   in any other case, he shall be liable to imprisonment for not more than three years.

(4)   No proceedings shall be instituted for an offence under subsection (1) above except by or with the consent of the Director of Public Prosecutions:

. . .

(5)–(7)   . . .

NOTES

Sub-s (1A): inserted by the Police and Criminal Evidence Act 1984, s 119, Sch 6, para 17.

Sub s (4): words omitted repealed by the Criminal Jurisdiction Act 1975, s 14(5), Sch 6, Part I.

Sub-s (5): repealed by the Criminal Law Act 1977, s 65, Sch 13.

Sub-s (6): repealed by the Extradition Act 1989, s 37(1), Sch 2.

Sub-s (7): repealed by the Theft Act 1968, s 33(3), Sch 3, Part III.

5 Penalties for concealing offences or giving false information

(1)   Where a person has committed an arrestable offence, any other person who, knowing or believing that the offence or some other arrestable offence has been committed, and that he has information which might be of material assistance in securing the prosecution or conviction of an offender for it, accepts or agrees to accept for not disclosing that information any consideration other than the making good of loss or injury caused by the offence, or the making of reasonable compensation for that loss or injury, shall be liable on conviction on indictment to imprisonment for not more than two years.

(2)   Where a person causes any wasteful employment of the police by knowingly making to any person a false report tending to show that an offence has been committed, or to give rise to apprehension for the safety of any persons or property, or tending to show that he has information material to any police inquiry, he shall be liable on summary conviction to imprisonment for not more than six months or to a fine of not more [level 4 on the standard scale] or to both.

(3)   No proceedings shall be instituted for an offence under this section except by or with the consent of the Director of Public Prosecutions.

(4)   . . .

(5)   The compounding of an offence other than treason shall not be an offence otherwise than under this section.

NOTES

Sub-s (2): reference to level on the standard scale substituted by virtue of the Criminal Justice Act 1982, ss 38, 46.

Sub-s (4): repealed by the Criminal Law Act 1977, s 65, Sch 13.

12 Commencement, savings, and other general provisions

(1)   This Part of this Act, except in so far as it enlarges the powers of the Parliament of Northern Ireland, shall not come into force until the 1st January 1968; and, in so far as it affects any matter of procedure or evidence or the jurisdiction or powers of any court in relation to offences, it shall have effect in relation to proceedings on indictment for an offence (except as provided by the following subsections) if, but only if, the person charged with the offence is arraigned on or after that day.

(2)   Where a person is arraigned after the commencement of this Part of this Act on an indictment for a felony committed before that commencement, then for purposes of his trial on that indictment the offence shall be deemed always to have been a misdemeanour and, notwithstanding that the indictment is framed as an indictment for felony, shall be deemed to be charged as a misdemeanour in the indictment.

(3)   On an indictment signed before the commencement of this Part of this Act, a person may be found guilty of any offence of which he could have been found guilty on that indictment if this Part of this Act had not been passed, but not of any other offence; and a person tried by a court-martial ordered or convened before that commencement may be found guilty of any offence of which he could have been found guilty if this Part of this Act had not been passed, but not of any other offence.

(4)   Where a person has been tried for or convicted of felony before the commencement of this Part of this Act, the trial or conviction may be proved in any manner in which it could have been proved if this Part of this Act had not been passed.

(5)   Subject to any express amendment or repeal made by this Act, the following provisions shall have effect in relation to any Act passed before this Act:—
  (a)   any enactment creating an offence by directing it to be felony shall be read as directing it to be an offence, and nothing in this Part of this Act shall affect the operation of any reference to an offence in the enactments specially relating to that offence by reason only of the reference being in terms no longer applicable after the commencement of this Part of this Act;
  (b)   any enactment referring to felonious stealing shall be read as referring merely to stealing;

(c) nothing in this Part of this Act shall affect the punishment provided for an offence by the enactments specially relating to that offence.

(6) In this Part of this Act references to felony shall not be taken as including treason; but the procedure on trials for treason or misprision of treason shall be the same as the procedure as altered by this Act on trials for murder.

(7) Any provision of this Part of this Act relating to proceedings on indictment shall, so far as applicable, apply also to proceedings on an inquisition.

PART III
SUPPLEMENTARY

15 Short title

This Act may be cited as the Criminal Law Act 1967.

Sexual Offences Act 1967

1967 CHAPTER 60

An Act to amend the law of England and Wales relating to homosexual acts
[27th July 1967]

1 Amendment of law relating to homosexual acts in private

(1) Notwithstanding any statutory or common law provision, . . .
  [(a)] a homosexual act in private shall not be an offence provided that the parties consent thereto and have attained the age of [sixteen] years; [and
  (b) a homosexual act by any person shall not be an offence if he is under the age of sixteen years and the other party has attained that age].

(2) An act which would otherwise be treated for the purposes of this Act as being done in private shall not be so treated if done—
  (a) when more than two persons take part or are present; or
  (b) in a lavatory to which the public have or are permitted to have access, whether on payment or otherwise.

(3) A man who is suffering from [severe mental handicap] cannot in law give any consent which, by virtue of subsection (1) of this section, would prevent a homosexual act from being an offence, but a person shall not be convicted, on account of the incapacity of such a man to consent, of an offence consisting of such an act if he proves that he did not know and had no reason to suspect that man to be suffering from [severe mental handicap].

[(3A) In subsection (3) of this section "severe mental handicap" means a state of arrested or incomplete development of mind which includes severe impairment of intelligence and social functioning.]

(4)   Section 128 of the Mental Health Act 1959 (prohibition on men on the staff of a hospital, or otherwise having responsibility for mental patients, having sexual intercourse with women patients) shall have effect as if any reference therein to having unlawful sexual intercourse with a woman included a reference to committing buggery or an act of gross indecency with another man.

(5)   . . .

(6)   It is hereby declared that where in any proceedings it is charged that a homosexual act is an offence the prosecutor shall have the burden of proving that the act was done otherwise than in private or otherwise than with the consent of the parties or that any of the parties had not attained the age of [sixteen] years.

(7)   For the purposes of this section a man shall be treated as doing a homosexual act if, and only if, he commits buggery with another man or commits an act of gross indecency with another man or is a party to the commission by a man of such an act.

NOTES

Sub-s (1): words omitted repealed by the Criminal Justice and Public Order Act 1994, s 168(3), Sch 11.

Sub-s (1): para (a) numbered as such by the Sexual Offences (Amendment) Act 2000, s 2(3)(a).

Date in force: 8 January 2001: see SI 2000/3303, art 2(1).

Sub-s (1): word "sixteen" in square brackets substituted by the Sexual Offences (Amendment) Act 2000, s 1(2)(a).

Date in force: 8 January 2001: see SI 2000/3303, art 2(1).

Sub-s (1): para (b) and word "and" immediately preceding it inserted by the Sexual Offences (Amendment) Act 2000, s 2(3)(b).

Date in force: 8 January 2001: see SI 2000/3303, art 2(1).

Sub-s (3): words in square brackets substituted by the Mental Health (Amendment) Act 1982, s 65(1), Sch 3, para 34.

Sub-s (3A): inserted by the Mental Health (Amendment) Act 1982, s 65(1), Sch 3, para 34.

Sub-s (5): repealed by the Criminal Justice and Public Order Act 1994, s 168(3), Sch 11.

Sub-s (6): word "sixteen" in square brackets substituted by the Sexual Offences (Amendment) Act 2000, s 1(2)(a).

Date in force: 8 January 2001: see SI 2000/3303, art 2(1).

11 Short title, citation, interpretation, saving and extent

(1)   This Act may be cited as the Sexual Offences Act 1967 and the Act of 1956 and this Act may be cited as the Sexual Offences Acts 1956 and 1967.

(2)   In this Act "the Act of 1952" means the Magistrates' Courts Act 1952 and "the Act of 1956" means the Sexual Offences Act 1956.

(3)   Section 46 of the Act of 1956 (interpretation of "man", "boy" and other expressions) shall apply for the purposes of the provisions of this Act as it applies for the purposes of the provisions of that Act.

(4)   References in this Act to any enactment shall, except in so far as the context otherwise requires, be construed as references to that enactment as amended or applied by or under any subsequent enactment including this Act.

(5) This Act shall not extend to Scotland or Northern Ireland.

Criminal Justice Act 1967

1967 CHAPTER 80

An Act to amend the law relating to the proceedings of criminal courts, including the law relating to evidence, and to the qualification of jurors, in such proceedings and to appeals in criminal cases; to reform existing methods and provide new methods of dealing with offenders; to make further provision for the treatment of offenders, the management of prisons and other institutions and the arrest of offenders unlawfully at large; to make further provision with respect to legal aid and advice in criminal proceedings; to amend the law relating to firearms and ammunition; to alter the penalties which may be imposed for certain offences; and for connected purposes

[27th July 1967]

PART I
CRIMINAL PROCEDURE, ETC

Miscellaneous provisions as to evidence, procedure and trial

8 Proof of criminal intent

A court or jury, in determining whether a person has committed an offence,—
  (a) shall not be bound in law to infer that he intended or foresaw a result of his actions by reason only of its being a natural and probable consequence of those actions; but
  (b) shall decide whether he did intend or foresee that result by reference to all the evidence, drawing such inferences from the evidence as appear proper in the circumstances.

PART VI
MISCELLANEOUS AND GENERAL

Miscellaneous

106 Short title, extent and commencement

(1) This Act may be cited as the Criminal Justice Act 1967.

(2) The following provisions of this Act shall extend to Scotland, that is to say—
  (a) so much of this Act as relates to courts-martial and appeals therefrom;
  (b) [section 102] and paragraphs 7, 10 to 12 and 14 of Schedule 5;
  (c) Part III (except sections 63, 65, 66, 67 and 71) and Schedule 2;
  (d) Part V;

(e)   section 92 and Schedule 3 so far as they amend any enactment which extends to Scotland;

[(ee) section 100;]

(f)   so much of section 103(1) and Schedule 6 as amends . . . . . .,the Criminal Justice Act 1961 and the Criminal Justice (Scotland) Act 1963; and

(g)   Part II of Schedule 7 and so much of section 103(2) as relates thereto;

but except as provided by this subsection and except so far as it relates to the interpretation or commencement of the said provisions this Act shall not extend to Scotland.

(3)   The following provisions of this Act shall extend to Northern Ireland that is to say—

(a)   so much of this Act as relates to courts-martial and appeals therefrom;

(b)   sections . . . 69 and 72;

(c)   so much of section 92 and Parts I and II of Schedule 3 as is extended to Northern Ireland by Part IV of that Schedule;

(d)   . . .

(e)   so much of section 103(1) and Schedule 6 as amends . . . the Criminal Justice Act 1961;

(f)   section 105; and

(g)   Part III of Schedule 7 and so much of section 103(2) as relates thereto;

but except as provided by this subsection and except so far as it relates to the interpretation or commencement of the said provisions this Act shall not extend to Northern Ireland.

(4)   Sections 69(1) and 92 of, and Schedule 3 to, this Act, so far as they amend any enactment which extends to the Channel Islands or the Isle of Man, shall extend to the Channel Islands or the Isle of Man, as the case may be.

(5)   This Act shall come into force on such day as the Secretary of State may by order appoint, and different days may be so appointed for different purposes of this Act, and any reference in any provision of this Act to the commencement of this Act shall be construed as a reference to the day so appointed for the coming into force of that provision, and any such reference to the commencement of a provision of this Act shall be construed as a reference to the day appointed for the coming into force of the provision referred to.

(6)   Without prejudice to Schedule 5 to this Act, any order under this section may make such transitional provision as appears to the Secretary of State to be necessary or expedient in connection with the provisions thereby brought into force, including such adaptations of those provisions or any provisions of this Act then in force as appear to him to be necessary or expedient in consequence of the partial operation of this Act (whether before or after the day appointed by the order).

NOTES

Sub-s (2): in para (b) words "section 102" in square brackets substituted by the Powers of Criminal Courts (Sentencing) Act 2000, s 165(1), Sch 9, para 27.

Date in force: 25 August 2000: see the Powers of Criminal Courts (Sentencing) Act 2000, s 168(1).

Sub-s (2): para (ee) inserted by the Criminal Justice Act 1982, s 33(c).

Sub-s (2): in para (f) first words omitted repealed by the Criminal Law Act 1977, s 65(7), Sch 13.

Sub-s (2): in para (f) second words omitted repealed by the Criminal Appeal Act 1968, s 54, Sch 7.

Sub-s (3): in para (b) numbers omitted repealed by the Powers of Criminal Courts Act 1973, s 56(2), Sch 6.

Sub-s (3): para (d) repealed by the Judicature (Northern Ireland) Act 1978, s 122(2), Sch 7, Pt I.

Sub-s (3): in para (e) words omitted repealed by the Criminal Appeal Act 1968, s 54, Sch 7.

Abortion Act 1967

1967 CHAPTER 87

An Act to amend and clarify the law relating to termination of pregnancy by registered medical practitioners

[27th October 1967]

1 Medical termination of pregnancy

(1) Subject to the provisions of this section, a person shall not be guilty of an offence under the law relating to abortion when a pregnancy is terminated by a registered medical practitioner if two registered medical practitioners are of the opinion, formed in good faith—

[(a) that the pregnancy has not exceeded its twenty-fourth week and that the continuance of the pregnancy would involve risk, greater than if the pregnancy were terminated, of injury to the physical or mental health of the pregnant woman or any existing children of her family; or

(b) that the termination is necessary to prevent grave permanent injury to the physical or mental health of the pregnant woman; or

(c) that the continuance of the pregnancy would involve risk to the life of the pregnant woman, greater than if the pregnancy were terminated; or

(d) that there is a substantial risk that if the child were born it would suffer from such physical or mental abnormalities as to be seriously handicapped].

(2) In determining whether the continuance of a pregnancy would involve such risk of injury to health as is mentioned in paragraph (a) [or (b)] of subsection (1) of this section, account may be taken of the pregnant woman's actual or reasonably foreseeable environment.

(3) Except as provided by subsection (4) of this section, any treatment for the termination of pregnancy must be carried out in a hospital vested in [the Secretary of State for the purposes of his functions under the National Health Service Act 1977 or the National Health Service (Scotland) Act 1978 [or in a hospital vested in [a Primary Care Trust or] a National Health Service trust] or in a place approved for the purposes of this section by the Secretary of State].

[(3A) The power under subsection (3) of this section to approve a place includes power, in relation to treatment consisting primarily in the use of such medicines as may be specified in the approval and carried out in such manner as may be so specified, to approve a class of places.]

(4)   Subsection (3) of this section, and so much of subsection (1) as relates to the opinion of two registered medical practitioners, shall not apply to the termination of a pregnancy by a registered medical practitioner in a case where he is of the opinion, formed in good faith, that the termination is immediately necessary to save the life or to prevent grave permanent injury to the physical or mental health of the pregnant woman.

NOTES

Sub-s (1): paras (a)–(d) substituted for paras (a), (b) as originally enacted by the Human Fertilisation and Embryology Act 1990, s 37(1).

Sub-s (2): words in square brackets inserted by the Human Fertilisation and Embryology Act 1990, s 37(2).

Sub-s (3): words from "the Secretary of State" to "the Secretary of State" in square brackets substituted by the Health Services Act 1980, Sch 1, para 17.

Sub-s (3): words "or in a hospital vested in a National Health Service trust" in square brackets inserted by the National Health Service and Community Care Act 1990, s 66(1), Sch 9, para 8.

Sub-s (3): words "a Primary Care Trust or" in square brackets inserted by SI 2000/90, art 3(1), Sch 1, para 6.

Date in force: 8 February 2000: see SI 2000/90, art 1.

Sub-s (3A): inserted by the Human Fertilisation and Embryology Act 1990, s 37(3).

2 Notification

(1)   The Minister of Health in respect of England and Wales, and the Secretary of State in respect of Scotland, shall by statutory instrument make regulations to provide—

(a)   for requiring any such opinion as is referred to in section 1 of this Act to be certified by the practitioners or practitioner concerned in such form and at such time as may be prescribed by the regulations, and for requiring the preservation and disposal of certificates made for the purposes of the regulations;

(b)   for requiring any registered medical practitioner who terminates a pregnancy to give notice of the termination and such other information relating to the termination as may be so prescribed;

(c)   for prohibiting the disclosure, except to such persons or for such purposes as may be so prescribed, of notices given or information furnished pursuant to the regulations.

(2)   The information furnished in pursuance of regulations made by virtue of paragraph (b) of subsection (1) of this section shall be notified solely to the [Chief Medical Officer of the [Department of Health], or of the Welsh Office, or of the [Scottish Administration]].

(3)   Any person who wilfully contravenes or wilfully fails to comply with the requirements of regulations under subsection (1) of this section shall be liable on summary conviction to a fine not exceeding [level 5 on the standard scale].

(4) Any statutory instrument made by virtue of this section shall be subject to annulment in pursuance of a resolution of either House of Parliament.

NOTES

Sub-s (2): words in square brackets beginning with the words "Chief Medical Officer" substituted by SI 1969/388, art 2, Sch 1.

Sub-s (2): words "Department of Health" in square brackets substituted by SI 1988/1843, art 5(4), Sch 3, para 3(a).

Sub-s (2): words "Scottish Administration" in square brackets substituted by SI 1999/1042, art 5, Sch 3, para 2.

Date in force: 1 July 1999: see SI 1999/1042, art 1(2)(c).

Sub-s (3): maximum fine increased by the Criminal Law Act 1977, s 31, Sch 6, and converted to a level on the standard scale by the Criminal Justice Act 1982, ss 37, 46.

4 Conscientious objection to participation in treatment

(1) Subject to subsection (2) of this section, no person shall be under any duty, whether by contract or by any statutory or other legal requirement, to participate in any treatment authorised by this Act to which he has a conscientious objection:

Provided that in any legal proceedings the burden of proof of conscientious objection shall rest on the person claiming to rely on it.

(2) Nothing in subsection (1) of this section shall affect any duty to participate in treatment which is necessary to save the life or to prevent grave permanent injury to the physical or mental health of a pregnant woman.

(3) In any proceedings before a court in Scotland, a statement on oath by any person to the effect that he has a conscientious objection to participating in any treatment authorised by this Act shall be sufficient evidence for the purpose of discharging the burden of proof imposed upon him by subsection (1) of this section.

5 Supplementary provisions

[(1) No offence under the Infant Life (Preservation) Act 1929 shall be committed by a registered medical practitioner who terminates a pregnancy in accordance with the provisions of this Act.]

(2) For the purposes of the law relating to abortion, anything done with intent to procure [a woman's miscarriage (or, in the case of a woman carrying more than one foetus, her miscarriage of any foetus) is unlawfully done unless authorised by section 1 of this Act and, in the case of a woman carrying more than one foetus, anything done with intent to procure her miscarriage of any foetus is authorised by that section if—

(a) the ground for termination of the pregnancy specified in subsection (1)(d) of that section applies in relation to any foetus and the thing is done for the purpose of procuring the miscarriage of that foetus, or

(b) any of the other grounds for termination of the pregnancy specified in that section applies].

Sub-s (1): substituted by the Human Fertilisation and Embryology Act 1990, s 37(4).
Sub-s (2): words in square brackets substituted by the Human Fertilisation and Embryology Act 1990, s 37(5).

6 Interpretation

In this Act, the following expressions have meanings hereby assigned to them:—
"the law relating to abortion" means sections 58 and 59 of the Offences against the Person Act 1861, and any rule of law relating to the procurement of abortion;
. . .

Definition omitted repealed by the Health Services Act 1980, s 25(4), Sch 7.

7 Short title, commencement and extent

(1)   This Act may be cited as the Abortion Act 1967.

(2)   This Act shall come into force on the expiration of the period of six months beginning with the date on which it is passed.

(3)   This Act does not extend to Northern Ireland.

Criminal Appeal Act 1968

1968 CHAPTER 19

An Act to consolidate certain enactments relating to appeals in criminal cases to the criminal division of the Court of Appeal, and thence to the House of Lords
[8th May 1968]

PART I
APPEAL TO COURT OF APPEAL IN CRIMINAL CASES

Appeal against conviction on indictment

[6 Substitution of finding of insanity or findings of unfitness to plead etc]

[(1)   This section applies where, on an appeal against conviction, the Court of Appeal, on the written or oral evidence of two or more registered medical practitioners at least one of whom is duly approved, are of opinion—
(a)   that the proper verdict would have been one of not guilty by reason of insanity; or

(b)   that the case is not one where there should have been a verdict of acquittal, but that there should have been findings that the accused was under a disability and that he did the act or made the omission charged against him.

(2)   Subject to subsection (3) below, the Court of Appeal shall either—
   (a)   make an order that the appellant be admitted, in accordance with the provisions of Schedule 1 to the Criminal Procedure (Insanity and Unfitness to Plead) Act 1991, to such hospital as may be specified by the Secretary of State; or
   (b)   where they have the power to do so by virtue of section 5 of that Act, make in respect of the appellant such one of the following orders as they think most suitable in all the circumstances of the case, namely—
      (i)   a guardianship order within the meaning of the Mental Health Act 1983;
      (ii)   a supervision and treatment order within the meaning of Schedule 2 to the said Act of 1991; and
      (iii) an order for his absolute discharge.

(3)   Paragraph (b) of subsection (2) above shall not apply where the offence to which the appeal relates is an offence the sentence for which is fixed by law.]

NOTES
Substituted by the Criminal Procedure (Insanity and Unfitness to Plead) Act 1991, s 4(1).

Appeal in cases of insanity

12 Appeal against verdict of not guilty by reason of insanity

A person in whose case there is returned a verdict of not guilty by reason of insanity may appeal to the Court of Appeal [against the verdict—
   (a)   with the leave of the Court of Appeal; or
   (b)   if the judge of the court of trial grants a certificate that the case if fit for appeal.]

NOTES
Words in square brackets substituted by the Criminal Appeal Act 1995, s 1(3).

[14 Substitution of findings of unfitness to plead etc]

[(1)   This section applies where, on an appeal under section 12 of this Act, the Court of Appeal, on the written or oral evidence of two or more registered medical practitioners at least one of whom is duly approved, are of opinion that—
   (a)   the case is not one where there should have been a verdict of acquittal; but
   (b)   there should have been findings that the accused was under a disability and that he did the act or made the omission charged against him.

(2)   Subject to subsection (3) below, the Court of Appeal shall either—
   (a)   make an order that the appellant be admitted, in accordance with the provisions of Schedule 1 to the Criminal Procedure (Insanity and Unfitness to Plead) Act 1991, to such hospital as may be specified by the Secretary of State; or

(b)   where they have the power to do so by virtue of section 5 of that Act, make in respect of the appellant such one of the following orders as they think most suitable in all the circumstances of the case, namely—

(i)   a guardianship order within the meaning of the Mental Health Act 1983;

(ii)   a supervision and treatment order within the meaning of Schedule 2 to the said Act of 1991; and

(iii)   an order for his absolute discharge.

(3)   Paragraph (b) of subsection (2) above shall not apply where the offence to which the appeal relates is an offence the sentence for which is fixed by law.]

NOTES

Substituted together with s 14A, for s 14 as originally enacted, by the Criminal Procedure (Insanity and Unfitness to Plead) Act 1991, s 4(2).

[14A Substitution of verdict of acquittal]

[(1)   This section applies where, in accordance with section 13(4)(b) of this Act, the Court of Appeal substitute a verdict of acquittal and the Court, on the written or oral evidence of two or more registered medical practitioners at least one of whom is duly approved, are of opinion—

(a)   that the appellant is suffering from mental disorder of a nature or degree which warrants his detention in a hospital for assessment (or for assessment followed by medical treatment) for at least a limited period; and

(b)   that he ought to be so detained in the interests of his own health or safety or with a view to the protection of other persons.

(2)   The Court of Appeal shall make an order that the appellant be admitted for assessment, in accordance with the provisions of Schedule 1 to the Criminal Procedure (Insanity and Unfitness to Plead) Act 1991, to such hospital as may be specified by the Secretary of State.]

NOTES

Substituted together with s 14, for s 14 as originally enacted, by the Criminal Procedure (Insanity and Unfitness to Plead) Act 1991, s 4.

PART III
MISCELLANEOUS AND GENERAL

55 Short title, commencement and extent

(1)   This Act may be cited as the Criminal Appeal Act 1968.

(2)   This Act shall come into force on the day appointed under section 106(5) of the Criminal Justice Act 1967 for the coming into force of section 98 of that Act.

(3)   So much of Schedule 5 to this Act as amends the Geneva Conventions Act 1957 shall extend to Scotland and Northern Ireland and the repeal by this Act of section 2(2) of the Administration of Justice Act 1960 shall extend to Northern Ireland; but except as aforesaid this Act shall not extend to Scotland or Northern Ireland.

Firearms Act 1968

1968 CHAPTER 27

An Act to consolidate the Firearms Acts 1937 and 1965, the Air Guns and Shot Guns, etc, Act 1962, Part V of the Criminal Justice Act 1967 and certain enactments amending the Firearms Act 1937

[30th May 1968]

PART I

PROVISIONS AS TO POSSESSION, HANDLING AND DISTRIBUTION OF WEAPONS AND AMMUNITION; PREVENTION OF CRIME AND MEASURES TO PROTECT PUBLIC SAFETY

General restrictions on possession and handling of firearms and ammunition

1 Requirement of firearm certificate

(1)   Subject to any exemption under this Act, it is an offence for a person—
  (a)   to have in his possession, or to purchase or acquire, a firearm to which this section applies without holding a firearm certificate in force at the time, or otherwise than as authorised by such a certificate;
  (b)   to have in his possession, or to purchase or acquire, any ammunition to which this section applies without holding a firearm certificate in force at the time, or otherwise than as authorised by such a certificate, or in quantities in excess of those so authorised.

(2)   It is an offence for a person to fail to comply with a condition subject to which a firearm certificate is held by him.

(3)   This section applies to every firearm except—
  [(a)   a shot gun within the meaning of this Act, that is to say a smooth-bore gun (not being an air gun) which—
    (i)   has a barrel not less than 24 inches in length and does not have any barrel with a bore exceeding 2 inches in diameter;
    (ii)   either has no magazine or has a non-detachable magazine incapable of holding more than two cartridges; and
    (iii)   is not a revolver gun; and,]
  (b)   an air weapon (that is to say, an air rifle, air gun or air pistol not of a type declared by rules made by the Secretary of State under section 53 of this Act to be specially dangerous).

[(3A)   A gun which has been adapted to have such a magazine as is mentioned in subsection (3)(a)(ii) above shall not be regarded as falling within that provision unless the magazine bears a mark approved by the Secretary of State for denoting that fact and that mark has been made, and the adaptation has been certified in writing as having been carried out in a manner approved by him, either by one of the two companies mentioned in section 58(1) of this Act or by such other person as may be approved by him for that purpose.]

(4)   This section applies to any ammunition for a firearm, except the following articles, namely:—

(a)   cartridges containing five or more shot, none of which exceeds .36 inch in diameter;

(b)   ammunition for an air gun, air rifle or air pistol; and

(c)   blank cartridges not more than one inch in diameter measured immediately in front of the rim or cannelure of the base of the cartridge.

NOTES

Sub-s (3): para (a) substituted by the Firearms (Amendment) Act 1988, s 2(2).
Sub-s (3A): inserted by the Firearms (Amendment) Act 1988, s 2(3).

2 Requirement of certificate for possession of shot guns

(1)   Subject to any exemption under this Act, it is an offence for a person to have in his possession, or to purchase or acquire, a shot gun without holding a certificate under this Act authorising him to possess shot guns.

(2)   It is an offence for a person to fail to comply with a condition subject to which a shot gun certificate is held by him.

3 Business and other transactions with firearms and ammunition

(1)   A person commits an offence if, by way of trade or business, he—

(a)   manufactures, sells, transfers, repairs, tests or proves any firearm or ammunition to which section 1 of this Act applies, or a shot gun; or

(b)   exposes for sale or transfer, or has in his possession for sale, transfer, repair, test or proof any such firearm or ammunition, or a shot gun,

without being registered under this Act as a firearms dealer.

(2)   It is an offence for a person to sell or transfer to any other person in the United Kingdom, other than a registered firearms dealer, any firearm or ammunition to which section 1 of this Act applies, or a shot gun, unless that other produces a firearm certificate authorising him to purchase or acquire it or, as the case may be, his shot gun certificate, or shows that he is by virtue of this Act entitled to purchase or acquire it without holding a certificate.

(3)   It is an offence for a person to undertake the repair, test or proof of a firearm or ammunition to which section 1 of this Act applies, or of a shot gun, for any other person in the United Kingdom other than a registered firearms dealer as such, unless that other produces or causes to be produced a firearm certificate authorising him to have possession of the firearm or ammunition or, as the case may be, his shot gun certificate, or shows that he is by virtue of this Act entitled to have possession of it without holding a certificate.

(4)   Subsections (1) to (3) above have effect subject to any exemption under subsequent provisions of this Part of this Act.

(5)   A person commits an offence if, with a view to purchasing or acquiring, or procuring the repair, test or proof of, any firearm or ammunition to which section 1 of this Act applies, or a shot gun, he produces a false certificate or a certificate in which any false entry has been made, or personates a person to whom a certificate has been granted, or [knowingly or recklessly makes a statement false in any material particular].

(6)   It is an offence for a pawnbroker to take in pawn any firearm or ammunition to which section 1 of this Act applies, or a shot gun.

NOTES

Sub-s (5): words in square brackets substituted by the Firearms (Amendment) Act 1997, s 52, Sch 2, para 2(1).

4 Conversion of weapons

(1)   Subject to this section, it is an offence to shorten the barrel of a shot gun to a length less than 24 inches.

(2)   It is not an offence under subsection (1) above for a registered firearms dealer to shorten the barrel of a shot gun for the sole purpose of replacing a defective part of the barrel so as to produce a barrel not less than 24 inches in length.

(3)   It is an offence for a person other than a registered firearms dealer to convert into a firearm anything which, though having the appearance of being a firearm, is so constructed as to be incapable of discharging any missile through its barrel.

(4)   A person who commits an offence under section 1 of this Act by having in his possession, or purchasing or acquiring, a shot gun which has been shortened contrary to subsection (1) above or a firearm which has been [converted as mentioned in subsection (3) above] (whether by a registered firearms dealer or not), without holding a firearm certificate authorising him to have it in his possession, or to purchase or acquire it, shall be treated for the purposes of provisions of this Act relating to the punishment of offences as committing that offence in an aggravated form.

NOTES

Sub-s (4): words in square brackets substituted by the Firearms (Amendment) Act 1988, s 23(1).

Prohibition of certain weapons and control of arms traffic

5 Weapons subject to general prohibition

(1)   A person commits an offence if, without the authority of [the Secretary of State] [or the Scottish Ministers (by virtue of provision made under section 63 of the Scotland Act 1998)], he has in his possession, or purchases or acquires, or manufactures, sells or transfers—

[(a)   any firearm which is so designed or adapted that two or more missiles can be successively discharged without repeated pressure on the trigger;

(ab) any self-loading or pump-action [rifled gun] other than one which is chambered for .22 rim-fire cartridges;

[(aba) any firearm which either has a barrel less than 30 centimetres in length or is less than 60 centimetres in length overall, other than an air weapon, . . ., a muzzle-loading gun or a firearm designed as signalling apparatus;]

(ac) any self-loading or pump-action smooth-bore gun which is not [an air weapon or] chambered for .22 rim-fire cartridges and either has a barrel less than 24 inches in length or . . . is less than 40 inches in length overall;

(ad) any smooth-bore revolver gun other than one which is chambered for 9mm rim-fire cartridges or [a muzzle-loading gun];

(ae) any rocket launcher, or any mortar, for projecting a stabilised missile, other than a launcher or mortar designed for line-throwing or pyrotechnic purposes or as signalling apparatus;]

(b) any weapon of whatever description designed or adapted for the discharge of any noxious liquid, gas or other thing; and

[(c) any cartridge with a bullet designed to explode on or immediately before impact, any ammunition containing or designed or adapted to contain any such noxious thing as is mentioned in paragraph (b) above and, if capable of being used with a firearm of any description, any grenade, bomb (or other like missile), or rocket or shell designed to explode as aforesaid].

[(1A) Subject to section 5A of this Act, a person commits an offence if, without the authority of the Secretary of State [or the Scottish Ministers (by virtue of provision made under section 63 of the Scotland Act 1998)], he has in his possession, or purchases or acquires or sells or transfers—

(a) any firearm which is disguised as another object;

(b) any rocket or ammunition not falling within paragraph (c) of subsection (1) of this section which consists in or incorporates a missile designed to explode on or immediately before impact and is for military use;

(c) any launcher or other projecting apparatus not falling within paragraph (ae) of that subsection which is designed to be used with any rocket or ammunition falling within paragraph (b) above or with ammunition which would fall within that paragraph but for its being ammunition falling within paragraph (c) of that subsection;

(d) any ammunition for military use which consists in or incorporates a missile designed so that a substance contained in the missile will ignite on or immediately before impact;

(e) any ammunition for military use which consists in or incorporates a missile designed, on account of its having a jacket and hard-core, to penetrate armour plating, armour screening or body armour;

[(f) any ammunition which incorporates a missile designed or adapted to expand on impact;]

(g) anything which is designed to be projected as a missile from any weapon and is designed to be, or has been, incorporated in—

(i) any ammunition falling within any of the preceding paragraphs; or

(ii) any ammunition which would fall within any of those paragraphs but for its being specified in subsection (1) of this section.]

(2)   The weapons and ammunition specified in [subsections (1) and (1A) of this section (including, in the case of ammunition, any missiles falling within subsection (1A)(g) of this section)] are referred to in this Act as "prohibited weapons" and "prohibited ammunition" respectively.

(3)   An authority given to a person by [the Secretary of State] [or the Scottish Ministers (by virtue of provision made under section 63 of the Scotland Act 1998)] under this section shall be in writing and be subject to conditions specified therein.

(4)   The conditions of the authority shall include such as [the Secretary of State] [or, where the authority is given by them (by virtue of provision made under section 63 of the Scotland Act 1998), the Scottish Ministers], having regard to the circumstances of each particular case, think fit to impose for the purpose of securing that the prohibited weapon or ammunition to which the authority relates will not endanger the public safety or the peace.

(5)   It is an offence for a person to whom an authority is given under this section to fail to comply with any condition of the authority.

(6)   [The Secretary of State] may at any time, if they think fit, revoke an authority given to a person under this section by notice in writing requiring him to deliver up the authority to such person as may be specified in the notice within twenty-one days from the date of the notice; and it is an offence for him to fail to comply with that requirement.

[(7)   For the purposes of this section and section 5A of this Act—
 (a) any rocket or ammunition which is designed to be capable of being used with a military weapon shall be taken to be for military use;
 (b) references to a missile designed so that a substance contained in the missile will ignite on or immediately before impact include references to any missile containing a substance that ignites on exposure to air; and
 (c) references to a missile's expanding on impact include references to its deforming in any predictable manner on or immediately after impact.]

[(8)   For the purposes of subsection (1)(aba) and (ac) above, any detachable, folding, retractable or other movable butt-stock shall be disregarded in measuring the length of any firearm.

(9)   Any reference in this section to a muzzle-loading gun is a reference to a gun which is designed to be loaded at the muzzle end of the barrel or chamber with a loose charge and a separate ball (or other missile).]

NOTES

Sub-s (1): words "the Secretary of State" in square brackets substituted by virtue of SI 1968/1200, arts 2, 3.

Sub-s (1): words "or the Scottish Ministers (by virtue of provision made under section 63 of the Scotland Act 1998)" in square brackets inserted by SI 1999/1750, art 6(1), Sch 5, para 3(1), (2)(a).

Date in force: 1 July 1999: see SI 1999/1750, art 1(1), and SI 1998/3178, art 3.

Sub-s (1): paras (a), (ab), (ac)–(ae) substituted, for para (a) as originally enacted, by the Firearms (Amendment) Act 1988, s 1(2).

Sub-s (1): in para (ab) words "rifled gun" in square brackets substituted by the Firearms (Amendment) Act 1997, s 1(3).

Sub-s (1): para (aba) inserted by the Firearms (Amendment) Act 1997, s 1(2).

Sub-s (1): in para (aba) words omitted repealed by the Firearms (Amendment) (No 2) Act 1997, ss 1, 2(7), Schedule.

Date in force: 1 February 1998 (with effect from 1 March 1998 in the case of certain certificate or permit holders and registered firearms dealers): see SI 1997/3114, arts 4, 5, Schedule, Pt II.

Sub-s (1): in para (ac) words "an air weapon or" in square brackets inserted by the Firearms (Amendment) Act 1997, s 1(4).

Sub-s (1): in para (ac) words omitted repealed by the Firearms (Amendment) Act 1997, s 52, Sch 3.

Sub-s (1): in para (ad) words "a muzzle-loading gun" in square brackets substituted by the Firearms (Amendment) Act 1997, s 1(5).

Sub-s (1): para (c) substituted by the Firearms (Amendment) Act 1988, s 1(3).

Sub-s (1A): inserted by SI 1992/2823, reg 3(1).

Sub-s (1A): words "or the Scottish Ministers (by virtue of provision made under section 63 of the Scotland Act 1998)" in square brackets inserted by SI 1999/1750, art 6(1), Sch 5, para 3(1), (2)(b).

Date in force: 1 July 1999: see SI 1999/1750, art 1(1), and SI 1998/3178, art 3.

Sub-s (1A): para (f) substituted by the Firearms (Amendment) Act 1997, s 9.

Sub-s (2): words from "subsections (1) and (1A) of this" to "subsection (1A)(g) of this section)" in square brackets substituted by SI 1992/2823, reg 3(2).

Sub-s (3): words "the Secretary of State" in square brackets substituted by virtue of SI 1968/1200, arts 2, 3.

Sub-s (3): words "or the Scottish Ministers (by virtue of provision made under section 63 of the Scotland Act 1998)" in square brackets inserted by SI 1999/1750, art 6(1), Sch 5, para 3(1), (2)(c).

Date in force: 1 July 1999: see SI 1999/1750, art 1(1), and SI 1998/3178, art 3.

Sub-s (4): words "the Secretary of State" in square brackets substituted by virtue of SI 1968/1200, arts 2, 3.

Sub-s (4): words "or, where the authority is given by them (by virtue of provision made under section 63 of the Scotland Act 1998), the Scottish Ministers" in square brackets inserted by SI 1999/1750, art 6(1), Sch 5, para 3(1), (2)(d).

Date in force: 1 July 1999: see SI 1999/1750, art 1(1), and SI 1998/3178, art 3.

Sub-s (6): words "The Secretary of State" in square brackets substituted by virtue of SI 1968/1200, arts 2, 3.

Sub-s (7): inserted by SI 1992/2823, reg 3(3).

Sub-ss (8), (9): inserted by the Firearms (Amendment) Act 1997, s 1(6).

Prevention of crime and preservation of public safety

16 Possession of firearm with intent to injure

It is an offence for a person to have in his possession any firearm or ammunition with intent by means thereof to endanger life . . . or to enable another person by means thereof to endanger life . . . whether any injury . . . has been caused or not.

NOTES

Words omitted repealed by the Criminal Damage Act 1971, s 11(8), Schedule, Part I.

[16A Possession of firearm with intent to cause fear of violence]

[It is an offence for a person to have in his possession any firearm or imitation firearm with intent—
(a)   by means thereof to cause, or
(b)   to enable another person by means thereof to cause,

any person to believe that unlawful violence will be used against him or another person.]

NOTES

Inserted by the Firearms (Amendment) Act 1994, s 1(1).

17 Use of firearm to resist arrest

(1)   It is an offence for a person to make or attempt to make any use whatsoever of a firearm or imitation firearm with intent to resist or prevent the lawful arrest or detention of himself or another person.

(2)   If a person, at the time of his committing or being arrested for an offence specified in Schedule 1 to this Act, has in his possession a firearm or imitation firearm, he shall be guilty of an offence under this subsection unless he shows that he had it in his possession for a lawful object.

(3)   . . .

(4)   For purposes of this section, the definition of "firearm" in section 57(1) of this Act shall apply without paragraphs (b) and (c) of that subsection, and "imitation firearm" shall be construed accordingly.

(5)   In the application of this section to Scotland, a reference to Schedule 2 to this Act shall be substituted for the reference in subsection (2) to Schedule 1 . . . .

NOTES

Sub-s (3): repealed by the Theft Act 1968, s 33(3), Sch 3, Part III.
Sub-s (5): words omitted repealed by the Theft Act 1968, s 33(3), Sch 3, Pt III.

18 Carrying firearm with criminal intent

(1)   It is an offence for a person to have with him a firearm or imitation firearm with intent to commit an indictable offence, or to resist arrest or prevent the arrest of another, in either case while he has the firearm or imitation firearm with him.

(2)   In proceedings for an offence under this section proof that the accused had a firearm or imitation firearm with him and intended to commit an offence, or to resist or prevent arrest, is evidence that he intended to have it with him while doing so.

(3)   In the application of this section to Scotland, for the reference to an indictable offence there shall be substituted a reference to any offence specified in paragraphs 1 to 18 of Schedule 2 to this Act.

19 Carrying a firearm in a public place

A person commits an offence if, without lawful authority or reasonable excuse (the proof whereof lies on him) he has with him in a public place a loaded shot gun or loaded air weapon, or any other firearm (whether loaded or not) together with ammunition suitable for use in that firearm.

PART IV
MISCELLANEOUS AND GENERAL

60 Short title, commencement and extent

(1)   This Act may be cited as the Firearms Act 1968.

(2)   This Act shall come into force on 1st August 1968.

(3)   This Act shall not extend to Northern Ireland.

Theft Act 1968

1968 CHAPTER 60

An Act to revise the law of England and Wales as to theft and similar or associated offences, and in connection therewith to make provision as to criminal proceedings by one party to a marriage against the other, and to make certain amendments extending beyond England and Wales in the Post Office Act 1953 and other enactments; and for other purposes connected therewith
[26th July 1968]

Definition of "Theft"

1 Basic definition of theft

(1)   A person is guilty of theft if he dishonestly appropriates property belonging to another with the intention of permanently depriving the other of it; and "thief" and "steal" shall be construed accordingly.

(2)   It is immaterial whether the appropriation is made with a view to gain, or is made for the thief's own benefit.

(3)   The five following sections of this Act shall have effect as regards the interpretation and operation of this section (and, except as otherwise provided by this Act, shall apply only for purposes of this section).

2 "Dishonestly"

(1)   A person's appropriation of property belonging to another is not to be regarded as dishonest—

(a) if he appropriates the property in the belief that he has in law the right to deprive the other of it, on behalf of himself or of a third person; or

(b) if he appropriates the property in the belief that he would have the other's consent if the other knew of the appropriation and the circumstances of it; or

(c) (except where the property came to him as trustee or personal representative) if he appropriates the property in the belief that the person to whom the property belongs cannot be discovered by taking reasonable steps.

(2) A person's appropriation of property belonging to another may be dishonest notwithstanding that he is willing to pay for the property.

3 "Appropriates"

(1) Any assumption by a person of the rights of an owner amounts to an appropriation, and this includes, where he has come by the property (innocently or not) without stealing it, any later assumption of a right to it by keeping or dealing with it as owner.

(2) Where property or a right or interest in property is or purports to be transferred for value to a person acting in good faith, no later assumption by him of rights which he believed himself to be acquiring shall, by reason of any defect in the transferor's title, amount to theft of the property.

4 "Property"

(1) "Property" includes money and all other property, real or personal, including things in action and other intangible property.

(2) A person cannot steal land, or things forming part of land and severed from it by him or by his directions, except in the following cases, that is to say—

(a) when he is a trustee or personal representative, or is authorised by power of attorney, or as liquidator of a company, or otherwise, to sell or dispose of land belonging to another, and he appropriates the land or anything forming part of it by dealing with it in breach of the confidence reposed in him; or

(b) when he is not in possession of the land and appropriates anything forming part of the land by severing it or causing it to be severed, or after it has been severed; or

(c) when, being in possession of the land under a tenancy, he appropriates the whole or part of any fixture or structure let to be used with the land.

For purposes of this subsection "land" does not include incorporeal hereditaments; "tenancy" means a tenancy for years or any less period and includes an agreement for such a tenancy, but a person who after the end of a tenancy remains in possession as statutory tenant or otherwise is to be treated as having possession under the tenancy, and "let" shall be construed accordingly.

(3) A person who picks mushrooms growing wild on any land, or who picks flowers, fruit or foliage from a plant wild on any land, does not (although not in possession of the land) steal what he picks, unless he does it for reward or for sale or other commercial purpose.

For purposes of this subsection "mushroom" includes any fungus, and "plant" includes any shrub or tree.

(4)   Wild creatures, tamed or untamed, shall be regarded as property; but a person cannot steal a wild creature not tamed nor ordinarily kept in captivity, or the carcase of any such creature, unless either it has been reduced into possession by or on behalf of another person and possession of it has not since been lost or abandoned, or another person is in course of reducing it into possession.

5 "Belonging to another"

(1)   Property shall be regarded as belonging to any person having possession or control of it, or having in it any proprietary right or interest (not being an equitable interest arising only from an agreement to transfer or grant an interest).

(2)   Where property is subject to a trust, the persons to whom it belongs shall be regarded as including any person having a right to enforce the trust, and an intention to defeat the trust shall be regarded accordingly as an intention to deprive of the property any person having that right.

(3)   Where a person receives property from or on account of another, and is under an obligation to the other to retain and deal with that property or its proceeds in a particular way, the property or proceeds shall be regarded (as against him) as belonging to the other.

(4)   Where a person gets property by another's mistake, and is under an obligation to make restoration (in whole or in part) of the property or its proceeds or of the value thereof, then to the extent of that obligation the property or proceeds shall be regarded (as against him) as belonging to the person entitled to restoration, and an intention not to make restoration shall be regarded accordingly as an intention to deprive that person of the property or proceeds.

(5)   Property of a corporation sole shall be regarded as belonging to the corporation notwithstanding a vacancy in the corporation.

6 "With the intention of permanently depriving the other of it"

(1)   A person appropriating property belonging to another without meaning the other permanently to lose the thing itself is nevertheless to be regarded as having the intention of permanently depriving the other of it if his intention is to treat the thing as his own to dispose of regardless of the other's rights; and a borrowing or lending of it may amount to so treating it if, but only if, the borrowing or lending is for a period and in circumstances making it equivalent to an outright taking or disposal.

(2)   Without prejudice to the generality of subsection (1) above, where a person, having possession or control (lawfully or not) of property belonging to another, parts with the property under a condition as to its return which he may not be able to perform, this (if done for purposes of his own and without the other's authority) amounts to treating the property as his own to dispose of regardless of the other's rights.

Theft, Robbery, Burglary, etc

7 Theft

A person guilty of theft shall on conviction on indictment be liable to imprisonment for a term not exceeding [seven years].

NOTES

Words in square brackets substituted by the Criminal Justice Act 1991, s 26(1).

8 Robbery

(1)   A person is guilty of robbery if he steals, and immediately before or at the time of doing so, and in order to do so, he uses force on any person or puts or seeks to put any person in fear of being then and there subjected to force.

(2)   A person guilty of robbery, or of an assault with intent to rob, shall on conviction on indictment be liable to imprisonment for life.

9 Burglary

(1)   A person is guilty of burglary if—
   (a)   he enters any building or part of a building as a trespasser and with intent to commit any such offence as is mentioned in subsection (2) below; or
   (b)   having entered any building or part of a building as a trespasser he steals or attempts to steal anything in the building or that part of it or inflicts or attempts to inflict on any person therein any grievous bodily harm.

(2)   The offences referred to in subsection (1)(a) above are offences of stealing anything in the building or part of a building in question, of inflicting on any person therein any grievous bodily harm or [raping any person] therein, and of doing unlawful damage to the building or anything therein.

[(3)   A person guilty of burglary shall on conviction on indictment be liable to imprisonment for a term not exceeding—
   (a)   where the offence was committed in respect of a building or part of a building which is a dwelling, fourteen years;
   (b)   in any other case, ten years.

(4)   References in subsections (1) and (2) above to a building, and the reference in subsection (3) above to a building which is a dwelling, shall apply also to an inhabited vehicle or vessel, and shall apply to any such vehicle or vessel at times when the person having a habitation in it is not there as well as at times when he is.]

NOTES

Sub-s (2): words in square brackets substituted by the Criminal Justice and Public Order Act 1994, s 168(2), Sch 10, para 26.
Sub-ss (3), (4): substituted by the Criminal Justice Act 1991, s 26(2).

10 Aggravated burglary

(1)   A person is guilty of aggravated burglary if he commits any burglary and at the time has with him any firearm or imitation firearm, any weapon of offence, or any explosive; and for this purpose—
- (a)   "firearm" includes an airgun or air pistol, and "imitation firearm" means anything which has the appearance of being a firearm, whether capable of being discharged or not; and
- (b)   "weapon of offence" means any article made or adapted for use for causing injury to or incapacitating a person, or intended by the person having it with him for such use; and
- (c)   "explosive" means any article manufactured for the purpose of producing a practical effect by explosion, or intended by the person having it with him for that purpose.

(2)   A person guilty of aggravated burglary shall on conviction on indictment be liable to imprisonment for life.

11 Removal of articles from places open to the public

(1)   Subject to subsections (2) and (3) below, where the public have access to a building in order to view the building or part of it, or a collection or part of a collection housed in it, any person who without lawful authority removes from the building or its grounds the whole or part of any article displayed or kept for display to the public in the building or that part of it or in its grounds shall be guilty of an offence.

For this purpose "collection" includes a collection got together for a temporary purpose, but references in this section to a collection do not apply to a collection made or exhibited for the purpose of effecting sales or other commercial dealings.

(2)   It is immaterial for purposes of subsection (1) above, that the public's access to a building is limited to a particular period or particular occasion; but where anything removed from a building or its grounds is there otherwise than as forming part of, or being on loan for exhibition with, a collection intended for permanent exhibition to the public, the person removing it does not thereby commit an offence under this section unless he removes it on a day when the public have access to the building as mentioned in subsection (1) above.

(3)   A person does not commit an offence under this section if he believes that he has lawful authority for the removal of the thing in question or that he would have it if the person entitled to give it knew of the removal and the circumstances of it.

(4)   A person guilty of an offence under this section shall, on conviction on indictment, be liable to imprisonment for a term not exceeding five years.

12 Taking motor vehicle or other conveyance without authority

(1)   Subject to subsections (5) and (6) below, a person shall be guilty of an offence if, without having the consent of the owner or other lawful authority, he takes any conveyance for his own or another's use or, knowing that any conveyance has been taken without such authority, drives it or allows himself to be carried in or on it.

(2)   A person guilty of an offence under subsection (1) above shall . . . [be liable on summary conviction to a fine not exceeding level 5 on the standard scale, to imprisonment for a term not exceeding six months, or to both.]

(3)   . . .

(4)   If on the trial of an indictment for theft the jury are not satisfied that the accused committed theft, but it is proved that the accused committed an offence under subsection (1) above, the jury may find him guilty of the offence under subsection (1) [and if he is found guilty of it, he shall be liable as he would have been liable under subsection (2) above on summary conviction].

[(4A)   Proceedings for an offence under subsection (1) above (but not proceedings of a kind falling within subsection (4) above) in relation to a mechanically propelled vehicle—
  (a)   shall not be commenced after the end of the period of three years beginning with the day on which the offence was committed; but
  (b)   subject to that, may be commenced at any time within the period of six months beginning with the relevant day.

(4B)   In subsection (4A)(b) above "the relevant day" means—
  (a)   in the case of a prosecution for an offence under subsection (1) above by a public prosecutor, the day on which sufficient evidence to justify the proceedings came to the knowledge of any person responsible for deciding whether to commence any such prosecution;
  (b)   in the case of a prosecution for an offence under subsection (1) above which is commenced by a person other than a public prosecutor after the discontinuance of a prosecution falling within paragraph (a) above which relates to the same facts, the day on which sufficient evidence to justify the proceedings came to the knowledge of the person who has decided to commence the prosecution or (if later) the discontinuance of the other prosecution;
  (c)   in the case of any other prosecution for an offence under subsection (1) above, the day on which sufficient evidence to justify the proceedings came to the knowledge of the person who has decided to commence the prosecution.

(4C)   For the purposes of subsection (4A)(b) above a certificate of a person responsible for deciding whether to commence a prosecution of a kind mentioned in subsection (4B)(a) above as to the date on which such evidence as is mentioned in the certificate came to the knowledge of any person responsible for deciding whether to commence any such prosecution shall be conclusive evidence of that fact.]

(5)   Subsection (1) above shall not apply in relation to pedal cycles; but, subject to subsection (6) below, a person who, without having the consent of the owner or other lawful authority, takes a pedal cycle for his own or another's use, or rides a pedal cycle knowing it to have been taken without such authority, shall on summary conviction be liable to a fine not exceeding [level 3 on the standard scale].

(6)   A person does not commit an offence under this section by anything done in the belief that he has lawful authority to do it or that he would have the owner's consent if the owner knew of his doing it and the circumstances of it.

(7)   For purposes of this section—

    (a)   "conveyance" means any conveyance constructed or adapted for the carriage of a person or persons whether by land, water or air, except that it does not include a conveyance constructed or adapted for use only under the control of a person not carried in or on it, and "drive" shall be construed accordingly; and

    (b)   "owner", in relation to a conveyance which is the subject of a hiring agreement or hire-purchase agreement, means the person in possession of the conveyance under that agreement.

NOTES

Sub-s (2): words omitted repealed by the Criminal Justice Act 1988, s 37(1).

Sub-s (2): words from "be liable on summary conviction" to "or to both" in square brackets substituted by the Criminal Justice Act 1988, s 37(1).

Sub-s (3): repealed by the Police and Criminal Evidence Act 1984, s 119, Sch 7, Part I.

Sub-s (4): words from "and if he is found guilty" to "on summary conviction" in square brackets inserted by the Criminal Justice Act 1988, s 37(1).

Sub-ss (4A)–(4C): inserted by the Vehicles (Crime) Act 2001, s 37(1).

Date in force: 1 October 2001 (in relation to offences committed on or after that date): see the Vehicles (Crime) Act 2001, s 37(2), and SI 2001/3215, art 2.

Sub-s (5): maximum fine increased and converted to a level on the standard scale by the Criminal Justice Act 1982, ss 37, 38, 46.

[12A Aggravated vehicle-taking]

[(1)   Subject to subsection (3) below, a person is guilty of aggravated taking of a vehicle if—

    (a)   he commits an offence under section 12(1) above (in this section referred to as a "basic offence") in relation to a mechanically propelled vehicle; and

    (b)   it is proved that, at any time after the vehicle was unlawfully taken (whether by him or another) and before it was recovered, the vehicle was driven, or injury or damage was caused, in one or more of the circumstances set out in paragraphs (a) to (d) of subsection (2) below.

(2)   The circumstances referred to in subsection (1)(b) above are—

    (a)   that the vehicle was driven dangerously on a road or other public place;

    (b)   that, owing to the driving of the vehicle, an accident occurred by which injury was caused to any person;

    (c)   that, owing to the driving of the vehicle, an accident occurred by which damage was caused to any property, other than the vehicle;

    (d)   that damage was caused to the vehicle.

(3)   A person is not guilty of an offence under this section if he proves that, as regards any such proven driving, injury or damage as is referred to in subsection (1)(b) above, either—

    (a)   the driving, accident or damage referred to in subsection (2) above occurred before he committed the basic offence; or

    (b)   he was neither in nor on nor in the immediate vicinity of the vehicle when that driving, accident or damage occurred.

(4)   A person guilty of an offence under this section shall be liable on conviction on indictment to imprisonment for a term not exceeding two years or, if it is proved that, in circumstances falling within subsection (2)(b) above, the accident caused the death of the person concerned, five years.

(5)   If a person who is charged with an offence under this section is found not guilty of that offence but it is proved that he committed a basic offence, he may be convicted of the basic offence.

(6)   If by virtue of subsection (5) above a person is convicted of a basic offence before the Crown Court, that court shall have the same powers and duties as a magistrates' court would have had on convicting him of such an offence.

(7)   For the purposes of this section a vehicle is driven dangerously if—
  (a)   it is driven in a way which falls far below what would be expected of a competent and careful driver; and
  (b)   it would be obvious to a competent and careful driver that driving the vehicle in that way would be dangerous.

(8)   For the purposes of this section a vehicle is recovered when it is restored to its owner or to other lawful possession or custody; and in this subsection "owner" has the same meaning as in section 12 above.]

NOTES
Inserted by the Aggravated Vehicle-Taking Act 1992, s 1(1).

13 Abstracting of electricity

A person who dishonestly uses without due authority, or dishonestly causes to be wasted or diverted, any electricity shall on conviction on indictment be liable to imprisonment for a term not exceeding five years.

Fraud and Blackmail

15 Obtaining property by deception

(1)   A person who by any deception dishonestly obtains property belonging to another, with the intention of permanently depriving the other of it, shall on conviction on indictment be liable to imprisonment for a term not exceeding ten years.

(2)   For purposes of this section a person is to be treated as obtaining property if he obtains ownership, possession or control of it, and "obtain" includes obtaining for another or enabling another to obtain or to retain.

(3)   Section 6 above shall apply for purposes of this section, with the necessary adaptation of the reference to appropriating, as it applies for purposes of section 1.

(4)   For purposes of this section "deception" means any deception (whether deliberate or reckless) by words or conduct as to fact or as to law, including a deception as to the present intentions of the person using the deception or any other person.

[15A Obtaining a money transfer by deception]

[(1)   A person is guilty of an offence if by any deception he dishonestly obtains a money transfer for himself or another.

(2)   A money transfer occurs when—
   (a)   a debit is made to one account,
   (b)   a credit is made to another, and
   (c)   the credit results from the debit or the debit results from the credit.

(3)   References to a credit and to a debit are to a credit of an amount of money and to a debit of an amount of money.

(4)   It is immaterial (in particular)—
   (a)   whether the amount credited is the same as the amount debited;
   (b)   whether the money transfer is effected on presentment of a cheque or by another method;
   (c)   whether any delay occurs in the process by which the money transfer is effected;
   (d)   whether any intermediate credits or debits are made in the course of the money transfer;
   (e)   whether either of the accounts is overdrawn before or after the money transfer is effected.

(5)   A person guilty of an offence under this section shall be liable on conviction on indictment to imprisonment for a term not exceeding ten years.]

NOTES
Inserted by the Theft (Amendment) Act 1996, s 1(1).

[15B Section 15A: supplementary]

[(1)   The following provisions have effect for the interpretation of section 15A of this Act.

(2)   "Deception" has the same meaning as in section 15 of this Act.

(3)   "Account" means an account kept with—
   (a)   a bank; or
   (b)   a person carrying on a business which falls within subsection (4) below.

(4)   A business falls within this subsection if—
   (a)   in the course of the business money received by way of deposit is lent to others; or
   (b)   any other activity of the business is financed, wholly or to any material extent, out of the capital of or the interest on money received by way of deposit;

. . ..

[(4A)   References in subsection (4) to a deposit must be read with—
   (a)   section 22 of the Financial Services and Markets Act 2000;
   (b)   any relevant order under that section; and
   (c)   Schedule 2 to that Act,

but any restriction on the meaning of deposit which arises from the identity of the person making it is to be disregarded.]

(5)   For the purposes of subsection (4) above—
   (a)   all the activities which a person carries on by way of business shall be regarded as a single business carried on by him; and
   (b)   "money" includes money expressed in a currency other than sterling or in the European currency unit (as defined in Council Regulation No 3320/ 94/EC or any Community instrument replacing it).]

NOTES

Inserted by the Theft (Amendment) Act 1996, s 1(1).
Sub-s (4): words omitted repealed by SI 2001/3649, art 278(1), (2).
Date in force: 1 December 2001: see SI 2001/3649, art 1.
Sub-s (4A): inserted by SI 2001/3649, art 278(1), (3).
Date in force: 1 December 2001: see SI 2001/3649, art 1.

16 Obtaining pecuniary advantage by deception

(1)   A person who by any deception dishonestly obtains for himself or another any pecuniary advantage shall on conviction on indictment be liable to imprisonment for a term not exceeding five years.

(2)   The cases in which a pecuniary advantage within the meaning of this section is to be regarded as obtained for a person are cases where—
   (a)   . . .
   (b)   he is allowed to borrow by way of overdraft, or to take out any policy of insurance or annuity contract, or obtains an improvement of the terms on which he is allowed to do so; or
   (c)   he is given the opportunity to earn remuneration or greater remuneration in an office or employment, or to win money by betting.

(3)   For purposes of this section "deception" has the same meaning as in section 15 of this Act.

NOTES

Sub-s (2): words omitted repealed by the Theft Act 1978, s 5(5).

17 False accounting

(1)   Where a person dishonestly, with a view to gain for himself or another or with intent to cause loss to another,—
   (a)   destroys, defaces, conceals or falsifies any account or any record or document made or required for any accounting purpose; or
   (b)   in furnishing information for any purpose produces or makes use of any account, or any such record or document as aforesaid, which to his knowledge is or may be misleading, false or deceptive in a material particular;

he shall, on conviction on indictment, be liable to imprisonment for a term not exceeding seven years.

(2)   For purposes of this section a person who makes or concurs in making in an account or other document an entry which is or may be misleading, false or deceptive in a material particular, or who omits or concurs in omitting a material particular from an account or other document, is to be treated as falsifying the account or document.

21 Blackmail

(1)   A person is guilty of blackmail if, with a view to gain for himself or another or with intent to cause loss to another, he makes any unwarranted demand with menaces; and for this purpose a demand with menaces is unwarranted unless the person making it does so in the belief—
  (a)   that he has reasonable grounds for making the demand; and
  (b)   that the use of the menaces is a proper means of reinforcing the demand.

(2)   The nature of the act or omission demanded is immaterial, and it is also immaterial whether the menaces relate to action to be taken by the person making the demand.

(3)   A person guilty of blackmail shall on conviction on indictment be liable to imprisonment for a term not exceeding fourteen years.

Offences relating to goods stolen etc

22 Handling stolen goods

(1)   A person handles stolen goods if (otherwise than in the course of the stealing) knowing or believing them to be stolen goods he dishonestly receives the goods, or dishonestly undertakes or assists in their retention, removal, disposal or realisation by or for the benefit of another person, or if he arranges to do so.

(2)   A person guilty of handling stolen goods shall on conviction on indictment be liable to imprisonment for a term not exceeding fourteen years.

24 Scope of offences relating to stolen goods

(1)   The provisions of this Act relating to goods which have been stolen shall apply whether the stealing occurred in England or Wales or elsewhere, and whether it occurred before or after the commencement of this Act, provided that the stealing (if not an offence under this Act) amounted to an offence where and at the time when the foods were stolen; and references to stolen goods shall be construed accordingly.

(2)   For purposes of those provisions references to stolen goods shall include, in addition to the goods originally stolen and parts of them (whether in their original state or not),—
  (a)   any other goods which directly or indirectly represent or have at any time represented the stolen goods in the hands of the thief as being the proceeds of any disposal or realisation of the whole or part of the goods stolen or of goods so representing the stolen goods; and
  (b)   any other goods which directly or indirectly represent or have at any time represented the stolen goods in the hands of a handler of the stolen goods or

any part of them as being the proceeds of any disposal or realisation of the whole or part of the stolen goods handled by him or of goods so representing them.

(3)   But no goods shall be regarded as having continued to be stolen goods after they have been restored to the person from whom they were stolen or to other lawful possession or custody, or after that person and any other person claiming through him have otherwise ceased as regards those goods to have any right to restitution in respect of the theft.

(4)   For purposes of the provisions of this Act relating to goods which have been stolen (including subsections (1) to (3) above) goods obtained in England or Wales or elsewhere either by blackmail or in the circumstances described in section 15(1) of this Act shall be regarded as stolen; and "steal", "theft" and "thief" shall be construed accordingly.

Possession of house breaking implements, etc

25 Going equipped for stealing, etc

(1)   A person shall be guilty of an offence if, when not at his place of abode, he has with him any article for use in the course of or in connection with any burglary, theft or cheat.

(2)   A person guilty of an offence under this section shall on conviction on indictment be liable to imprisonment for a term not exceeding three years.

(3)   Where a person is charged with an offence under this section, proof that he had with him any article made or adapted for use in committing a burglary, theft or cheat shall be evidence that he had it with him for such use.

(4)   Any person may arrest without warrant anyone who is, or whom he, with reasonable cause, suspects to be, committing an offence under this section.

(5)   For purposes of this section an offence under section 12(1) of this Act of taking a conveyance shall be treated as theft, and "cheat" means an offence under section 15 of this Act.

Supplementary

35 Commencement and transitional provisions

(1)   This Act shall come into force on the 1st January 1969 and, save as otherwise provided by this Act, shall have effect only in relation to offences wholly or partly committed on or after that date.

(2)   [Section 27 of this Act and section 148 of the Powers of Criminal Courts (Sentencing) Act 2000] shall apply in relation to proceedings for an offence committed before the commencement of this Act as they would apply in relation to proceedings for a corresponding offence under this Act, and shall so apply in place of any corresponding enactment repealed by this Act.

(3)   Subject to subsection (2) above, no repeal or amendment by this Act of any enactment relating to procedure or evidence, or to the jurisdiction or powers of any court, or to the effect of a conviction, shall affect the operation of the enactment in relation to offences committed before the commencement of this Act or to proceedings for any such offence.

NOTES

Sub-s (2): words "Section 27 of this Act and section 148 of the Powers of Criminal Courts (Sentencing) Act 2000" in square brackets substituted by the Powers of Criminal Courts (Sentencing) Act 2000, s 165(1), Sch 9, para 35.

Date in force: 25 August 2000: see the Powers of Criminal Courts (Sentencing) Act 2000, s 168(1).

36 Short title, and general provisions as to Scotland and Northern Ireland

(1)   This Act may be cited as the Theft Act 1968.

(2)   . . .

(3)   This Act does not extend to Scotland or, . . . to Northern Ireland, except as regards any amendment or repeal which in accordance with section 33 above is to extend to Scotland or Northern Ireland.

NOTES

Sub-ss (2), (3): words omitted repealed by the Northern Ireland Constitution Act 1973, s 41(1), Sch 6, Part I.

Misuse of Drugs Act 1971

1971 CHAPTER 38

An Act to make new provision with respect to dangerous or otherwise harmful drugs and related matters, and for purposes therewith

[27th May 1971]

Controlled drugs and their classification

2 Controlled drugs and their classification for purposes of this Act

(1)   In this Act—
  (a)   the expression "controlled drug" means any substance or product for the time being specified in Part I, II, or III of Schedule 2 to this Act; and
  (b)   the expressions "Class A drug", "Class B drug" and "Class C drug" mean any of the substances and products for the time being specified respectively in Part I, Part II and Part III of that Schedule;

and the provisions of Part IV of that Schedule shall have effect with respect to the meanings of expressions used in that Schedule.

(2)   Her Majesty may by Order in Council make such amendments in Schedule 2 to this Act as may be requisite for the purpose of adding any substance or product to, or removing any substance or product from, any of Parts I to III of that Schedule, including amendments for securing that no substance or product is for the time being specified in a particular one of those Parts or for inserting any substance or product into any of those Parts in which no substance or product is for the time being specified.

(3)   An Order in Council under this section may amend Part IV of Schedule 2 to this Act, and may do so whether or not it amends any other Part of that Schedule.

(4)   An Order in Council under this section may be varied or revoked by a subsequent Order in Council thereunder.

(5)   No recommendation shall be made to Her Majesty in Council to make an Order under this section unless a draft of the Order has been laid before Parliament and approved by a resolution of each House of Parliament; and the Secretary of State shall not lay a draft of such an Order before Parliament except after consultation with or on the recommendation of the Advisory Council.

Restrictions relating to controlled drugs etc

3 Restriction of importation and exportation of controlled drugs

(1)   Subject to subsection (2) below—
  (a)   the importation of a controlled drug; and
  (b)   the exportation of a controlled drug,

are hereby prohibited.

(2)   Subsection (1) above does not apply—
  (a)   to the importation or exportation of a controlled drug which is for the time being excepted from paragraph (a) or, as the case may be, paragraph (b) of subsection (1) above by regulations under section 7 of this Act; or
  (b)   to the importation or exportation of a controlled drug under and in accordance with the terms of a licence issued by the Secretary of State and in compliance with any conditions attached thereto.

4 Restriction of production and supply of controlled drugs

(1)   Subject to any regulations under section 7 of this Act for the time being in force, it shall not be lawful for a person—
  (a)   to produce a controlled drug; or
  (b)   to supply or offer to supply a controlled drug to another.

(2)   Subject to section 28 of this Act, it is an offence for a person—
  (a)   to produce a controlled drug in contravention of subsection (1) above; or
  (b)   to be concerned in the production of such a drug in contravention of that subsection by another.

(3)   Subject to section 28 of this Act, it is an offence for a person—

(a) to supply or offer to supply a controlled drug to another in contravention of subsection (1) above; or

(b) to be concerned in the supplying of such a drug to another in contravention of that subsection; or

(c) to be concerned in the making to another in contravention of that subsection of an offer to supply such a drug.

5 Restriction of possession of controlled drugs

(1) Subject to any regulations under section 7 of this Act for the time being in force, it shall not be lawful for a person to have a controlled drug in his possession.

(2) Subject to section 28 of this Act and to subsection (4) below, it is an offence for a person to have a controlled drug in his possession in contravention of subsection (1) above.

(3) Subject to section 28 of this Act, it is an offence for a person to have a controlled drug in his possession, whether lawfully or not, with intent to supply it to another in contravention of section 4(1) of this Act.

(4) In any proceedings for an offence under subsection (2) above in which it is proved that the accused had a controlled drug in his possession, it shall be a defence for him to prove—

(a) that, knowing or suspecting it to be a controlled drug, he took possession of it for the purpose of preventing another from committing or continuing to commit an offence in connection with that drug and that as soon as possible after taking possession of it he took all such steps as were reasonably open to him to destroy the drug or to deliver it into the custody of a person lawfully entitled to take custody of it; or

(b) that, knowing or suspecting it to be a controlled drug, he took possession of it for the purpose of delivering it into the custody of a person lawfully entitled to take custody of it and that as soon as possible after taking possession of it he took all such steps as were reasonably open to him to deliver it into the custody of such a person.

(5) . . .

(6) Nothing in subsection (4) . . . above shall prejudice any defence which it is open to a person charged with an offence under this section to raise apart from that subsection.

NOTES

Sub-ss (5), (6): words omitted repealed by the Criminal Attempts Act 1981, s 10, Schedule, Part I.

6 Restrictions of cultivation of cannabis plant

(1) Subject to any regulations under section 7 of this Act for the time being in force, it shall not be lawful for a person to cultivate any plant of the genus *Cannabis.*

(2)   Subject to section 28 of this Act, it is an offence to cultivate any such plant in contravention of subsection (1) above.

Miscellaneous offences involving controlled drugs etc

8 Occupiers etc of premises to be punishable for permitting certain activities to take place there

A person commits an offence if, being the occupier or concerned in the management of any premises, he knowingly permits or suffers any of the following activities to take place on those premises, that is to say—

(a)   producing or attempting to produce a controlled drug in contravention of section 4(1) of this Act;

(b)   supplying or attempting to supply a controlled drug to another in contravention of section 4(1) of this Act, or offering to supply a controlled drug to another in contravention of section 4(1);

(c)   preparing opium for smoking;

(d)   *smoking cannabis, cannabis resin or prepared opium*

[(d)   administering or using a controlled drug which is unlawfully in any person's possession at or immediately before the time when it is administered or used].

9 Prohibition of certain activities etc. relating to opium

Subject to section 28 of this Act, it is an offence for a person—

(a)   to smoke or otherwise use prepared opium; or

(b)   to frequent a place used for the purpose of opium smoking; or

(c)   to have in his possession

(i)   any pipes or other utensils made or adapted for use in connection with the smoking of opium, being pipes or utensils which have been used by him or with his knowledge and permission in that connection or which he intends to use or permit others to use in that connection; or

(ii)   any utensils which have been used by him or with his knowledge and permission in connection with the preparation of opium for smoking.

[9A Prohibition of supply etc of articles for administering or preparing controlled drugs]

[(1)   A person who supplies or offers to supply any article which may be used or adapted to be used (whether by itself or in combination with another article or other articles) in the administration by any person of a controlled drug to himself or another, believing that the article (or the article as adapted) is to be so used in circumstances where the administration is unlawful, is guilty of an offence.

(2)   It is not an offence under subsection (1) above to supply or offer to supply a hypodermic syringe, or any part of one.

(3)   A person who supplies or offers to supply any article which may be used to prepare a controlled drug for administration by any person to himself or another believing that the article is to be so used in circumstances where the administration is unlawful is guilty of an offence.

(4)   For the purposes of this section, any administration of a controlled drug is unlawful except—
>   (a)   the administration by any person of a controlled drug to another in circumstances where the administration of the drug is not unlawful under section 4(1) of this Act, or
>   (b)   the administration by any person of a controlled drug to himself in circumstances where having the controlled drug in his possession is not unlawful under section 5(1) of this Act.

(5)   In this section, references to administration by any person of a controlled drug to himself include a reference to his administering it to himself with the assistance of another.]

NOTES
Inserted by the Drug Trafficking Offences Act 1986, s 9(1).

Miscellaneous and supplementary provisions

28 Proof of lack of knowledge etc to be a defence in proceedings for certain offences

(1)   This section applies to offences under any of the following provisions of this Act, that is to say section 4(2) and (3), section 5(2) and (3), section 6(2) and section 9.

(2)   Subject to subsection (3) below, in any proceedings for an offence to which this section applies it shall be a defence for the accused to prove that he neither knew of nor suspected nor had reason to suspect the existence of some fact alleged by the prosecution which it is necessary for the prosecution to prove if he is to be convicted of the offence charged.

(3)   Where in any proceedings for an offence to which this section applies it is necessary, if the accused is to be convicted of the offence charged, for the prosecution to prove that some substance or product involved in the alleged offence was the controlled drug which the prosecution alleges it to have been, and it is proved that the substance or product in question was that controlled drug, the accused—
>   (a)   shall not be acquitted of the offence charged by reason only of proving that he neither knew nor suspected nor had reason to suspect that the substance or product in question was the particular controlled drug alleged; but
>   (b)   shall be acquitted thereof—

(i)   if he proves that he neither believed nor suspected nor had reason to suspect that the substance or product in question was a controlled drug; or

(ii) if he proves that he believed the substance or product in question to be a controlled drug, or a controlled drug of a description, such that, if it had in fact been that controlled drug or a controlled drug of that description, he would not at the material time have been committing any offence to which this section applies.

(4)   Nothing in this section shall prejudice any defence which it is open to a person charged with an offence to which this section applies to raise apart from this section.

40 Short title, extent and commencement

(1)   This Act may be cited as the Misuse of Drugs Act 1971.

(2)   This Act extends to Northern Ireland.

(3)   This Act shall come into operation on such day as the Secretary of State may by order made by statutory instrument appoint, and different dates may be appointed under this subsection for different purposes.

Criminal Damage Act 1971

1971 CHAPTER 48

An Act to revise the law of England and Wales as to offences of damage to property, and to repeal or amend as respects the United Kingdom certain enactments relating to such offences; and for connected purposes

[14th July 1971]

1 Destroying or damaging property

(1)   A person who without lawful excuse destroys or damages any property belonging to another intending to destroy or damage any such property or being reckless as to whether any such property would be destroyed or damaged shall be guilty of an offence.

(2)   A person who without lawful excuse destroys or damages any property, whether belonging to himself or another—
  (a) intending to destroy or damage any property or being reckless as to whether any property would be destroyed or damaged; and
  (b) intending by the destruction or damage to endanger the life of another or being reckless as to whether the life of another would be thereby endangered;

shall be guilty of an offence.

(3)   An offence committed under this section by destroying or damaging property by fire shall be charged as arson.

2 Threats to destroy or damage property

A person who without lawful excuse makes to another a threat, intending that that other would fear it would be carried out,—

(a) to destroy or damage any property belonging to that other or a third person; or

(b) to destroy or damage his own property in a way which he knows is likely to endanger the life of that other or a third person;

shall be guilty of an offence.

3 Possessing anything with intent to destroy or damage property

A person who has anything in his custody or under his control intending without lawful excuse to use it or cause or permit another to use it—

(a) to destroy or damage any property belonging to some other person; or

(b) to destroy or damage his own or the user's property in a way which he knows is likely to endanger the life of some other person;

shall be guilty of an offence.

4 Punishment of offences

(1) A person guilty of arson under section 1 above or of an offence under section 1(2) above (whether arson or not) shall on conviction on indictment be liable to imprisonment for life.

(2) A person guilty of any other offence under this Act shall on conviction on indictment be liable to imprisonment for a term not exceeding ten years.

5 "Without lawful excuse"

(1) This section applies to any offence under section 1(1) above and any offence under section 2 or 3 above other than one involving a threat by the person charged to destroy or damage property in a way which he knows is likely to endanger the life of another or involving an intent by the person charged to use or cause or permit the use of something in his custody or under his control so to destroy or damage property.

(2) A person charged with an offence to which this section applies shall, whether or not he would be treated for the purposes of this Act as having a lawful excuse apart from this subsection, be treated for those purposes as having a lawful excuse—

(a) if at the time of the act or acts alleged to constitute the offence he believed that the person or persons whom he believed to be entitled to consent to the destruction of or damage to the property in question had so consented, or would have so consented to it if he or they had known of the destruction or damage and its circumstances; or

(b) if he destroyed or damaged or threatened to destroy or damage the property in question or, in the case of a charge of an offence under section 3 above, intended to use or cause or permit the use of something to destroy or damage it, in order to protect property belonging to himself or another or a right or interest in property which was or which he believed to be vested in himself or another, and at the time of the act or acts alleged to constitute the offence he believed—

(i) that the property, right or interest was in immediate need of protection; and

(ii) that the means of protection adopted or proposed to be adopted were or would be reasonable having regard to all the circumstances.

(3) For the purposes of this section it is immaterial whether a belief is justified or not if it is honestly held.

(4) For the purposes of subsection (2) above a right or interest in property includes any right or privilege in or over land, whether created by grant, licence or otherwise.

(5) This section shall not be construed as casting doubt on any defence recognised by law as a defence to criminal charges.

10 Interpretation

(1) In this Act "property" means property of a tangible nature, whether real or personal, including money and—

(a) including wild creatures which have been tamed or are ordinarily kept in captivity, and any other wild creatures or their carcasses if, but only if, they have been reduced into possession which has not been lost or abandoned or are in the course of being reduced into possession; but

(b) not including mushrooms growing wild on any land or flowers, fruit or foliage of a plant growing wild on any land.

For the purposes of this subsection "mushroom" includes any fungus and "plant" includes any shrub or tree.

(2) Property shall be treated for the purposes of this Act as belonging to any person—

(a) having the custody or control of it;

(b) having in it any proprietary right or interest (not being an equitable interest arising only from an agreement to transfer or grant an interest); or

(c) having a charge on it.

(3) Where property is subject to a trust, the persons to whom it belongs shall be so treated as including any person having a right to enforce the trust.

(4) Property of a corporation sole shall be so treated as belonging to the corporation notwithstanding a vacancy in the corporation.

12 Short title and extent

(1) This Act shall come into force at the expiration of the period of three months beginning with the day on which it is passed.

(2) This Act may be cited as the Criminal Damage Act 1971.

(3) Except as provided by subsections (4) to (6) below, this Act does not extend to Scotland or Northern Ireland.

(4), (5) . . .

(6)   Part II of the Schedule to this Act and so much of section 11(8) above as relates thereto extend to Scotland; and section 11(2) of this Act, Part III of that Schedule and so much of section 11(8) as relates thereto extend to Scotland and Northern Ireland.

NOTES

Sub-ss (4), (5): repealed by the Statute Law (Repeals) Act 1993.

Bail Act 1976

1976 CHAPTER 63

An Act to make provision in relation to bail in or in connection with criminal proceedings in England and Wales, to make it an offence to agree to indemnify sureties in criminal proceedings, to make provision for legal aid limited to questions of bail in certain cases and for legal aid for persons kept in custody for inquiries or reports, to extend the powers of coroners to grant bail and for connected purposes

[15th November 1976]

Supplementary

6 Offence of absconding by person released on bail

(1)   If a person who has been released on bail in criminal proceedings fails without reasonable cause to surrender to custody he shall be guilty of an offence.

(2)   If a person who—
   (a)   has been released on bail in criminal proceedings, and
   (b)   having reasonable cause therefor, has failed to surrender to custody,

fails to surrender to custody at the appointed place as soon after the appointed time as is reasonably practicable he shall be guilty of an offence.

(3)   It shall be for the accused to prove that he had reasonable cause for his failure to surrender to custody.

(4)   A failure to give to a person granted bail in criminal proceedings a copy of the record of the decision shall not constitute a reasonable cause for that person's failure to surrender to custody.

(5)   An offence under subsection (1) or (2) above shall be punishable either on summary conviction or as if it were a criminal contempt of court.

(6)   Where a magistrates' court convicts a person of an offence under subsection (1) or (2) above the court may, if it thinks—
   (a)   that the circumstances of the offence are such that greater punishment should be inflicted for that offence than the court has power to inflict, or

    (b)   in a case where it commits that person for trial to the Crown Court for another offence, that it would be appropriate for him to be dealt with for the offence under subsection (1) or (2) above by the court before which he is tried for the other offence,

commit him in custody or on bail to the Crown Court for sentence.

(7)   A person who is convicted summarily of an offence under subsection (1) or (2) above and is not committed to the Crown Court for sentence shall be liable to imprisonment for a term not exceeding 3 months or to a fine not exceeding [level 5 on the standard scale] or to both and a person who is so committed for sentence or is dealt with as for such a contempt shall be liable to imprisonment for a term not exceeding 12 months or to a fine or to both.

(8)   In any proceedings for an offence under subsection (1) or (2) above a document purporting to be a copy of the part of the prescribed record which relates to the time and place appointed for the person specified in the record to surrender to custody and to be duly certified to be a true copy of that part of the record shall be evidence of the time and place appointed for that person to surrender to custody.

(9)   For the purposes of subsection (8) above—
    (a)   "the prescribed record" means the record of the decision of the court, officer or constable made in pursuance of section 5(1) of this Act;
    (b)   the copy of the prescribed record is duly certified if it is certified by the appropriate officer of the court or, as the case may be, by the constable who took the decision or a constable designated for the purpose by the officer in charge of the police station from which the person to whom the record relates was released;
    (c)   "the appropriate officer" of the court is—
        (i)   in the case of a magistrates' court, the justices' [chief executive];
        (ii)   in the case of the Crown Court, such officer as may be designated for the purpose in accordance with arrangements made by the Lord Chancellor;
        (iii)   in the case of the High Court, such officer as may be designated for the purpose in accordance with arrangements made by the Lord Chancellor;
        (iv)   in the case of the Court of Appeal, the registrar of criminal appeals or such other officer as may be authorised by him to act for the purpose;
        (v)   in the case of the Courts-Martial Appeal Court, the registrar or such other officer as may be authorised by him to act for the purpose.

NOTES

Sub-s (7): maximum fine increased and converted to a level on the standard scale by virtue of the Criminal Justice Act 1982, ss 37, 38, 46.

Sub-s (9): in para (c)(i) words "chief executive" in square brackets substituted by the Access to Justice Act 1999, s 90(1), Sch 13, para 89.

Date in force: 1 April 2001: see SI 2001/916, art 2(a)(ii).

Miscellaneous

9 Offence of agreeing to indemnify sureties in criminal proceedings

(1)   If a person agrees with another to indemnify that other against any liability which that other may incur as a surety to secure the surrender to custody of a person accused or convicted of or under arrest for an offence, he and that other person shall be guilty of an offence.

(2)   An offence under subsection (1) above is committed whether the agreement is made before or after the person to be indemnified becomes a surety and whether or not he becomes a surety and whether the agreement contemplates compensation in money or in money's worth.

(3)   Where a magistrates' court convicts a person of an offence under subsection (1) above the court may, if it thinks—
   (a)   that the circumstances of the offence are such that greater punishment should be inflicted for that offence than the court has power to inflict, or
   (b)   in a case where it commits that person for trial to the Crown Court for another offence, that it would be appropriate for him to be dealt with for the offence under subsection (1) above by the court before which he is tried for the other offence,

commit him in custody or on bail to the Crown Court for sentence.

(4)   A person guilty of an offence under subsection (1) above shall be liable—
   (a)   on summary conviction, to imprisonment for a term not exceeding 3 months or to a fine not exceeding [the prescribed sum] or to both; or
   (b)   on conviction on indictment or if sentenced by the Crown Court on committal for sentence under subsection (3) above, to imprisonment for a term not exceeding 12 months or to a fine or to both.

(5)   No proceedings for an offence under subsection (1) above shall be instituted except by or with the consent of the Director of Public Prosecutions.

NOTES

Sub-s (4): words in square brackets substituted by virtue of the Magistrates' Courts Act 1980, s 32(2).

13 Short title, commencement, application and extent

(1)   This Act may be cited as the Bail Act 1976.

(2)   This Act (except this section) shall come into force on such day as the Secretary of State may by order in a statutory instrument appoint.

(3)   Section 1 of this Act applies to bail grantable by the Courts-Martial Appeal Court when sitting outside England and Wales and accordingly section 6 of this Act applies to a failure outside England and Wales by a person granted bail by that Court to surrender to custody.

(4)   Except as provided by subsection (3) above and with the exception of so much of section 8 as relates to entering into recognizances in Scotland and paragraphs 31 and 46 of Schedule 2 to this Act, this Act does not extend beyond England and Wales.

Sexual Offences (Amendment) Act 1976

1976 CHAPTER 82

An Act to amend the law relating to rape

[22nd November 1976]

1 Meaning of "rape" etc

(1)   . . .

(2)   It is hereby declared that if at a trial for a rape offence the jury has to consider whether a man believed that a woman [or man] was consenting to sexual intercourse, the presence or absence of reasonable grounds for such a belief is a matter to which the jury is to have regard, in conjunction with any other relevant matters, in considering whether he so believed.

NOTES

Sub-s (1): repealed by the Criminal Justice and Public Order Act 1994, s 168(3), Sch 11.

Sub-s (2): words in square brackets inserted by the Criminal Justice and Public Order Act 1994, s 168(2), Sch 10, para 35(2).

7 Citation, interpretation, commencement and extent

(1)   This Act may be cited as the Sexual Offences (Amendment) Act 1976, and this Act and the Sexual Offences Acts 1956 and 1967 may be cited together as the Sexual Offences Acts 1956 to 1976.

(2)   In this Act—

"a rape offence" means any of the following, namely rape, attempted rape, aiding, abetting, counselling and procuring rape or attempted rape, [incitement to rape, conspiracy to rape and burglary with intent to rape]; and

. . . ;

[section 46 of the Sexual Offences Act 1956] (which relates to the meaning of "man" and "woman" in that Act) shall have effect as if the reference to that Act included a reference to this Act.

(3)   In relation to such a trial as is mentioned in subsection (2) of section 1 of this Act which is a trial by court-martial or a summary trial by a magistrates' court, references to the jury in that subsection shall be construed as references to the court.

(4)   This Act shall come into force on the expiration of the period of one month beginning with the date on which it is passed, *except that sections 5(1)(b) < . . . > shall come into force on such day as the Secretary of State may appoint by order made by statutory instrument.*

(5)   *Sections 2 and 3 of this Act shall not have effect in relation to a trial or inquiry which begins before the expiration of that period and sections 4 < . . . > of this Act shall not have effect in relation to an accusation alleging a rape offence which is made before the expiration of that period.*

(6)   This Act, except so far as it relates to courts-martial and the Courts-Martial Appeal Court, shall not extend to Scotland *and this Act, except so far as it relates to courts-martial and the Courts-Martial Appeal Court [and to such a publication or [in, or such an inclusion of matter in a relevant programme for reception in,] in Northern Ireland as is mentioned in section 4(1) as adapted by section 5(1)(b)]* < . . . > , *shall not extend to Northern Ireland* [or Northern Ireland].

NOTES

Sub-s (2): in definition of "a rape offence" words in square brackets substituted by the Criminal Justice Act 1988, s 158(1), (6); words omitted repealed and final words in square brackets substituted, by the Criminal Justice and Public Order Act 1994, s 168(2), (3), Sch 10, para 35(4), Sch 11.

Sub-s (4): words from "except that" to "by statutory instrument" in italics repealed by the Youth Justice and Criminal Evidence Act 1999, s 67(3), Sch 6.

Date in force: to be appointed: see the Youth Justice and Criminal Evidence Act 1999, s 68(3).

Sub-s (4): words omitted repealed by the Criminal Justice Act 1988, s 170(2), Sch 16.

Sub-s (5): repealed by the Youth Justice and Criminal Evidence Act 1999, s 67(3), Sch 6.

Date in force: to be appointed: see the Youth Justice and Criminal Evidence Act 1999, s 68(3).

Sub-s (5): words omitted repealed by the Criminal Justice Act 1988, s 170(2), Sch 16.

Sub-s (6): words from "and this Act," to "extend to Northern Ireland" in italics repealed and subsequent words in square brackets substituted by the Youth Justice and Criminal Evidence Act 1999, s 48, Sch 2, paras 4(1), (3).

Date in force: to be appointed: see the Youth Justice and Criminal Evidence Act 1999, s 68(3).

Sub-s (6): words from "and to such" to "section 5(1)(b)" in square brackets substitiuted by the Criminal Justice Act 1988, s 170, Sch 15, para 53(1), (3), Sch 16.

Sub-s (6): words from "in, or such an inclusion" to "for reception in," in square brackets substituted by the Broadcasting Act 1990, s 203(1), Sch 20, para 26(3).

Sub-s (6): words omitted repealed by the Criminal Justice Act 1988, s 170, Sch 15, para 53(1), (3), Sch 16.

Criminal Law Act 1977

1977 CHAPTER 45

An Act to amend the law of England and Wales with respect to criminal conspiracy; to make new provision in that law, in place of the provisions of the common law and the Statutes of Forcible Entry, for restricting the use or threat of violence for securing entry into any premises and for penalising unauthorised entry or remaining on premises in certain circumstances; otherwise to amend the criminal law, including the law with respect to the administration of criminal justice; to provide for the alteration of certain pecuniary and other limits; to amend section 9(4) of the Administration of Justice Act 1973, the Legal Aid Act 1974, the Rabies Act 1974 and the Diseases of Animals (Northern Ireland) Order 1975 and the law about juries and coroners' inquests; and for connected purposes

[29th July 1977]

PART I
CONSPIRACY

1 The offence of conspiracy

[(1)   Subject to the following provisions of this part of this Act, if a person agrees with any other person or persons that a course of conduct shall be pursued which, if the agreement is carried out in accordance with their intentions, either—
  (a)   will necessarily amount to or involve the commission of any offence or offences by one or more of the parties to the agreement, or
  (b)   would do so but for the existence of facts which render the commission of the offence or any of the offences impossible,

he is guilty of conspiracy to commit the offence or offences in question.]

[(1A)   . . .

(1B)   . . .]

(2)   Where liability for any offence may be incurred without knowledge on the part of the person committing it of any particular fact or circumstance necessary for the commission of the offence, a person shall nevertheless not be guilty of conspiracy to commit that offence by virtue of subsection (1) above unless he and at least one other party to the agreement intend or know that that fact or circumstance shall or will exist at the time when the conduct constituting the offence is to take place.

(3)   . . .

(4)   In this Part of this Act "offence" means an offence triable in England and Wales, . . .

[(5)   . . .

(6)   . . .]

NOTES

Sub-s (1): substituted by the Criminal Attempts Act 1981, s 5(1), except as to agreements entered into before 27 August 1981 when the conspiracy continued to exist after that date.

Sub-ss (1A), (1B), (5), (6): inserted by the Computer Misuse Act 1990, s 7(1), (2).

Sub-ss (1A), (1B): inserted by the Computer Misuse Act 1990, s 7(1), (2); repealed by the Criminal Justice (Terrorism and Conspiracy) Act 1998, s 9(1), (2), Sch 1, para 4(a), Sch 2, Pt II.

Date in force: 4 September 1998: (no specific commencement provision).

Sub-s (3): repealed by the Trade Union and Labour Relations (Consolidation) Act 1992, s 300(1), Sch 1.

Sub-s (4): words omitted repealed by the Criminal Justice (Terrorism and Conspiracy) Act 1998, s 9(1), (2), Sch 1, para 4(b), Sch 2, Pt II.

Date in force: 4 September 1998: (no specific commencement provision).

Sub-ss (5), (6): inserted by the Computer Misuse Act 1990, s 7(1), (2); repealed by the Criminal Justice (Terrorism and Conspiracy) Act 1998, s 9(1), (2), Sch 1, para 4(c), Sch 2, Pt II.

Date in force: 4 September 1998: (no specific commencement provision).

[1A Conspiracy to commit offences outside the United Kingdom]

[(1)   Where each of the following conditions is satisfied in the case of an agreement, this Part of this Act has effect in relation to the agreement as it has effect in relation to an agreement falling within section 1(1) above.

(2)   The first condition is that the pursuit of the agreed course of conduct would at some stage involve—

   (a)   an act by one or more of the parties, or

   (b)   the happening of some other event,

intended to take place in a country or territory outside the United Kingdom.

(3)   The second condition is that that act or other event constitutes an offence under the law in force in that country or territory.

(4)   The third condition is that the agreement would fall within section 1(1) above as an agreement relating to the commission of an offence but for the fact that the offence would not be an offence triable in England and Wales if committed in accordance with the parties' intentions.

(5)   The fourth condition is that—

   (a)   a party to the agreement, or a party's agent, did anything in England and Wales in relation to the agreement before its formation, or

   (b)   a party to the agreement became a party in England and Wales (by joining it either in person or through an agent), or

   (c)   a party to the agreement, or a party's agent, did or omitted anything in England and Wales in pursuance of the agreement.

(6)   In the application of this Part of this Act to an agreement in the case of which each of the above conditions is satisfied, a reference to an offence is to be read as a reference to what would be the offence in question but for the fact that it is not an offence triable in England and Wales.

(7) Conduct punishable under the law in force in any country or territory is an offence under that law for the purposes of this section, however it is described in that law.

(8) Subject to subsection (9) below, the second condition is to be taken to be satisfied unless, not later than rules of court may provide, the defence serve on the prosecution a notice—

    (a)   stating that, on the facts as alleged with respect to the agreed course of conduct, the condition is not in their opinion satisfied,

    (b)   showing their grounds for that opinion, and

    (c)   requiring the prosecution to show that it is satisfied.

(9) The court may permit the defence to require the prosecution to show that the second condition is satisfied without the prior service of a notice under subsection (8) above.

(10) In the Crown Court the question whether the second condition is satisfied shall be decided by the judge alone, and shall be treated as a question of law for the purposes of—

    (a)   section 9(3) of the Criminal Justice Act 1987 (preparatory hearing in fraud cases), and

    (b)   section 31(3) of the Criminal Procedure and Investigations Act 1996 (preparatory hearing in other cases).

(11) Any act done by means of a message (however communicated) is to be treated for the purposes of the fourth condition as done in England and Wales if the message is sent or received in England and Wales.

(12) In any proceedings in respect of an offence triable by virtue of this section, it is immaterial to guilt whether or not the accused was a British citizen at the time of any act or other event proof of which is required for conviction of the offence.

(13) References in any enactment, instrument or document (except those in this Part of this Act) to an offence of conspiracy to commit an offence include an offence triable in England and Wales as such a conspiracy by virtue of this section (without prejudice to subsection (6) above).

(14) Nothing in this section—

    (a)   applies to an agreement entered into before the day on which the Criminal Justice (Terrorism and Conspiracy) Act 1998 was passed, or

    (b)   imposes criminal liability on any person acting on behalf of, or holding office under, the Crown.]

NOTES

Inserted by the Criminal Justice (Terrorism and Conspiracy) Act 1998, s 5(1).
Date in force: 4 September 1998: (no specific commencement provision).

2 Exemptions from liability for conspiracy

(1) A person shall not by virtue of section 1 above be guilty of conspiracy to commit any offence if he is an intended victim of that offence.

(2)   A person shall not by virtue of section 1 above be guilty of conspiracy to commit any offence or offences if the only other person or persons with whom he agrees are (both initially and at all times during the currency of the agreement) persons of any one or more of the following descriptions, that is to say—

(a)   his spouse;

(b)   a person under the age of criminal responsibility; and

(c)   an intended victim of that offence or of each of those offences.

(3)   A person is under the age of criminal responsibility for the purposes of subsection (2)(b) above so long as it is conclusively presumed, by virtue of section 50 of the Children and Young Persons Act 1933, that he cannot be guilty of any offence.

3 Penalties for conspiracy

(1)   A person guilty by virtue of section 1 above of conspiracy to commit any offence or offences shall be liable on conviction on indictment—

(a)   in a case falling within subsection (2) or (3) below, to imprisonment for a term related in accordance with that subsection to the gravity of the offence or offences in question (referred to below in this section as the relevant offence or offences); and

(b)   in any other case, to a fine.

Paragraph (b) above shall not be taken as prejudicing the application of [section 127 of the Powers of Criminal Courts (Sentencing) Act 2000] (general power of court to fine offender convicted on indictment) in a case falling within subsection (2) or (3) below.

(2)   Where the relevant offence or any of the relevant offences is an offence of any of the following descriptions, that is to say—

(a)   murder, or any other offence the sentence for which is fixed by law;

(b)   an offence for which a sentence extending to imprisonment for life is provided; or

(c)   an indictable offence punishable with imprisonment for which no maximum term of imprisonment is provided,

the person convicted shall be liable to imprisonment for life.

(3)   Where in a case other than one to which subsection (2) above applies the relevant offence or any of the relevant offences is punishable with imprisonment, the person convicted shall be liable to imprisonment for a term not exceeding the maximum term provided for that offence or (where more than one such offence is in question) for any one of those offences (taking the longer or the longest term as the limit for the purposes of this section where the terms provided differ).

In the case of an offence triable either way the references above in this subsection to the maximum term provided for that offence are references to the maximum term so provided on conviction on indictment.

NOTES

Sub-s (1): words "section 127 of the Powers of Criminal Courts (Sentencing) Act 2000" in square brackets substituted by the Powers of Criminal Courts (Sentencing) Act 2000, s 165(1), Sch 9, para 55.

Date in force: 25 August 2000: see the Powers of Criminal Courts (Sentencing) Act 2000, s 168(1).

4 Restrictions on the institution of proceedings for conspiracy

(1)   Subject to subsection (2) below proceedings under section 1 above for conspiracy to commit any offence or offences shall not be instituted against any person except by or with the consent of the Director of Public Prosecutions if the offence or (as the case may be) each of the offences in question is a summary offence.

(2)   In relation to the institution of proceedings under section 1 above for conspiracy to commit—
  (a)   an offence which is subject to a prohibition by or under any enactment on the institution of proceedings otherwise than by, or on behalf or with the consent of, the Attorney General, or
  (b)   two or more offences of which at least one is subject to such a prohibition,

subsection (1) above shall have effect with the substitution of a reference to the Attorney General for the reference to the Director of Public Prosecutions.

(3)   Any prohibition by or under any enactment on the institution of proceedings for any offence which is not a summary offence otherwise than by, or on behalf or with the consent of, the Director of Public Prosecutions or any other person shall apply also in relation to proceedings under section 1 above for conspiracy to commit that offence.

(4)   Where—
  (a)   an offence has been committed in pursuance of any agreement; and
  (b)   proceedings may not be instituted for that offence because any time limit applicable to the institution of any such proceedings has expired,

proceedings under section 1 above for conspiracy to commit that offence shall not be instituted against any person on the basis of that agreement.

[(5)

Subject to subsection (6) below, no proceedings for an offence triable by virtue of section 1A above may be instituted except by or with the consent of the Attorney General.

(6)   The Secretary of State may by order provide that subsection (5) above shall not apply, or shall not apply to any case of a description specified in the order.

(7)   An order under subsection (6) above—
  (a)   shall be made by statutory instrument, and
  (b)   shall not be made unless a draft has been laid before, and approved by resolution of, each House of Parliament.]

NOTES
Sub-ss (5), (6), (7): inserted by the Criminal Justice (Terrorism and Conspiracy) Act 1998, s 5(2).
Date in force: 4 September 1998: (no specific commencement provision).

5 Abolitions, savings, transitional provisions, consequential amendment and repeals

(1)   Subject to the following provisions of this section, the offence of conspiracy at common law is hereby abolished.

(2)   Subsection (1) above shall not affect the offence of conspiracy at common law so far as relates to conspiracy to defraud . . .

(3)   Subsection (1) above shall not affect the offence of conspiracy at common law if and in so far as it may be committed by entering into an agreement to engage in conduct which—
   (a)   tends to corrupt public morals or outrages public decency; but
   (b)   would not amount to or involve the commission of an offence if carried out by a single person otherwise than in pursuance of an agreement.

(4)   Subsection (1) above shall not affect—
   (a)   any proceedings commenced before the time when this Part of this Act comes into force;
   (b)   any proceedings commenced after that time against a person charged with the same conspiracy as that charged in any proceedings commenced before that time; or
   (c)   any proceedings commenced after that time in respect of a trespass committed before that time;

but a person convicted of conspiracy to trespass in any proceedings brought by virtue of paragraph (c) above shall not in respect of that conviction be liable to imprisonment for a term exceeding six months.

(5)   Sections 1 and 2 above shall apply to things done before as well as to things done after the time when this Part of this Act comes into force, but in the application of section 3 above to a case where the agreement in question was entered into before that time—
   (a)   subsection (2) shall be read without the reference to murder in paragraph (a); and
   (b)   any murder intended under the agreement shall be treated as an offence for which a maximum term of imprisonment of ten years is provided.

(6)   The rules laid down by sections 1 and 2 above shall apply for determining whether a person is guilty of an offence of conspiracy under any enactment other than section 1 above, but conduct which is an offence under any such other enactment shall not also be an offence under section 1 above.

(7)   Incitement . . . to commit the offence of conspiracy (whether the conspiracy incited . . . would be an offence at common law or under section 1 above or any other enactment) shall cease to be offences.

(8)   The fact that the person or persons who, so far as appears from the indictment on which any person has been convicted of conspiracy, were the only other parties to the agreement on which his conviction was based have been acquitted of conspiracy by reference to that agreement (whether after being tried with the person convicted or separately) shall not be a ground for quashing his conviction unless under all the circumstances of the case his conviction is inconsistent with the acquittal of the other person or persons in question.

(9)   Any rule of law or practice inconsistent with the provisions of subsection (8) above is hereby abolished.

(10), (11)   . . .

NOTES

Sub-s (2): words omitted repealed by the Criminal Justice Act 1987, s 12(2).

Sub-s (7): words omitted repealed by the Criminal Attempts Act 1981, s 10, Schedule, Part I.

Sub-s (10): amends the Offences against the Person Act 1861, s 4.

Sub-s (11): repealed by the Trade Union and Labour Relations (Consolidation) Act 1992, s 300(1), Sch 1.

PART II
OFFENCES RELATING TO ENTERING AND REMAINING ON PROPERTY

6 Violence for securing entry

(1)   Subject to the following provisions of this section, any person who, without lawful authority, uses or threatens violence for the purpose of securing entry into any premises for himself or for any other person is guilty of an offence, provided that—
  (a)   there is someone present on those premises at the time who is opposed to the entry which the violence is intended to secure; and
  (b)   the person using or threatening the violence knows that that is the case.

[(1A)   Subsection (1) above does not apply to a person who is a displaced residential occupier or a protected intending occupier of the premises in question or who is acting on behalf of such an occupier; and if the accused adduces sufficient evidence that he was, or was acting on behalf of, such an occupier he shall be presumed to be, or to be acting on behalf of, such an occupier unless the contrary is proved by the prosecution.]

(2)   [Subject to subsection (1A) above,] the fact that a person has any interest in or right to possession or occupation of any premises shall not for the purposes of subsection (1) above constitute lawful authority for the use or threat of violence by him or anyone else for the purpose of securing his entry into those premises.

(3)   . . .

(4)   It is immaterial for the purposes of this section—
  (a)   whether the violence in question is directed against the person or against property; and
  (b)   whether the entry which the violence is intended to secure is for the purpose of acquiring possession of the premises in question or for any other purpose.

(5)   A person guilty of an offence under this section shall be liable on summary conviction to imprisonment for a term not exceeding six months or to a fine not exceeding [level 5 on the standard scale] or to both.

(6)   A constable in uniform may arrest without warrant anyone who is, or whom he, with reasonable cause, suspects to be, guilty of an offence under this section.

(7)   Section 12 below contains provisions which apply for determining when any person is to be regarded for the purposes of this Part of this Act as a displaced residential occupier of any premises or of any access to any premises [and section 12A below contains provisions which apply for determining when any person is to be regarded for the purposes of this Part of this Act as a protected intending occupier of any premises or of any access to any premises.]

NOTES

Sub-s (1A): inserted by the Criminal Justice and Public Order Act 1994, s 72(2).

Sub-ss (2), (7): words in square brackets inserted by the Criminal Justice and Public Order Act 1994, s 72(3), (5).

Sub-s (3): repealed by the Criminal Justice and Public Order Act 1994, ss 72(4), 168(3), Sch 11.

Sub-s (5): maximum fine converted to a level on the standard scale by virtue of the Criminal Justice Act 1982, ss 37, 38, 46.

[7 Adverse occupation of residential premises]

[(1)   Subject to the following provisions of this section and to section 12A(9) below, any person who is on any premises as a trespasser after having entered as such is guilty of an offence if he fails to leave those premises on being required to do so by or on behalf of—

(a)   a displaced residential occupier of the premises; or

(b)   an individual who is a protected intending occupier of the premises.

(2)   In any proceedings for an offence under this section it shall be a defence for the accused to prove that he believed that the person requiring him to leave the premises was not a displaced residential occupier or protected intending occupier of the premises or a person acting on behalf of a displaced residential occupier or protected intending occupier.

(3)   In any proceedings for an offence under this section it shall be a defence for the accused to prove—

(a)   that the premises in question are or form part of premises used mainly for non-residential purposes; and

(b)   that he was not on any part of the premises used wholly or mainly for residential purposes.

(4)   Any reference in the preceding provisions of this section to any premises includes a reference to any access to them, whether or not any such access itself constitutes premises, within the meaning of this Part of this Act.

(5)   A person guilty of an offence under this section shall be liable on summary conviction to imprisonment for a term not exceeding six months or to a fine not exceeding level 5 on the standard scale or to both.

(6)   A constable in uniform may arrest without warrant anyone who is, or whom he, with reasonable cause, suspects to be, guilty of an offence under this section.

(7)   Section 12 below contains provisions which apply for determining when any person is to be regarded for the purposes of this Part of this Act as a displaced residential occupier of any premises or of any access to any premises and section 12A below contains provisions which apply for determining when any person is to be regarded for the purposes of this Part of this Act as a protected intending occupier of any premises or of any access to any premises.]

NOTES

Substituted by the Criminal Justice and Public Order Act 1994, s 73.

8 Trespassing with a weapon of offence

(1)   A person who is on any premises as a trespasser, after having entered as such, is guilty of an offence if, without lawful authority or reasonable excuse, he has with him on the premises any weapon of offence.

(2)   In subsection (1) above "weapon of offence" means any article made or adapted for use for causing injury to or incapacitating a person, or intended by the person having it with him for such use.

(3)   A person guilty of an offence under this section shall be liable on summary conviction to imprisonment for a term not exceeding three months or to a fine not exceeding [level 5 on the standard scale] or to both.

(4)   A constable in uniform may arrest without warrant anyone who is, or whom he, with reasonable cause, suspects to be, in the act of committing an offence under this section.

NOTES

Sub-s (3): maximum fine converted to a level on the standard scale by the Criminal Justice Act 1982, ss 37, 46.

9 Trespassing on premises of foreign missions, etc

(1)   Subject to subsection (3) below, a person who enters or is on any premises to which this section applies as a trespasser is guilty of an offence.

(2)   This section applies to any premises which are or form part of—
  (a)   the premises of a diplomatic mission within the meaning of the definition in Article 1(i) of the Vienna Convention on Diplomatic Relations signed in 1961 as that Article has effect in the United Kingdom by virtue of section 2 of and Schedule 1 to the Diplomatic Privileges Act 1964;
  [(aa) the premises of a closed diplomatic mission;]
  (b)   consular premises within the meaning of the definition in paragraph 1(j) of Article 1 of the Vienna Convention on Consular Relations signed in 1963 as that Article has effect in the United Kingdom by virtue of section 1 of and Schedule 1 to the Consular Relations Act 1968;
  [(bb)the premises of a closed consular post;]

(c) any other premises in respect of which any organisation or body is entitled to inviolability by or under any enactment; and

(d) any premises which are the private residence of a diplomatic agent (within the meaning of Article 1(e) of the Convention mentioned in paragraph (a) above) or of any other person who is entitled to inviolability of residence by or under any enactment.

[(2A) In subsection (2) above—

"the premises of a closed diplomatic mission" means premises which fall within Article 45 of the Convention mentioned in subsection (2)(a) above (as that Article has effect in the United Kingdom by virtue of the section and Schedule mentioned in that paragraph); and

"the premises of a closed consular post" means premises which fall within Article 27 of the Convention mentioned in subsection (2)(b) above (as that Article has effect in the United Kingdom by virtue of the section and Schedule mentioned in that paragraph).]

(3) In any proceedings for an offence under this section it shall be a defence for the accused to prove that he believed that the premises in question were not premises to which this section applies.

(4) In any proceedings for an offence under this section a certificate issued by or under the authority of the Secretary of State stating that any premises were or formed part of premises of any description mentioned in paragraphs (a) to (d) of subsection (2) above at the time of the alleged offence shall be conclusive evidence that the premises were or formed part of premises of that description at that time.

(5) A person guilty of an offence under this section shall be liable on summary conviction to imprisonment for a term not exceeding six months or to a fine not exceeding [level 5 on the standard scale] or to both.

(6) Proceedings for an offence under this section shall not be instituted against any person except by or with the consent of the Attorney General.

(7) A constable in uniform may arrest without warrant anyone who is, or whom he, with reasonable cause, suspects to be, in the act of committing an offence under this section.

NOTES

Sub-s (2): paras (aa), (bb) inserted by the Diplomatic and Consular Premises Act 1987, s 7.
Sub-s (2A): inserted by the Diplomatic and Consular Premises Act 1987, s 7.
Sub-s (5): maximum fine converted to a level on the standard scale by virtue of the Criminal Justice Act 1982, ss 37, 38, 46.

12 Supplementary provisions

(1) In this Part of this Act—
(a) "premises" means any building, any part of a building under separate occupation, any land ancillary to a building, the site comprising any building or buildings together with any land ancillary thereto, and (for the purposes only of sections 10 and 11 above) any other place; and

(b)   "access" means, in relation to any premises, any part of any site or building within which those premises are situated which constitutes an ordinary means of access to those premises (whether or not that is its sole or primary use).

(2)   References in this section to a building shall apply also to any structure other than a movable one, and to any movable structure, vehicle or vessel designed or adapted for use for residential purposes; and for the purposes of subsection (1) above—

(a)   part of a building is under separate occupation if anyone is in occupation or entitled to occupation of that part as distinct from the whole; and

(b)   land is ancillary to a building if it is adjacent to it and used (or intended for use) in connection with the occupation of that building or any part of it.

(3)   Subject to subsection (4) below, any person who was occupying any premises as a residence immediately before being excluded from occupation by anyone who entered those premises, or any access to those premises, as a trespasser is a displaced residential occupier of the premises for the purposes of this Part of this Act so long as he continues to be excluded from occupation of the premises by the original trespasser or by any subsequent trespasser.

(4)   A person who was himself occupying the premises in question as a trespasser immediately before being excluded from occupation shall not by virtue of subsection (3) above be a displaced residential occupier of the premises for the purposes of this Part of this Act.

(5)   A person who by virtue of subsection (3) above is a displaced residential occupier of any premises shall be regarded for the purposes of this Part of this Act as a displaced residential occupier also of any access to those premises.

(6)   Anyone who enters or is on or in occupation of any premises by virtue of—

(a)   any title derived from a trespasser; or

(b)   any licence or consent given by a trespasser or by a person deriving title from a trespasser,

shall himself be treated as a trespasser for the purposes of this Part of this Act (without prejudice to whether or not he would be a trespasser apart from this provision); and references in this Part of this Act to a person's entering or being on or occupying any premises as a trespasser shall be construed accordingly.

(7)   Anyone who is on any premises as a trespasser shall not cease to be a trespasser for the purposes of this Part of this Act by virtue of being allowed time to leave the premises, nor shall anyone cease to be a displaced residential occupier of any premises by virtue of any such allowance of time to a trespasser.

(8)   No rule of law ousting the jurisdiction of magistrates' courts to try offences where a dispute of title to property is involved shall preclude magistrates' courts from trying offences under this Part of this Act.

[12A Protected intending occupiers: supplementary provisions]

[(1)   For the purposes of this Part of this Act an individual is a protected intending occupier of any premises at any time if at that time he falls within subsection (2), (4) or (6) below.

(2)   An individual is a protected intending occupier of any premises if—
  (a)   he has in those premises a freehold interest or a leasehold interest with not less than two years still to run;
  (b)   he requires the premises for his own occupation as a residence;
  (c)   he is excluded from occupation of the premises by a person who entered them, or any access to them, as a trespasser; and
  (d)   he or a person acting on his behalf holds a written statement—
    (i)   which specifies his interest in the premises;
    (ii)   which states that he requires the premises for occupation as a residence for himself; and
    (iii)   with respect to which the requirements in subsection (3) below are fulfilled.

(3)   The requirements referred to in subsection (2)(d)(iii) above are—
  (a)   that the statement is signed by the person whose interest is specified in it in the presence of a justice of the peace or commissioner for oaths; and
  (b)   that the justice of the peace or commissioner for oaths has subscribed his name as a witness to the signature.

(4)   An individual is also a protected intending occupier of any premises if—
  (a)   he has a tenancy of those premises (other than a tenancy falling within subsection (2)(a) above or (6)(a) below) or a licence to occupy those premises granted by a person with a freehold interest or a leasehold interest with not less than two years still to run in the premises;
  (b)   he requires the premises for his own occupation as a residence;
  (c)   he is excluded from occupation of the premises by a person who entered them, or any access to them, as a trespasser; and
  (d)   he or a person acting on his behalf holds a written statement—
    (i)   which states that he has been granted a tenancy of those premises or a licence to occupy those premises;
    (ii)   which specifies the interest in the premises of the person who granted that tenancy or licence to occupy ("the landlord");
    (iii)   which states that he requires the premises for occupation as a residence for himself; and
    (iv)   with respect to which the requirements in subsection (5) below are fulfilled.

(5)   The requirements referred to in subsection (4)(d)(iv) above are—
  (a)   that the statement is signed by the landlord and by the tenant or licensee in the presence of a justice of the peace or commissioner for oaths;
  (b)   that the justice of the peace or commissioner for oaths has subscribed his name as a witness to the signatures.

(6)   An individual is also a protected intending occupier of any premises if—
   (a)   he has a tenancy of those premises (other than a tenancy falling within subsection (2)(a) or (4)(a) above) or a licence to occupy those premises granted by an authority to which this subsection applies;
   (b)   he requires the premises for his own occupation as a residence;
   (c)   he is excluded from occupation of the premises by a person who entered the premises, or any access to them, as a trespasser; and
   (d)   there has been issued to him by or on behalf of the authority referred to in paragraph (a) above a certificate stating that—
      (i)   he has been granted a tenancy of those premises or a licence to occupy those premises as a residence by the authority; and
      (ii)   the authority which granted that tenancy or licence to occupy is one to which this subsection applies, being of a description specified in the certificate.

(7)   Subsection (6) above applies to the following authorities—
   (a)   any body mentioned in section 14 of the Rent Act 1977 (landlord's interest belonging to local authority etc);
   (b)   the Housing Corporation;
   (c)   . . . and
   [(d)   a registered social landlord within the meaning of the Housing Act 1985 (see section 5(4) and (5) of that Act)].

[(7A)   Subsection (6) also applies to the Secretary of State if the tenancy or licence is granted by him under Part III of the Housing Associations Act 1985.]

(8)   A person is guilty of an offence if he makes a statement for the purposes of subsection (2)(d) or (4)(d) above which he knows to be false in a material particular or if he recklessly makes such a statement which is false in a material particular.

(9)   In any proceedings for an offence under section 7 of this Act where the accused was requested to leave the premises by a person claiming to be or to act on behalf of a protected intending occupier of the premises—
   (a)   it shall be a defence for the accused to prove that, although asked to do so by the accused at the time the accused was requested to leave, that person failed at that time to produce to the accused such a statement as is referred to in subsection (2)(d) or (4)(d) above or such a certificate as is referred to in subsection (6)(d) above; and
   (b)   any document purporting to be a certificate under subsection (6)(d) above shall be received in evidence and, unless the contrary is proved, shall be deemed to have been issued by or on behalf of the authority stated in the certificate.

(10)   A person guilty of an offence under subsection (8) above shall be liable on summary conviction to imprisonment for a term not exceeding six months or to a fine not exceeding level 5 on the standard scale or to both.

(11)   A person who is a protected intending occupier of any premises shall be regarded for the purposes of this Part of this Act as a protected intending occupier also of any access to those premises.]

NOTES
Inserted by the Criminal Justice and Public Order Act 1994, s 74.
Sub-s (7): para (c) repealed by the Government of Wales Act 1998, ss 140, 152, Sch 16, para 3(2), Sch 18, Pt VI.
Date in force: 1 November 1998: see SI 1998/2244, art 5.
Sub-s (7): para (d) substituted by SI 1996/2325, art 5(1), Sch 2, para 8.
Sub-s (7A): inserted by the Government of Wales Act 1998, s 140, Sch 16, para 3(3).
Date in force: 1 November 1998: see SI 1998/2244, art 5.

PART IV
MISCELLANEOUS PROVISIONS

51 Bomb hoaxes

(1)   A person who—
(a)   places any article in any place whatever; or
(b)   dispatches any article by post, rail or any other means whatever of sending things from one place to another,

with the intention (in either case) of inducing in some other person a belief that it is likely to explode or ignite and thereby cause personal injury or damage to property is guilty of an offence.

In this subsection "article" includes substance.

(2)   A person who communicates any information which he knows or believes to be false to another person with the intention of inducing in him or any other person a false belief that a bomb or other thing liable to explode or ignite is present in any place or location whatever is guilty of an offence.

(3)   For a person to be guilty of an offence under subsection (1) or (2) above it is not necessary for him to have any particular person in mind as the person in whom he intends to induce the belief mentioned in that subsection.

(4)   A person guilty of an offence under this section shall be liable—
(a)   on summary conviction, to imprisonment for a term not exceeding [six months] or to a fine not exceeding [the prescribed sum], or both;
(b)   on conviction on indictment, to imprisonment for a term not exceeding [seven years].

NOTES
Sub-s (4): first and final words in square brackets substituted by the Criminal Justice Act 1991, s 26; reference to "the prescribed sum" substituted by virtue of the Magistrates' Courts Act 1980, s 32(2).

54 Inciting girl under sixteen to have incestuous sexual intercourse

(1)   It is an offence for a man to incite to have sexual intercourse with him a girl under the age of sixteen whom he knows to be his grand-daughter, daughter or sister.

(2) In the preceding subsection "man" includes boy, "sister" includes half-sister, and for the purposes of that subsection any expression importing a relationship between two people shall be taken to apply notwithstanding that the relationship is not traced through lawful wedlock.

(3) The following provisions of section 1 of the Indecency with Children Act 1960, namely—

. . .

subsection (3) (references in Children and Young Persons Act 1933 to the offences mentioned in Schedule 1 to that Act to include offences under that section);

subsection (4) (offences under that section to be deemed offences against the person for the purpose of section 3 of the Visiting Forces Act 1952),

shall apply in relation to offences under this section.

(4) A person guilty of an offence under this section shall be liable—
  (a) on summary conviction, to imprisonment for a term not exceeding six months or to a fine not exceeding [the prescribed sum], or both;
  (b) on conviction on indictment, to imprisonment for a term not exceeding two years.

NOTES

Sub-s (3): words omitted repealed by the Police and Criminal Evidence Act 1984, s 119, Sch 7, Part V.

Sub-s (4): reference to "the prescribed sum" substituted by virtue of the Magistrates' Courts Act 1980, s 32(2).

PART VI
SUPPLEMENTARY

65 Citation, etc

(1) This Act may be cited as the Criminal Law Act 1977.

(2) The provisions of sections [15] to 32 and 48 above, so far as they relate to proceedings before magistrates' courts, shall be construed as one with the [Magistrates' Courts Act 1980] except that in those provisions "fine" shall include any pecuniary penalty.

(3) Except where the context otherwise requires, any reference in this Act to any enactment is a reference to it as amended, and includes a reference to it as extended or applied, by or under any other enactment, including this Act.

(4) The enactments specified in Schedule 12 to this Act shall have effect subject to the amendments there specified, being minor amendments and amendments consequential on the provisions of this Act.

(5) Subject to the transitional provisions contained in this Act, the enactments specified in Schedule 13 to this Act (which include certain spent provisions) are hereby repealed to the extent specified in the third column of that Schedule.

(6)   There shall be defrayed out of money provided by Parliament any increase attributable to the provisions of this Act in the sums payable out of such money under any other Act.

(7)   This Act shall come into force on such day as the Secretary of State may appoint by order made by statutory instrument, and different days may be so appointed for different purposes.

(8)   Without prejudice to any other transitional provision contained in this Act, the transitional provisions contained in Schedule 14 to this Act shall have effect.

(9)   Without prejudice to Schedule 14 or any other transitional provision contained in this Act, an order under subsection (7) above may make such transitional provision as appears to the Secretary of State to be necessary or expedient in connection with the provisions thereby brought into force.

(10)   In this Act—
- (a)   Part V and, so far as there provided, the provisions mentioned in section 63(2) above extend to Scotland;
- (b)   the following provisions extend to Northern Ireland namely—
  sections 38 to 40,
  . . .
  section 52,
  . . .
  subsections (1), (3) and (6) to (10) of this section,
  Schedule 7,
  in Schedule 14, paragraph 5;
- (c)   section 31 and Schedule 6, so far as they amend any enactment which extends to the Channel Islands or the Isle of Man, extend to the Channel Islands or the Isle of Man, as the case may be;
- (d)   subsections (4) and (5) above and Schedules 12 and 13, so far as they relate to—
  - (i)   section 45 of the Prison Act 1952 (in its application to persons for the time being in Northern Ireland or in the Channel Islands or the Isle of Man);
  - (ii)   Part III and section 39(1) of the Criminal Justice Act 1961; and
  - (iii)   sections 60 and 63 of the Criminal Justice Act 1967 (in their application to persons for the time being in Northern Ireland or in the Channel Islands or the Isle of Man),
  extend to Northern Ireland, the Channel Islands and the Isle of Man (as well as, by virtue of paragraph (a) above, to Scotland);
- (e)   section 32(3) extends to all places (except Scotland) to which section 2 of the European Communities Act 1972 extends (as well as, by virtue of paragraph (a) above, to Scotland) . . .

but save as aforesaid, this Act extends to England and Wales only.

NOTES

Sub-s (2): words in square brackets substituted by the Magistrates' Courts Act 1980, s 154(1), Sch 7, para 153.

Sub-s (10): first words omitted from para (b) repealed by the Criminal Appeal (Northern

Ireland) Act 1980, s 51(2), Sch 5, second words omitted from para (b) repealed by the Diseases of Animals (Northern Ireland) Order 1981, SI 1981/1115; words omitted from para (e) repealed by the Magistrates' Courts Act 1980, s 154(3), Sch 9.

Theft Act 1978

1978 CHAPTER 31

An Act to replace section 16(2)(a) of the Theft Act 1968 with other provision against fraudulent conduct; and for connected purposes

[20th July 1978]

1 Obtaining services by deception

(1)   A person who by any deception dishonestly obtains services from another shall be guilty of an offence.

(2)   It is an obtaining of services where the other is induced to confer a benefit by doing some act, or causing or permitting some act to be done, on the understanding that the benefit has been or will be paid for.

[(3)   Without prejudice to the generality of subsection (2) above, it is an obtaining of services where the other is induced to make a loan, or to cause or permit a loan to be made, on the understanding that any payment (whether by way of interest or otherwise) will be or has been made in respect of the loan.]

NOTES

Sub-s (3): inserted by the Theft (Amendment) Act 1996, s 4(1).

2 Evasion of liability by deception

(1)   Subject to subsection (2) below, where a person by any deception—
  (a)   dishonestly secures the remission of the whole or part of any existing liability to make a payment, whether his own liability or another's; or
  (b)   with intent to make permanent default in whole or in part on any existing liability to make a payment, or with intent to let another do so, dishonestly induces the creditor or any person claiming payment on behalf of the creditor to wait for payment (whether or not the due date for payment is deferred) or to forgo payment; or
  (c)   dishonestly obtains any exemption from or abatement of liability to make a payment;

he shall be guilty of an offence.

(2)   For purposes of this section "liability" means legally enforceable liability; and subsection (1) shall not apply in relation to a liability that has not been accepted or established to pay compensation for a wrongful act or omission.

(3)   For purposes of subsection (1)(*b*) a person induced to take in payment a cheque or other security for money by way of conditional satisfaction of a pre-existing liability is to be treated not as being paid but as being induced to wait for payment.

(4)   For purposes of subsection (1)(*c*) "obtains" includes obtaining for another or enabling another to obtain.

3 Making off without payment

(1)   Subject to subsection (3) below, a person who, knowing that payment on the spot for any goods supplied or service done is required or expected from him, dishonestly makes off without having paid as required or expected and with intent to avoid payment of the amount due shall be guilty of an offence.

(2)   For purposes of this section "payment on the spot" includes payment at the time of collecting goods on which work has been done or in respect of which service has been provided.

(3)   Subsection (1) above shall not apply where the supply of the goods or the doing of the service is contrary to law, or where the service done is such that payment is not legally enforceable.

(4)   Any person may arrest without warrant anyone who is, or whom he, with reasonable cause, suspects to be, committing or attempting to commit an offence under this section.

4 Punishments

(1)   Offences under this Act shall be punishable either on conviction on indictment or on summary conviction.

(2)   A person convicted on indictment shall be liable—
   (a)   for an offence under section 1 or section 2 of this Act, to imprisonment for a term not exceeding five years; and
   (b)   for an offence under section 3 of this Act, to imprisonment for a term not exceeding two years.

(3)   A person convicted summarily of any offence under this Act shall be liable—
   (a)   to imprisonment for a term not exceeding six months; or
   (b)   to a fine not exceeding the prescribed sum for the purposes of [section 32 of the Magistrates' Courts Act 1980] (punishment on summary conviction of offences triable either way: £1,000 or other sum substituted by order under that Act),

or to both.

NOTES

Amended by the Magistrates' Courts Act 1980, Sch 7 para 170.

5 Supplementary

(1) For purposes of sections 1 and 2 above "deception" has the same meaning as in section 15 of the Theft Act 1968, that is to say, it means any deception (whether deliberate or reckless) by words or conduct as to fact or as to law, including a deception as to the present intentions of the person using the deception or any other person; and section 18 of that Act (liability of company officers for offences by the company) shall apply in relation to sections 1 and 2 above as it applies in relation to section 15 of that Act.

(2) Sections 30(1) (husband and wife), 31(1) (effect on civil proceedings) and 34 (interpretation) of the Theft Act 1968, so far as they are applicable in relation to this Act, shall apply as they apply in relation to that Act.

(3)–(5) . . .

NOTES

Sub-s (3): repealed by the Extradition Act 1989, s 37(1), Sch 2.
Sub-s (4): amends the Visiting Forces Act 1952, Schedule.
Sub-s (5): repeals the Theft Act 1968, s 16(2)(a).

7 Short title, commencement and extent

(1) This Act may be cited as the Theft Act 1978.

(2) This Act shall come into force at the expiration of three months beginning with the date on which it is passed.

(3) This Act except section 5(3), shall not extend to Scotland; and except for that subsection, and subject also to section 6, it shall not extend to Northern Ireland.

Protection of Children Act 1978

1978 CHAPTER 37

An Act to prevent the exploitation of children by making indecent photographs of them; and to penalise the distribution, showing and advertisement of such indecent photographs

[20th July 1978]

1 Indecent photographs of children

(1) It is an offence for a person—
  (a) to take, or permit to be taken [or to make], any indecent photograph [or pseudo-photograph] of a child . . . ; or
  (b) to distribute or show such indecent photographs [or pseudo-photographs]; or
  (c) to have in his possession such indecent photographs [or pseudo-photographs], with a view to their being distributed or shown by himself or others; or

(d) to publish or cause to be published any advertisement likely to be understood as conveying that the advertiser distributes or shows such indecent photographs [or pseudo-photographs], or intends to do so.

(2) For purposes of this Act, a person is to be regarded as distributing an indecent photograph [or pseudo-photograph] if he parts with possession of it to, or exposes or offers it for acquisition by, another person.

(3) Proceedings for an offence under this Act shall not be instituted except by or with the consent of the Director of Public Prosecutions.

(4) Where a person is charged with an offence under subsection (1)(b) or (c), it shall be a defence for him to prove—

(a) that he had a legitimate reason for distributing or showing the photographs [or pseudo-photographs] or (as the case may be) having them in his possession; or

(b) that he had not himself seen the photographs [or pseudo-photographs] and did not know, nor had any cause to suspect, them to be indecent.

(5) References in the Children and Young Persons Act 1933 (except in sections 15 and 99) to the offences mentioned in Schedule 1 to that Act shall include an offence under subsection (1)(a) above.

(6), (7)   . . .

NOTES

Sub-s (1): words in square brackets inserted and words omitted repealed by the Criminal Justice and Public Order Act 1994, ss 84(2)(a), (b), 168(3), Sch 11.

Sub-ss (2), (4): words in square brackets inserted by the Criminal Justice and Public Order Act 1994, s 84(2)(c), (d).

Sub-s (6): repealed by the Extradition Act 1989, s 37(1), Sch 2.

Sub-s (7): amends the Visiting Forces Act 1952, Schedule.

9 Short title, extent and commencement

(1) This Act may be cited as the Protection of Children Act 1978.

(2) This Act except section 1(6) shall not extend to Scotland and except for that subsection, and subject also to section 8 shall not extend to Northern Ireland.

(3) Section 8 of this Act shall come into force forthwith, but otherwise this Act shall come into force at the expiration of one month beginning with the date it is passed.

Magistrates' Courts Act 1980

1980 CHAPTER 43

An Act to consolidate certain enactments relating to the jurisdiction of, and the practice and procedure before, magistrates' courts and the functions of justices' clerks, and to matters connected therewith, with amendments to give effect to recommendations of the Law Commission

[1st August 1980]

PART I
CRIMINAL JURISDICTION AND PROCEDURE

Miscellaneous

44 Aiders and abettors

(1) A person who aids, abets, counsels or procures the commission by another person of a summary offence shall be guilty of the like offence and may be tried (whether or not he is charged as a principal) either by a court having jurisdiction to try that other person or by a court having by virtue of his own offence jurisdiction to try him.

(2) Any offence consisting in aiding, abetting, counselling or procuring the commission of an offence triable either way (other than an offence listed in Schedule 1 to this Act) shall by virtue of this subsection be triable either way.

PART VII
MISCELLANEOUS AND SUPPLEMENTARY

Repeals, short title, etc

155 Short title, extent and commencement

(1) This Act may be cited as the Magistrates' Courts Act 1980.

(2) The following provisions of this Act extend to Scotland—
   (a) sections 8 (except subsection (9)), [12(13)], 83(3), 90 and 91 and this section; and
   (b) section 154 and Schedules 7, 8 and 9 so far as they relate to any enactment extending to Scotland.

(3) The following provisions of this Act extend to Northern Ireland—
   (a) sections 83(3), 90 and 91 and this section; and
   (b) section 154 and Schedules 7, 8 and 9 so far as they relate to any enactment extending to Northern Ireland.

(4) The provisions of section 126 above have the same extent as the sections of the Indictable Offences Act 1848 to which they refer.

(5)   . . .

(6)   Except as stated in subsections (2) to (5) above, and except so far as relates to the interpretation or commencement of the provisions mentioned in those subsections, this Act extends to England and Wales only.

(7)   This Act shall come into force on such date as the Secretary of State may appoint by order made by statutory instrument.

NOTES

Sub-s (2): in para (a) number in square brackets substituted by the Criminal Justice and Public Order Act 1994, s 45, Sch 5, para 3(4).
Sub-s (5): repealed by the Statute Law (Repeals) Act 1993.

Indecent Displays (Control) Act 1981

1981 CHAPTER 42

An Act to make fresh provision with respect to the public display of indecent matter; and for purposes connected therewith

[27th July 1981]

1 Indecent displays

(1)   If any indecent matter is publicly displayed the person making the display and any person causing or permitting the display to be made shall be guilty of an offence.

(2)   Any matter which is displayed in or so as to be visible from any public place shall, for the purposes of this section, be deemed to be publicly displayed.

(3)   In subsection (2) above, "public place", in relation to the display of any matter, means any place to which the public have or are permitted to have access (whether on payment or otherwise) while that matter is displayed except—
  (a)   a place to which the public are permitted to have access only on payment which is or includes payment for that display; or
  (b)   a shop or any part of a shop to which the public can only gain access by passing beyond an adequate warning notice;

but the exclusions contained in paragraphs (a) and (b) above shall only apply where persons under the age of 18 years are not permitted to enter while the display in question is continuing.

(4)   Nothing in this section applies in relation to any matter—
  [(a)   included by any person in a television broadcasting service or other television programme service (within the meaning of Part I of the Broadcasting Act 1990);] or
  (b)   included in the display of an art gallery or museum and visible only from within the gallery or museum; or

(c)   displayed by or with the authority of, and visible only from within a building occupied by, the Crown or any local authority; or

(d)   included in a performance of a play (within the meaning of the Theatres Act 1968); or

[(e) included in a film exhibition as defined in the Cinemas Act 1985—

    (i)   given in a place which as regards that exhibition is required to be licensed under section 1 of that Act or by virtue only of section 5, 7 or 8 of that Act is not required to be so licensed; or

    (ii) which is an exhibition to which section 6 of that Act applies given by an exempted organisation as defined by subsection (6) of that section].

(5)   In this section "matter" includes anything capable of being displayed, except that it does not include an actual human body or any part thereof; and in determining for the purpose of this section whether any displayed matter is indecent—

(a)   there shall be disregarded any part of that matter which is not exposed to view; and

(b)   account may be taken of the effect of juxtaposing one thing with another.

(6)   A warning notice shall not be adequate for the purposes of this section unless it complies with the following requirements—

(a)   The warning notice must contain the following words, and no others—

"WARNING

Persons passing beyond this notice will find material on display which they may consider indecent. No admittance to persons under 18 years of age."

(b)   The word "WARNING" must appear as a heading.

(c)   No pictures or other matter shall appear on the notice.

(d)   The notice must be so situated that no one could reasonably gain access to the shop or part of the shop in question without being aware of the notice and it must be easily legible by any person gaining such access.

NOTES

Sub-s (4): para (a) substituted by the Broadcasting Act 1990, s 203(1), Sch 20, para 30; para (e) substituted by the Cinemas Act 1985, s 24(1), Sch 2, para 13.

5 Short title, repeal, extent and commencement

(1)   This Act may be cited as the Indecent Displays (Control) Act 1981.

(2)   The enactments mentioned in the Schedule to this Act are hereby repealed to the extent specified in the third column of that Schedule.

(3)   This Act does not extend to Northern Ireland.

(4)   As respects Scotland, nothing in this Act (except to the extent provided by it) affects—

(a)   any rule of law relating to shameless indecency or to the publication of obscene works; or

[(b) section 51 of the Civic Government (Scotland) Act 1982].

(5)   This Act shall come into force at the expiration of a period of three months, beginning with the day on which this Act is passed.

NOTES

Sub-s (4): para (b) substituted by the Civic Government (Scotland) Act 1982, s 51(7).

Forgery and Counterfeiting Act 1981

1981 CHAPTER 45

An Act to make fresh provision for England and Wales and Northern Ireland with respect to forgery and kindred offences; to make fresh provision for Great Britain and Northern Ireland with respect to the counterfeiting of notes and coins and kindred offences; to amend the penalties for offences under section 63 of the Post Office Act 1953; and for connected purposes

[27th July 1981]

PART I
FORGERY AND KINDRED OFFENCES

Offences

1 The offence of forgery

A person is guilty of forgery if he makes a false instrument, with the intention that he or another shall use it to induce somebody to accept it as genuine, and by reason of so accepting it to do or not to do some act to his own or any other person's prejudice.

2 The offence of copying a false instrument

It is an offence for a person to make a copy of an instrument which is, and which he knows or believes to be, a false instrument, with the intention that he or another shall use it to induce somebody to accept it as a copy of a genuine instrument, and by reason of so accepting it to do or not to do some act to his own or any other person's prejudice.

3 The offence of using a false instrument

It is an offence for a person to use an instrument which is, and which he knows or believes to be, false, with the intention of inducing somebody to accept it as genuine, and by reason of so accepting it to do or not to do some act to his own or any other person's prejudice.

4 The offence of using a copy of a false instrument

It is an offence for a person to use a copy of an instrument which is, and which he knows or believes to be, a false instrument, with the intention of inducing somebody to accept it as a copy of a genuine instrument, and by reason of so accepting it to do or not to do some act to his own or any other person's prejudice.

5 Offences relating to money orders, share certificates, passports, etc

(1) It is an offence for a person to have in his custody or under his control an instrument to which this section applies which is, and which he knows or believes to be, false, with the intention that he or another shall use it to induce somebody to accept it as genuine, and by reason of so accepting it to do or not to do some act to his own or any other person's prejudice.

(2) It is an offence for a person to have in his custody or under his control, without lawful authority or excuse, an instrument to which this section applies which is, and which he knows or believes to be, false.

(3) It is an offence for a person to make or to have in his custody or under his control a machine or implement, or paper or any other material, which to his knowledge is or has been specially designed or adapted for the making of an instrument to which this section applies, with the intention that he or another shall make an instrument to which this section applies which is false and that he or another shall use the instrument to induce somebody to accept it as genuine, and by reason of so accepting it to do or not to do some act to his own or any other person's prejudice.

(4) It is an offence for a person to make or to have in his custody or under his control any such machine, implement, paper or material, without lawful authority or excuse.

(5) The instruments to which this section applies are—
  (a) money orders;
  (b) postal orders;
  (c) United Kingdom postage stamps;
  (d) Inland Revenue stamps;
  (e) share certificates;
  (f) passports and documents which can be used instead of passports;
  (g) cheques;
  (h) travellers' cheques;
  (j) cheque cards;
  (k) credit cards;
  (l) certified copies relating to an entry in a register of births, adoptions, marriages or deaths and issued by the Registrar General, the Registrar General for Northern Ireland, a registration officer or a person lawfully authorised to register marriages; and
  (m) certificates relating to entries in such registers.

(6)   In subsection (5)(e) above "share certificate" means an instrument entitling or evidencing the title of a person to a share or interest—
- (a)   in any public stock, annuity, fund or debt of any government or state, including a state which forms part of another state; or
- (b)   in any stock, fund or debt of a body (whether corporate or unincorporated) established in the United Kingdom or elsewhere.

Interpretation of Part I

8 Meaning of "instrument"

(1)   Subject to subsection (2) below, in this Part of this Act "instrument" means—
- (a)   any document, whether of a formal or informal character;
- (b)   any stamp issued or sold by [a postal operator];
- (c)   any Inland Revenue stamp; and
- (d)   any disc, tape, sound track or other device on or in which information is recorded or stored by mechanical, electronic or other means.

(2)   A currency note within the meaning of Part II of this Act is not an instrument for the purposes of this Part of this Act.

(3)   A mark denoting payment of postage which [a postal operator authorises] to be used instead of an adhesive stamp is to be treated for the purposes of this Part of this Act as if it were a stamp issued by [the postal operator concerned].

[(3A)   In this section "postal operator" has the same meaning as in the Postal Services Act 2000.]

(4)   In this Part of this Act "Inland Revenue stamp" means a stamp as defined in section 27 of the Stamp Duties Management Act 1891.

NOTES

Sub-s (1): in para (b) words "a postal operator" in square brackets substituted by SI 2001/1149, art 3(1), Sch 1, para 50(1), (2).
Date in force: 26 March 2001: see SI 2001/1149, art 1(2).
Sub-s (3): words "a postal operator authorises" in square brackets substituted by SI 2001/1149, art 3(1), Sch 1, para 50(1), (3)(a).
Date in force: 26 March 2001: see SI 2001/1149, art 1(2).
Sub-s (3): words "the postal operator concerned" in square brackets substituted by SI 2001/1149, art 3(1), Sch 1, para 50(1), (3)(b).
Date in force: 26 March 2001: see SI 2001/1149, art 1(2).
Sub-s (3A): inserted by SI 2001/1149, art 3(1), Sch 1, para 50(1), (4).
Date in force: 26 March 2001: see SI 2001/1149, art 1(2).

9 Meaning of "false" and "making"

(1)   An instrument is false for the purposes of this Part of this Act—
- (a)   if it purports to have been made in the form in which it is made by a person who did not in fact make it in that form; or
- (b)   if it purports to have been made in the form in which it is made on the authority of a person who did not in fact authorise its making in that form; or

(c) if it purports to have been made in the terms in which it is made by a person who did not in fact make it in those terms; or

(d) if it purports to have been made in the terms in which it is made on the authority of a person who did not in fact authorise its making in those terms; or

(e) if it purports to have been altered in any respect by a person who did not in fact alter it in that respect; or

(f) if it purports to have been altered in any respect on the authority of a person who did not in fact authorise the alteration in that respect; or

(g) if it purports to have been made or altered on a date on which, or at a place at which, or otherwise in circumstances in which, it was not in fact made or altered; or

(h) if it purports to have been made or altered by an existing person but he did not in fact exist.

(2) A person is to be treated for the purposes of this Part of this Act as making a false instrument if he alters an instrument so as to make it false in any respect (whether or not it is false in some other respect apart from that alteration).

10 Meaning of "prejudice" and "induce"

(1) Subject to subsections (2) and (4) below, for the purposes of this Part of this Act an act or omission intended to be induced is to a person's prejudice if, and only if, it is one which, if it occurs—

(a) will result—
   (i) in his temporary or permanent loss of property; or
   (ii) in his being deprived of an opportunity to earn remuneration or greater remuneration; or
   (iii) in his being deprived of an opportunity to gain a financial advantage otherwise than by way of remuneration; or

(b) will result in somebody being given an opportunity—
   (i) to earn remuneration or greater remuneration from him; or
   (ii) to gain a financial advantage from him otherwise than by way of remuneration; or

(c) will be the result of his having accepted a false instrument as genuine, or a copy of a false instrument as a copy of a genuine one, in connection with his performance of any duty.

(2) An act which a person has an enforceable duty to do and an omission to do an act which a person is not entitled to do shall be disregarded for the purposes of this Part of this Act.

(3) In this Part of this Act references to inducing somebody to accept a false instrument as genuine, or a copy of a false instrument as a copy of a genuine one, include references to inducing a machine to respond to the instrument or copy as if it were a genuine instrument or, as the case may be, a copy of a genuine one.

(4) Where subsection (3) above applies, the act or omission intended to be induced by the machine responding to the instrument or copy shall be treated as an act or omission to a person's prejudice.

(5) In this section "loss" includes not getting what one might get as well as parting with what one has.

Miscellaneous

PART III
MISCELLANEOUS AND GENERAL

Extent

32 Northern Ireland

It is hereby declared that this Act extends to Northern Ireland.

Commencement and short title

33 Commencement

This Act shall come into force on the expiration of the period of three months from the date on which it is passed.

34 Citation

This Act may be cited as the Forgery and Counterfeiting Act 1981.

Criminal Attempts Act 1981

(C 47)

An Act to amend the law of England and Wales as to attempts to commit offences and as to cases of conspiring to commit offences which, in the circumstances, cannot be committed; to repeal the provisions of section 4 of the Vagrancy Act 1824 which apply to suspected persons and reputed thieves; to make provision against unauthorised interference with vehicles; and for connected purposes

[27 July 1981]

PART I
ATTEMPTS ETC

Attempt

1 Attempting to commit an offence

(1) If, with intent to commit an offence to which this section applies, a person does an act which is more than merely preparatory to the commission of the offence, he is guilty of attempting to commit the offence.

[(1A)   Subject to section 8 of the Computer Misuse Act 1990 (relevance of external law), if this subsection applies to an act, what the person doing it had in view shall be treated as an offence to which this section applies.

(1B)   Subsection (1A) above applies to an act if—
   (a)   it is done in England and Wales; and
   (b)   it would fall within subsection (1) above as more than merely preparatory to the commission of an offence under section 3 of the Computer Misuse Act 1990 but for the fact that the offence, if completed, would not be an offence triable in England and Wales.]

(2)   A person may be guilty of attempting to commit an offence to which this section applies even though the facts are such that the commission of the offence is impossible.

(3)   In any case where—
   (a)   apart from this subsection a person's intention would not be regarded as having amounted to an intent to commit an offence; but
   (b)   if the facts of the case had been as he believed them to be, his intention would be so regarded,

then, for the purposes of subsection (1) above, he shall be regarded as having had an intent to commit that offence.

(4)   This section applies to any offence which, if it were completed, would be triable in England and Wales as an indictable offence, other than—
   (a)   conspiracy (at common law or under section 1 of the Criminal Law Act 1977 or any other enactment);
   (b)   aiding, abetting, counselling, procuring or suborning the commission of an offence;
   (c)   offences under section 4(1) (assisting offenders) or 5(1) (accepting or agreeing to accept consideration for not disclosing information about an arrestable offence) of the Criminal Law Act 1967.

NOTES

Sub-ss (1A), (1B): inserted by the Computer Misuse Act 1990, s 7(3).

[1A Extended jurisdiction in relation to certain attempts]

[(1)   If this section applies to an act, what the person doing the act had in view shall be treated as an offence to which section 1(1) above applies.

(2)   This section applies to an act if—
   (a)   it is done in England and Wales, and
   (b)   it would fall within section 1(1) above as more than merely preparatory to the commission of a Group A offence but for the fact that that offence, if completed, would not be an offence triable in England and Wales.

(3)   In this section "Group A offence" has the same meaning as in Part I of the Criminal Justice Act 1993.

(4)   Subsection (1) above is subject to the provisions of section 6 of the Act of 1993 (relevance of external law).

(5) Where a person does any act to which this section applies, the offence which he commits shall for all purposes be treated as the offence of attempting to commit the relevant Group A offence.]

NOTES

Inserted by the Criminal Justice Act 1993, s 5(2).
Date in force: 1 June 1999: see SI 1999/1189, art 2.

Trial etc of offences of attempt

4 Trial and penalties

(1) A person guilty by virtue of section 1 above of attempting to commit an offence shall—
  (a) if the offence attempted is murder or any other offence the sentence for which is fixed by law, be liable on conviction on indictment to imprisonment for life; and
  (b) if the offence attempted is indictable but does not fall within paragraph (a) above, be liable on conviction on indictment to any penalty to which he would have been liable on conviction on indictment of that offence; and
  (c) if the offence attempted is triable either way, be liable on summary conviction to any penalty to which he would have been liable on summary conviction of that offence.

(2) In any case in which a court may proceed to summary trial of an information charging a person with an offence and an information charging him with an offence under section 1 above of attempting to commit it or an attempt under a special statutory provision, the court may, without his consent, try the informations together.

(3) Where, in proceedings against a person for an offence under section 1 above, there is evidence sufficient in law to support a finding that he did an act falling within subsection (1) of that section, the question whether or not his act fell within that subsection is a question of fact.

(4) Where, in proceedings against a person for an attempt under a special statutory provision, there is evidence sufficient in law to support a finding that he did an act falling within subsection (3) of section 3 above, the question whether or not his act fell within that subsection is a question of fact.

(5) Subsection (1) above shall have effect—
  (a) subject to section 37 of and Schedule 2 to the Sexual Offences Act 1956 (mode of trial of and penalties for attempts to commit certain offences under that Act); and
  (b) notwithstanding anything—

    (i)   in section 32(1) (no limit to fine on conviction on indictment) of the Criminal Law Act 1977; or

    (ii) in [section 78(1) and (2)] (maximum of six months' imprisonment on summary conviction unless express provision made to the contrary) of [the Powers of Criminal Courts (Sentencing) Act 2000].

NOTES

Sub-s (5): in para (b)(ii) words "section 78(1) and (2)" in square brackets substituted by the Powers of Criminal Courts (Sentencing) Act 2000, s 165(1), Sch 9, para 82(a).

Date in force: 25 August 2000: see the Powers of Criminal Courts (Sentencing) Act 2000, s 168(1).

Sub-s (5): in para (b)(ii) words "the Powers of Criminal Courts (Sentencing) Act 2000" in square brackets substituted by the Powers of Criminal Courts (Sentencing) Act 2000, s 165(1), Sch 9, para 82(b).

Date in force: 25 August 2000: see the Powers of Criminal Courts (Sentencing) Act 2000, s 168(1).

Supplementary

6 Effect of Part I on common law

(1)   The offence of attempt at common law and any offence at common law of procuring materials for crime are hereby abolished for all purposes not relating to acts done before the commencement of this Act.

(2)   Except as regards offences committed before the commencement of this Act, references in any enactment passed before this Act which fall to be construed as references to the offence of attempt at common law shall be construed as references to the offence under section 1 above.

PART II
SUSPECTED PERSONS ETC

9 Interference with vehicles

(1)   A person is guilty of the offence of vehicle interference if he interferes with a motor vehicle or trailer or with anything carried in or on a motor vehicle or trailer with the intention that an offence specified in subsection (2) below shall be committed by himself or some other person.

(2)   The offences mentioned in subsection (1) above are—
   (a)   theft of the motor vehicle or trailer or part of it;
   (b)   theft of anything carried in or on the motor vehicle or trailer; and
   (c)   an offence under section 12(1) of the Theft Act 1968 (taking and driving away without consent);

and, if it is shown that a person accused of an offence under this section intended that one of those offences should be committed, it is immaterial that it cannot be shown which it was.

(3) A person guilty of an offence under this section shall be liable on summary conviction to imprisonment for a term not exceeding three months or to a fine not exceeding [level 4 on the standard scale] or to both.

(4) . . .

(5) In this section "motor vehicle" and "trailer" have the meanings assigned to them by [section 185(1) of the Road Traffic Act 1988].

NOTES

Sub-s (3): maximum fine converted to a level on the standard scale by the Criminal Justice Act 1982, ss 38, 46(1).

Sub-s (4): repealed by the Police and Criminal Evidence Act 1984, s 119(2), Sch 7, Part I.

Sub-s (5): words in square brackets substituted by the Road Traffic (Consequential Provisions) Act 1988, s 4, Sch 3, para 23.

PART III
GENERAL AND SUPPLEMENTARY

11 Commencement and extent

(1) This Act shall come into force at the expiry of the period of one month beginning with the day on which it is passed.

(2) Section 7(1) in its application to each of the enactments which it amends extends to any place to which that enactment extends; but save as aforesaid, this Act extends to England and Wales only.

12 Short title

This Act may be cited as the Criminal Attempts Act 1981.

Child Abduction Act 1984

1984 CHAPTER 37

An Act to amend the criminal law relating to the abduction of children

[12th July 1984]

PART I
OFFENCES UNDER LAW OF ENGLAND AND WALES

1 Offence of abduction of child by parent, etc

(1) Subject to subsections (5) and (8) below, a person connected with a child under the age of sixteen commits an offence if he takes or sends the child out of the United Kingdom without the appropriate consent.

[(2) A person is connected with a child for the purposes of this section if—

(a) he is a parent of the child; or

(b) in the case of a child whose parents were not married to each other at the time of his birth, there are reasonable grounds for believing that he is the father of the child; or

(c) he is a guardian of the child; or

(d) he is a person in whose favour a residence order is in force with respect to the child; or

(e) he has custody of the child.

(3) In this section "the appropriate consent", in relation to a child means—

   (a) the consent of each of the following—

      (i) the child's mother;

      (ii) the child's father, if he has parental responsibility for him;

      (iii) any guardian of the child;

      (iv) any person in whose favour a residence order is in force with respect to the child;

      (v) any person who has custody of the child; or

   (b) the leave of the court granted under or by virtue of any provision of Part II of the Children Act 1989; or

   (c) if any person has custody of the child, the leave of the court which awarded custody to him.

(4) A person does not commit an offence under this section by taking or sending a child out of the United Kingdom without obtaining the appropriate consent if—

   (a) he is a person in whose favour there is a residence order in force with respect to the child, and

   (b) he takes or sends him out of the United Kingdom for a period of less than one month.

(4A) Subsection (4) above does not apply if the person taking or sending the child out of the United Kingdom does so in breach of an order under Part II of the Children Act 1989.]

(5) A person does not commit an offence under this section by doing anything without the consent of another person whose consent is required under the foregoing provisions if—

   (a) he does it in the belief that the other person—

      (i) has consented; or

      (ii) would consent if he was aware of all the relevant circumstances; or

   (b) he has taken all reasonable steps to communicate with the other person but has been unable to communicate with him; or

   (c) the other person has unreasonably refused to consent,

. . .

[(5A) Subsection (5)(c) above does not apply if—

   (a) the person who refused to consent is a person—

      (i)   in whose favour there is a residence order in force with respect to the child; or

      (ii) who has custody of the child; or

  (b)   the person taking or sending the child out of the United Kingdom is, by so acting, in breach of an order made by a court in the United Kingdom.]

(6)   Where, in proceedings for an offence under this section, there is sufficient evidence to raise an issue as to the application of subsection (5) above, it shall be for the prosecution to prove that that subsection does not apply.

[(7)   For the purposes of this section—

  (a)   "guardian of a child", "residence order" and "parental responsibility" have the same meaning as in the Children Act 1989; and

  (b)   a person shall be treated as having custody of a child if there is in force an order of a court in the United Kingdom awarding him (whether solely or jointly with another person) custody, legal custody or care and control of the child.]

(8)   This section shall have effect subject to the provisions of the Schedule to this Act in relation to a child who is in the care of a local authority [detained in a place of safety, remanded to a local authority accommodation or the subject of] proceedings or an order relating to adoption.

NOTES

Sub-ss (2)–(4A): substituted, for sub-ss (2)–(4) as originally enacted, by the Children Act 1989, s 108(4), Sch 12, para 37(2).

Sub-s (5A): substituted for words omitted from sub-s (5) by the Children Act 1989, s 108(4), Sch 12, para 37(3).

Sub-s (7): substituted by the Children Act 1989, s 108(4), Sch 12, para 37(4).

Sub-s (8): words in square brackets substituted by the Children Act 1989, s 108(4), Sch 12, para 37(5).

2 Offence of abduction of child by other persons

(1)   [Subject to subsection (3) below, a person, other than one mentioned in subsection (2) below,] commits an offence if, without lawful authority or reasonable excuse, he takes or detains a child under the age of sixteen—

  (a)   so as to remove him from the lawful control of any person having lawful control of the child; or

  (b)   so as to keep him out of the lawful control of any person entitled to lawful control of the child.

[(2)   The persons are—

  (a)   where the father and mother of the child in question were married to each other at the time of his birth, the child's father and mother;

  (b)   where the father and mother of the child in question were not married to each other at the time of his birth, the child's mother; and

  (c)   any other person mentioned in section 1(2)(c) to (e) above.

(3)   In proceedings against any person for an offence under this section, it shall be a defence for that person to prove—

(a) where the father and mother of the child in question were not married to each other at the time of his birth—
   (i) that he is the child's father; or
   (ii) that, at the time of the alleged offence, he believed, on reasonable grounds, that he was the child's father; or
(b) that, at the time of the alleged offence, he believed that the child had attained the age of sixteen.]

NOTES

Sub-s (1): words in square brackets substituted by the Children Act 1989, s 108(4), Sch 12, para 38(1).

Sub-ss (2), (3): substituted, for sub-s (2) as originally enacted, by the Children Act 1989, s 108(4), Sch 12, para 38(2).

3 Construction of references to taking, sending and detaining

For the purposes of this Part of this Act—
(a) a person shall be regarded as taking a child if he causes or induces the child to accompany him or any other person or causes the child to be taken;
(b) a person shall be regarded as sending a child if he causes the child to be sent; . . .
(c) a person shall be regarded as detaining a child if he causes the child to be detained or induces the child to remain with him or any other person [and
(d) references to a child's parents and to a child whose parents were (or were not) married to each other at the time of his birth shall be construed in accordance with section 1 of the Family Law Reform Act 1987 (which extends their meaning).].

NOTES

Word omitted from para (b) repealed, and para (d) and preceding word "and" inserted, by the Children Act 1989, s 108(4), (7), Sch 12, para 39, Sch 15.

4 Penalties and prosecutions

(1) A person guilty of an offence under this Part of this Act shall be liable—
(a) on summary conviction, to imprisonment for a term not exceeding six months or to a fine not exceeding the statutory maximum, . . . , or to both such imprisonment and fine;
(b) on conviction on indictment, to imprisonment for a term not exceeding seven years.

(2) No prosecution for an offence under section 1 above shall be instituted except by or with the consent of the Director of Public Prosecutions.

NOTES

Sub-s (1): words omitted repealed by the Statute Law (Repeals) Act 1993.

5 Restriction on prosecutions for offence of kidnapping

Except by or with the consent of the Director of Public Prosecutions no prosecution shall be instituted for an offence of kidnapping if it was committed—

    (a)   against a child under the age of sixteen; and

    (b)   by a person connected with the child, within the meaning of section 1 above.

PART III

SUPPLEMENTARY

13 Short title, commencement and extent

(1)   This Act may be cited as the Child Abduction Act 1984.

(2)   This Act shall come into force at the end of the period of three months beginning with the day on which it is passed.

(3)   Part I of this Act extends to England and Wales only, Part II extends to Scotland only and in Part III section 11(1) and (5)(a) and section 12 do not extend to Scotland and section 11(1), (2) and (5)(a) and (c) does not extend to Northern Ireland.

SCHEDULE

MODIFICATIONS OF SECTION 1 FOR CHILDREN IN CERTAIN CASES

Section 1(8)

Children in care of local authorities and voluntary organisations

1   (1)   This paragraph applies in the case of a child who is in the care of a local authority [within the meaning of the Children Act 1989] in England or Wales.

(2)   Where this paragraph applies, section 1 of this Act shall have effect as if—

    (a)   the reference in subsection (1) to the appropriate consent were a reference to the consent of the local authority in whose care the child is; and

    (b)   subsections (3) to (6) were omitted.

Children in places of safety

2   [(1)   This paragraph applies in the case of a child who is—

    (a)   detained in a place of safety under [paragraph 7(4) of Schedule 7 to the Powers of Criminal Courts (Sentencing) Act 2000]; or

    (b)   remanded to local authority accommodation under section 23 of [the Children and Young Persons Act 1969].]

(2)   Where this paragraph applies, section 1 of this Act shall have effect as if—

    (a)   the reference in subsection (1) to the appropriate consent were a reference to the leave of any magistrates' court acting for the area in which the place of safety is; and

    (b)   subsections (3) to (6) were omitted.

Adoption and custodianship

3   (1)   This paragraph applies in the case of a child—

    (a)   who is the subject of an order under [section 18 of the Adoption Act 1976] freeing him for adoption; or

(b) who is the subject of a pending application for such an order; or

(c) who is the subject of a pending application for an adoption order; or

(d) who is the subject of an order under [section 55 of the Adoption Act 1976] relating to adoption abroad or of a pending application for such an order; or

(e) . . .

(2) Where this paragraph applies, section 1 of this Act shall have effect as if—

(a) the reference in subsection (1) to the appropriate consent were a reference—

(i) in a case within sub-paragraph (1)(a) above, to the consent of the adoption agency which made the application for the [section 18 order or, if the section 18 order has been varied under section 21 of that Act so as to give parental responsibility to another agency], to the consent of that other agency;

(ii) in a case within sub-paragraph (1)(b), [or (c)] above, to the leave of the court to which the application was made; and

(iii) in a case within sub-paragraph (1)(d) above, to the leave of the court which made the order or, as the case may be, to which the application was made; and

(b) subsections (3) to (6) were omitted.

[(3) Sub-paragraph (2) above shall be construed as if the references to the court included, in any case where the court is a magistrates' court, a reference to any magistrates' court acting for the same area as that court.]

Cases within paragraphs 1 and 3

4 In the case of a child falling within both paragraph 1 and paragraph 3 above, the provisions of paragraph 3 shall apply to the exclusion of those in paragraph 1.

Interpretation

[**5** In this Schedule—

(a) "adoption agency" and "adoption order" have the same meaning as in the Adoption Act 1976; and

(b) "area", in relation to a magistrates' court, means the petty sessions area . . . for which the court is appointed.]

NOTES

Para 1: in sub-para (1) words "within the meaning of the Children Act 1989" in square brackets substituted by the Children Act 1989, s 108(4), Sch 12, para 40(1), (2).

Para 2: sub-para (1) substituted by the Children Act 1989, s 108(4), Sch 12, para 40(1), (3).

Para 2: in sub-para (1)(a) words "paragraph 7(4) of Schedule 7 to the Powers of Criminal Courts (Sentencing) Act 2000" in square brackets substituted by the Powers of Criminal Courts (Sentencing) Act 2000, s 165(1), Sch 9, para 93(a).

Date in force: 25 August 2000: see the Powers of Criminal Courts (Sentencing) Act 2000, s 168(1).

Para 2: in sub-para (1)(b) words "the Children and Young Persons Act 1969" in square brackets substituted by the Powers of Criminal Courts (Sentencing) Act 2000, s 165(1), Sch 9, para 93(b).

Date in force: 25 August 2000: see the Powers of Criminal Courts (Sentencing) Act 2000, s 168(1).

Para 3: in sub-para (1)(a) words "section 18 of the Adoption Act 1976" in square brackets substituted by the Children Act 1989, s 108(4), Sch 12, para 40(1), (4)(a).

Para 3: in sub-para (1)(d) words "section 55 of the Adoption Act 1976" in square brackets substituted by the Children Act 1989, s 108(4), Sch 12, para 40(1), (4)(b).

Para 3: sub-para (1)(c) repealed by the Children Act 1989, s 108(7), Sch 15.

Para 3: in sub-para (2)(a)(i) words from "section 18 order or," to "responsibility to another agency" in square brackets substituted by the Children Act 1989, s 108(4), Sch 12, para 40(1), (5)(a).

Para 3: in sub-para (2)(a)(ii) words "or (c)" in square brackets substituted by the Children Act 1989, s 108(4), Sch 12, para 40(1), (5)(b).

Para 3: sub-para (3) substituted by the Children Act 1989, s 108(4), Sch 12, para 40(1), (6).

Para 5: substituted by the Children Act 1989, s 108(4), Sch 12, para 40.

Para 5: in sub-para (b) words omitted repealed by the Access to Justice Act 1999, s 106, Sch 15, Pt V, Table (1).

Date in force: 27 September 1999: see the Access to Justice Act 1999, s 108(3)(f).

Police and Criminal Evidence Act 1984

1984 CHAPTER 60

An Act to make further provision in relation to the powers and duties of the police, persons in police detention, criminal evidence, police discipline and complaints against the police; to provide for arrangements for obtaining the views of the community on policing and for a rank of deputy chief constable; to amend the law relating to the Police Federations and Police Forces and Police Cadets in Scotland; and for connected purposes

[31st October 1984]

PART III
ARREST

24 Arrest without warrant for arrestable offences

(1) The powers of summary arrest conferred by the following subsections shall apply—

(a) to offences for which the sentence is fixed by law;

(b) to offences for which a person of *21* [18] years of age or over (not previously convicted) may be sentenced to imprisonment for a term of five years (or might be so sentenced but for the restrictions imposed by section 33 of the Magistrates' Courts Act 1980); and

(c) to the offences to which subsection (2) below applies,

and in this Act "arrestable offence" means any such offence.

(2) The offences to which this subsection applies are—

(a) offences for which a person may be arrested under the customs and excise Acts, as defined in section 1(1) of the Customs and Excise Management Act 1979;

(b) offences under [the Official Secrets Act 1920] that are not arrestable offences by virtue of the term of imprisonment for which a person may be sentenced in respect of them;

[(bb) offences under any provision of the Official Secrets Act 1989 except section 8(1), (4) or (5);]

(c)   offences under section . . . 22 (causing prostitution of women) or 23 (procuration of girl under 21) of the Sexual Offences Act 1956;

[(ca) an offence under section 46 of the Criminal Justice and Police Act 2001;]

(d)   offences under section 12(1) (taking motor vehicle or other conveyance without authority etc.) or 25(1) (going equipped for stealing, etc.) of the Theft Act 1968; and

[(e)   any offence under the Football (Offences) Act 1991.]

[(f)   an offence under section 2 of the Obscene Publications Act 1959 (publication of obscene matter);

(g)   an offence under section 1 of the Protection of Children Act 1978 (indecent photographs and pseudo-photographs of children);]

[(ga) an offence under section 1 of the Sexual Offences Act 1985 (c 44) (kerb-crawling);

(gb) an offence under subsection (4) of section 170 of the Road Traffic Act 1988 (c 52) (failure to stop and report an accident) in respect of an accident to which that section applies by virtue of subsection (1)(a) of that section (accidents causing personal injury);]

[(h)   an offence under section 166 of the Criminal Justice and Public Order Act 1994 (sale of tickets by unauthorised persons);]

[(i)   an offence under section 19 of the Public Order Act 1986 (publishing, etc material intended or likely to stir up racial hatred);]

[(j)   an offence under section 167 of the Criminal Justice and Public Order Act 1994 (touting for hire car services);]

[(k)   an offence under section 1(1) of the Prevention of Crime Act 1953 (prohibition of the carrying of offensive weapons without lawful authority or reasonable excuse);

(l)   an offence under section 139(1) of the Criminal Justice Act 1988 (offence of having article with blade or point in public place);

(m)   an offence under section 139A(1) or (2) of the Criminal Justice Act 1988 (offence of having article with blade or point (or offensive weapon) on school premises)];

[(n)   an offence under section 2 of the Protection from Harassment Act 1997 (harassment).]

[(o)   an offence under [section 60AA(7)] of the Criminal Justice and Public Order Act 1994 (failing to comply with requirement to remove mask etc);]

[(p)   an offence falling within section 32(1)(a) of the Crime and Disorder Act 1998 ([racially or religiously aggravated] harassment);]

[(q)   an offence under section 14J or 21C of the Football Spectators Act 1989 (failure to comply with requirements imposed by or under a banning order or a notice under section 21B);]

[(qa) an offence under section 12(4) of the Criminal Justice and Police Act 2001;]

[(r)   . . .]

[(s)   an offence under section 1(1) or (2) or 6 of the Wildlife and Countryside Act 1981 (taking, possessing, selling etc of wild birds) in respect of a bird included in Schedule 1 to that Act or any part of, or anything derived from, such a bird;

(t)   an offence under any of the following provisions of the Wildlife and Countryside Act 1981—

      (i)   section 1(5) (disturbance of wild birds),

      (ii) section 9 or 13(1)(a) or (2) (taking, possessing, selling etc of wild animals or plants),

      (iii) section 14 (introduction of new species etc)];

  [(u) an offence under section 21C(1) or 21D(1) of the Aviation Security Act 1982 (c 36) (unauthorised presence in restricted zone or on aircraft);

  (v) an offence under section 39(1) of the Civil Aviation Act 1982 (c 16) (trespass on aerodrome)].

(3)   Without prejudice to section 2 of the Criminal Attempts Act 1981, the powers of summary arrest conferred by the following subsections shall also apply to the offences of—

  (a) conspiring to commit any of the offences mentioned in subsection (2) above;

  (b) attempting to commit any such offence [other than an offence under section 12(1) of the Theft Act 1968];

  (c) inciting, aiding, abetting, counselling or procuring the commission of any such offence;

and such offences are also arrestable offences for the purposes of this Act.

(4)   Any person may arrest without a warrant—

  (a) anyone who is in the act of committing an arrestable offence;

  (b) anyone whom he has reasonable grounds for suspecting to be committing such an offence.

(5)   Where an arrestable offence has been committed, any person may arrest without a warrant—

  (a) anyone who is guilty of the offence;

  (b) anyone whom he has reasonable grounds for suspecting to be guilty of it.

(6)   Where a constable has reasonable grounds for suspecting that an arrestable offence has been committed, he may arrest without a warrant anyone whom he has reasonable grounds for suspecting to be guilty of the offence.

(7)   A constable may arrest without a warrant—

  (a) anyone who is about to commit an arrestable offence;

  (b) anyone whom he has reasonable grounds for suspecting to be about to commit an arrestable offence.

NOTES

Sub-s (1): in para (b) number "21" in italics repealed and subsequent number in square brackets substituted by the Criminal Justice and Court Services Act 2000, s 74, Sch 7, Pt II, paras 76, 77.

Date in force: to be appointed: see the Criminal Justice and Court Services Act 2000, s 80(1).

Sub-s (2): in para (b) words "the Official Secrets Act 1920" in square brackets substituted by the Official Secrets Act 1989, s 11(1).

Sub-s (2): para (bb) inserted by the Official Secrets Act 1989, s 11(1).

Sub-s (2): in para (c) words omitted repealed by the Sexual Offences Act 1985, s 5(3), Schedule.

Sub-s (2): para (ca) inserted by the Criminal Justice and Police Act 2001, s 46(6).

Date in force: 1 September 2001: see SI 2001/2223, art 4(c).

Sub-s (2): para (e) as originally enacted repealed by the Criminal Justice Act 1988, s 170(2), Sch 16, new para (e) inserted by the Football Offences Act 1991, s 5(1).

Sub-s (2): paras (f), (g) inserted by the Criminal Justice and Public Order Act 1994, s 85(2).

Sub-s (2): paras (ga), (gb) inserted by the Criminal Justice and Police Act 2001, s 71.

Date in force: 1 October 2001: see SI 2001/3150, art 2(a).

Sub-s (2): para (h) inserted by the Criminal Justice and Public Order Act 1994, s 166(4).

Sub-s (2): para (i) inserted by the Criminal Justice and Public Order Act 1994, s 155.

Sub-s (2): para (j) inserted by the Criminal Justice and Public Order Act 1994, s 167(7).

Sub-s (2): paras (k)–(m) inserted by the Offensive Weapons Act 1996, s 1(1).

Sub-s (2): para (n) inserted by the Protection from Harassment Act 1997, s 2(3).

Sub-s (2): para (o) inserted by the Crime and Disorder Act 1998, s 27(1).

Date in force: 1 March 1999: see SI 1998/3263, art 4.

Sub-s (2): in para (o) words "section 60AA(7)" in square brackets substituted by the Anti-terrorism, Crime and Security Act 2001, s 94(3).

Date in force: 14 December 2001: see the Anti-terrorism, Crime and Security Act 2001, s 127(2)(d).

Sub-s (2): para (p) inserted by the Crime and Disorder Act 1998, s 32(2).

Date in force: 30 September 1998: see SI 1998/2327, art 2(1)(g).

Sub-s (2): in para (p) words "racially or religiously aggravated" in square brackets substituted by the Anti-terrorism, Crime and Security Act 2001, s 39(8).

Date in force: 14 December 2001 (except in relation to anything done before that date): see the Anti-terrorism, Crime and Security Act 2001, ss 42, 127(2)(a).

Sub-s (2): para (q) (as originally inserted by the Crime and Disorder Act 1998, s 84(2)) substituted by the Football (Disorder) Act 2000, s 1, Sch 2, para 2.

Date in force: 28 August 2000: see the Football (Disorder) Act 2000, s 5(1), and SI 2000/2125, art 2.

Sub-s (2): para (qa) inserted by the Criminal Justice and Police Act 2001, s 12(6).

Date in force: 1 September 2001: see SI 2001/2223, art 4(a).

Sub-s (2): para (r) inserted by the Football (Offences and Disorder) Act 1999, s 8(3).

Date in force: 27 September 1999, except in relation to offences committed, or orders made before that date: see the Football (Offences and Disorder) Act 1999, s 12(2), (3).

Sub-s (2): para (r) repealed by the Football (Disorder) Act 2000, s 1, Sch 2, para 2, Sch 3.

Date in force: 28 August 2000: see the Football (Disorder) Act 2000, s 5(1), and SI 2000/2125, art 2.

Sub-s (2): paras (s), (t) inserted by the Countryside and Rights of Way Act 2000, s 81(1), Sch 12, para 13.

Date in force: 30 January 2001: see the Countryside and Rights of Way Act 2000, s 103(2).

Sub-s (2): paras (u), (v) inserted by the Anti-terrorism, Crime and Security Act 2001, s 82(1).

Date in force: 14 February 2002 (in relation to an offence committed or alleged to have been committed after that date): see the Anti-terrorism, Crime and Security Act 2001, ss 82(4), 127(2)(c).

Sub-s (3): in para (b) words in square brackets inserted by the Criminal Justice Act 1988, s 170(1), Sch 15, paras 97, 98.

25 General arrest conditions

(1) Where a constable has reasonable grounds for suspecting that any offence which is not an arrestable offence has been committed or attempted, or is being committed or attempted, he may arrest the relevant person if it appears to him that service of a summons is impracticable or inappropriate because any of the general arrest conditions is satisfied.

(2)   In this section "the relevant person" means any person whom the constable has reasonable grounds to suspect of having committed or having attempted to commit the offence or of being in the course of committing or attempting to commit it.

(3)   The general arrest conditions are—
  (a)   that the name of the relevant person is unknown to, and cannot be readily ascertained by, the constable;
  (b)   that the constable has reasonable grounds for doubting whether a name furnished by the relevant person as his name is his real name;
  (c)   that—
      (i)   the relevant person has failed to furnish a satisfactory address for service; or
      (ii)   the constable has reasonable grounds for doubting whether an address furnished by the relevant person is a satisfactory address for service;
  (d)   that the constable has reasonable grounds for believing that arrest is necessary to prevent the relevant person—
      (i)   causing physical injury to himself or any other person;
      (ii)   suffering physical injury;
      (iii)   causing loss of or damage to property;
      (iv)   committing an offence against public decency; or
      (v)   causing an unlawful obstruction of the highway;
  (e)   that the constable has reasonable grounds for believing that arrest is necessary to protect a child or other vulnerable person from the relevant person.

(4)   For the purposes of subsection (3) above an address is a satisfactory address for service if it appears to the constable—
  (a)   that the relevant person will be at it for a sufficiently long period for it to be possible to serve him with a summons; or
  (b)   that some other person specified by the relevant person will accept service of a summons for the relevant person at it.

(5)   Nothing in subsection (3)(d) above authorises the arrest of a person under sub-paragraph (iv) of that paragraph except where members of the public going about their normal business cannot reasonably be expected to avoid the person to be arrested.

(6)   This section shall not prejudice any power of arrest conferred apart from this section.

PART XI
MISCELLANEOUS AND SUPPLEMENTARY

120 Extent

(1)   Subject to the following provisions of this section, this Act extends to England and Wales only.

(2)-(11) . . .

Sub-ss (2)-(11): outside the scope of this work.

121 Commencement

(1) This Act, except section 120 above, this section and section 122 below, shall come into foperation on such day as the Secretary of State may by order made by statutory instrument appoint, and different days may be so appointed for different provisions and for different purposes.

(2)-(4) . . .

Sub-ss (2)-(4): outside the scope of this work.

122 Short title

This Act may be cited as the Police and Criminal Evidence Act 1984.

Companies Act 1985

1985 CHAPTER 6

An Act to consolidate the greater part of the Companies Acts

[11th March 1985]

PART XVI
FRAUDULENT TRADING BY A COMPANY

458 Punishment for fraudulent trading

If any business of a company is carried on with intent to defraud creditors of the company or creditors of any other person, or for any fraudulent purpose, every person who was knowingly a party to the carrying on of the business in that manner is liable to imprisonment or a fine, or both.

This applies whether or not the company has been, or is in the course of being, wound up.

PART XXVII
FINAL PROVISIONS

746 Commencement

. . . this Act comes into force on 1st July 1985.

Words omitted repealed by the Companies Act 1989, s 212, Sch 24.

747 Citation

This Act may be cited as the Companies Act 1985.

Intoxicating Substances (Supply) Act 1985

1985 CHAPTER 26

An Act to prohibit the supply to persons under the age of eighteen of certain substances which may cause intoxication if inhaled

[13th June 1985]

1 Offence of supplying intoxicating substance

(1)   It is an offence for a person to supply or offer to supply a substance other than a controlled drug—

  (a)   to a person under the age of eighteen whom he knows, or has reasonable cause to believe, to be under that age; or

  (b)   to a person—
      (i)   who is acting on behalf of a person under that age; and
      (ii)   whom he knows, or has reasonable cause to believe, to be acting,

if he knows or has reasonable cause to believe that the substance is, or its fumes are, likely to be inhaled by the person under the age of eighteen for the purpose of causing intoxication.

(2)   In proceedings against any person for an offence under subsection (1) above it is a defence for him to show that at the time he made the supply or offer he was under the age of eighteen and was acting otherwise than in the course or furtherance of a business.

(3)   A person guilty of an offence under this section shall be liable on summary conviction to imprisonment for a term not exceeding six months or to a fine not exceeding level 5 on the standard scale . . . , or to both.

(4)   In this section "controlled drug" has the same meaning as in the Misuse of Drugs Act 1971.

Sub-s (3): words omitted repealed by the Statute Law (Repeals) Act 1993.

2 Short title, commencement and extent

(1)   This Act may be cited as the Intoxicating Substances (Supply) Act 1985.

(2) This Act shall come into force at the end of the period of two months beginning with the day on which it is passed.

(3) This Act extends to Northern Ireland but not to Scotland.

Sexual Offences Act 1985

1985 CHAPTER 44

An Act to make, as respect England and Wales, provision for penalising in certain circumstances the soliciting of women for sexual purposes by men, and to increase the penalties under the Sexual Offences Act 1956 for certain offences against women

[16th July 1985]

Soliciting of women by men

1 Kerb-crawling

(1) A man commits an offence if he solicits a woman (or different women) for the purpose of prostitution—
  (a) from a motor vehicle while it is in a street or public place; or
  (b) in a street or public place while in the immediate vicinity of a motor vehicle that he has just got out of or off,

persistently or, . . . , in such manner or in such circumstances as to be likely to cause annoyance to the woman (or any of the women) solicited, or nuisance to other persons in the neighbourhood.

(2) A person guilty of an offence under this section shall be liable on summary conviction to a fine not exceeding level 3 on the standard scale . . .

(3) In this section "motor vehicle" has the same meaning as in [the Road Traffic Act 1988].

NOTES

Sub-ss (1), (2): words omitted repealed by the Statute Law (Repeals) Act 1993.

Sub-s (3): words in square brackets substituted by the Road Traffic (Consequential Provisions) Act 1988, s 4, Sch 3, para 29.

2 Persistent soliciting of women for the purpose of prostitution

(1) A man commits an offence if in a street or public place he persistently solicits a woman (or different women) for the purpose of prostitution.

(2) A person guilty of an offence under this section shall be liable on summary conviction to a fine not exceeding level 3 on the standard scale . . .

NOTES

Sub-s (2): words omitted repealed by the Statute Law (Repeals) Act 1993.

Supplementary

4 Interpretation

(1)   References in this Act to a man soliciting a woman for the purpose of prostitution are references to his soliciting her for the purpose of obtaining her services as a prostitute.

(2)   The use in any provision of this Act of the word "man" without the addition of the word "boy" shall not prevent the provision applying to any person to whom it would have applied if both words had been used, and similarly with the words "woman" and "girl".

(3)   Paragraphs (*a*) and (*b*) of section 6 of the Interpretation Act 1978 (words importing the masculine gender to include the feminine, and vice versa) do not apply to this Act.

(4)   For the purposes of this Act "street" includes any bridge, road, lane, footway, subway, square, court, alley or passage, whether a thoroughfare or not, which is for the time being open to the public; and the doorways and entrances of premises abutting on a street (as hereinbefore defined), and any ground adjoining and open to a street, shall be treated as forming part of the street.

5 Short title, commencement etc

(1)   This Act may be cited as the Sexual Offences Act 1985.

(2)   . . .

(3)   The enactments mentioned in the Schedule to this Act are hereby repealed to the extent specified in the third column of that Schedule.

(4)   This Act shall come into force at the end of the period of two months beginning with the day on which it is passed.

(5)   Nothing in this Act shall apply in relation to any offence committed or act done before this Act comes into force.

(6)   . . .

(7)   This Act extends to England and Wales only.

NOTES

Sub-s (2): amends the Indecency with Children Act 1960, s 2.
Sub-s (6): repealed by the Statute Law (Repeals) Act 1993.

Public Order Act 1986

1986 CHAPTER 64

An Act to abolish the common law offences of riot, rout, unlawful assembly and affray and certain statutory offences relating to public order; to create new offences relating to public order; to control public processions and assemblies; to control the stirring up of racial hatred; to provide for the exclusion of certain offenders from sporting events; to create a new offence relating to the contamination of or interference with goods; to confer power to direct certain trespassers to leave land; to amend section 7 of the Conspiracy and Protection of Property Act 1875, section 1 of the Prevention of Crime Act 1953, Part V of the Criminal Justice (Scotland) Act 1980 and the Sporting Events (Control of Alcohol etc) Act 1985; to repeal certain obsolete or unnecessary enactments; and for connected purposes

[7th November 1986]

PART I
NEW OFFENCES

1 Riot

(1) Where 12 or more persons who are present together use or threaten unlawful violence for a common purpose and the conduct of them (taken together) is such as would cause a person of reasonable firmness present at the scene to fear for his personal safety, each of the persons using unlawful violence for the common purpose is guilty of riot.

(2) It is immaterial whether or not the 12 or more use or threaten unlawful violence simultaneously.

(3) The common purpose may be inferred from conduct.

(4) No person of reasonable firmness need actually be, or be likely to be, present at the scene.

(5) Riot may be committed in private as well as in public places.

(6) A person guilty of riot is liable on conviction on indictment to imprisonment for a term not exceeding ten years or a fine or both.

2 Violent Disorder

(1) Where 3 or more persons who are present together use or threaten unlawful violence and the conduct of them (taken together) is such as would cause a person of reasonable firmness present at the scene to fear for personal safety, each of the persons using or threatening unlawful violence is guilty of violent disorder.

(2) It is immaterial whether or not the 3 or more use or threaten unlawful violence simultaneously.

(3)   No person of reasonable firmness need actually be, or be likely to be, present at the scene.

(4)   Violent disorder may be committed in private as well as in public places.

(5)   A person guilty of violent disorder is liable on conviction on indictment to imprisonment for a term not exceeding 5 years or a fine or both, or on summary conviction to imprisonment for a term not exceeding 6 months or a fine not exceeding the statutory maximum or both.

3 Affray

(1)   A person is guilty of affray if he uses or threatens unlawful violence towards another and his conduct is such as would cause a person of reasonable firmness present at the scene to fear for his personal safety.

(2)   Where 2 or more persons use or threaten the unlawful violence, it is the conduct of them taken together that must be considered for the purposes of subsection (1).

(3)   For the purposes of this section a threat cannot be made by the use of words alone.

(4)   No person of reasonable firmness need actually be, or be likely to be, present at the scene.

(5)   Affray may be committed in private as well as in public places.

(6)   A constable may arrest without warrant anyone he reasonably suspects is committing affray.

(7)   A person guilty of affray is liable on conviction on indictment to imprisonment for a term not exceeding 3 years or a fine or both, or on summary conviction to imprisonment for a term not exceeding 6 months or a fine not exceeding the statutory maximum or both.

4 Fear or provocation of violence

(1)   A person is guilty of an offence if he—
  (a)   uses towards another person threatening, abusive or insulting words or behaviour, or
  (b)   distributes or displays to another person any writing, sign or other visible representation which is threatening, abusive or insulting,

with intent to cause that person to believe that immediate unlawful violence will be used against him or another by any person, or to provoke the immediate use of unlawful violence by that person or another, or whereby that person is likely to believe that such violence will be used or it is likely that such violence will be provoked.

(2)   An offence under this section may be committed in a public or a private place, except that no offence is committed where the words or behaviour are used, or the writing, sign or other visible representation is distributed or displayed, by a person inside a dwelling and the other person is also inside that or another dwelling.

(3)   A constable may arrest without warrant anyone he reasonably suspects is committing an offence under this section.

(4)   A person guilty of an offence under this section is liable on summary conviction to imprisonment for a term not exceeding 6 months or a fine not exceeding level 5 on the standard scale or both.

[4A Intentional harassment, alarm or distress]

[(1)   A person is guilty of an offence if, with intent to cause a person harassment, alarm or distress, he—
  (a)   uses threatening, abusive or insulting words or behaviour, or disorderly behaviour, or
  (b)   displays any writing, sign or other visible representation which is threatening, abusive or insulting,

thereby causing that or another person harassment, alarm or distress.

(2)   An offence under this section may be committed in a public or a private place, except that no offence is committed where the words or behaviour are used, or the writing, sign or other visible representation is displayed, by a person inside a dwelling and the person who is harassed, alarmed or distressed is also inside that or another dwelling.

(3)   It is a defence for the accused to prove—
  (a)   that he was inside a dwelling and had no reason to believe that the words or behaviour used, or the writing, sign or other visible representation displayed, would be heard or seen by a person outside that or any other dwelling, or
  (b)   that his conduct was reasonable.

(4)   A constable may arrest without warrant anyone he reasonably suspects is committing an offence under this section.

(5)   A person guilty of an offence under this section is liable on summary conviction to imprisonment for a term not exceeding 6 months or a fine not exceeding level 5 on the standard scale or both.]

NOTES
Inserted by the Criminal Justice and Public Order Act 1994, s 154.

5 Harassment, alarm or distress

(1)   A person is guilty of an offence if he—
  (a)   uses threatening, abusive or insulting words or behaviour, or disorderly behaviour, or
  (b)   displays any writing, sign or other visible representation which is threatening, abusive or insulting,

within the hearing or sight of a person likely to be caused harassment, alarm or distress thereby.

(2)   An offence under this section may be committed in a public or a private place, except that no offence is committed where the words or behaviour are used, or the

writing, sign or other visible representation is displayed, by a person inside a dwelling and the other person is also inside that or another dwelling.

(3) It is a defence for the accused to prove—
   (a) that he had no reason to believe that there was any person within hearing or sight who was likely to be caused harassment, alarm or distress, or
   (b) that he was inside a dwelling and had no reason to believe that the words or behaviour used, or the writing, sign or other visible representation displayed, would be heard or seen by a person outside that or any other dwelling, or
   (c) that his conduct was reasonable.

(4) A constable may arrest a person without warrant if—
   (a) he engages in offensive conduct which [a] constable warns him to stop, and
   (b) he engages in further offensive conduct immediately or shortly after the warning.

(5) In subsection (4) "offensive conduct" means conduct the constable reasonably suspects to constitute an offence under this section, and the conduct mentioned in paragraph (a) and the further conduct need not be of the same nature.

(6) A person guilty of an offence under this section is liable on summary conviction to a fine not exceeding level 3 on the standard scale.

NOTES

Sub-s (4): word in square brackets in para (a) substituted by the Public Order (Amendment) Act 1996, s 1.

6 Mental element: miscellaneous

(1) A person is guilty of riot only if he intends to use violence or is aware that his conduct may be violent.

(2) A person is guilty of violent disorder or affray only if he intends to use or threaten violence or is aware that his conduct may be violent or threaten violence.

(3) A person is guilty of an offence under section 4 only if he intends his words or behaviour, or the writing, sign or other visible representation, to be threatening, abusive or insulting, or is aware that it may be threatening, abusive or insulting.

(4) A person is guilty of an offence under section 5 only if he intends his words or behaviour, or the writing, sign or other visible representation, to be threatening, abusive or insulting, or is aware that it may be threatening, abusive or insulting or (as the case may be) he intends his behaviour to be or is aware that it may be disorderly.

(5) For the purposes of this section a person whose awareness is impaired by intoxication shall be taken to be aware of that of which he would be aware if not intoxicated, unless he shows either that his intoxication was not self-induced or that it was caused solely by the taking or administration of a substance in the course of medical treatment.

(6) In subsection (5) "intoxication" means any intoxication, whether caused by drink, drugs or other means, or by a combination of means.

(7)   Subsections (1) and (2) do not affect the determination for the purposes of riot or violent disorder of the number of persons who use or threaten violence.

7 Procedure: miscellaneous

(1)   No prosecution for an offence of riot or incitement to riot may be instituted except by or with the consent of the Director of Public Prosecutions.

(2)   For the purposes of the rules against charging more than one offence in the same count or information, each of sections 1 to 5 creates one offence.

(3)   If on the trial on indictment of a person charged with violent disorder or affray the jury find him not guilty of the offence charged, they may (without prejudice to section 6(3) of the Criminal Law Act 1967) find him guilty of an offence under section 4.

(4)   The Crown Court has the same powers and duties in relation to a person who is by virtue of subsection (3) convicted before it of an offence under section 4 as a magistrates' court would have on convicting him of the offence.

8 Interpretation

(1)   In this Part—
    "dwelling" means any structure or part of a structure occupied as a person's home or as other living accommodation (whether the occupation is separate or shared with others) but does not include any part not so occupied, and for his purpose "structure" includes a tent, caravan, vehicle, vessel or other temporary or movable structure;
    "violence" means any violent conduct, so that—
    (a)   except in the context of affray, it includes violent conduct towards property as well as violent conduct towards persons, and
    (b)   it is not restricted to conduct causing or intended to cause injury or damage but includes any other violent conduct (for example, throwing at or towards a person a missile of a kind capable of causing injury which does not hit or falls short).

PART III
RACIAL HATRED

Meaning of "racial hatred"

17 Meaning of "racial hatred"

In this Part "racial hatred" means hatred against a group of persons . . . defined by reference to colour, race, nationality (including citizenship) or ethnic or national origins.

NOTES

    Words omitted repealed by the Anti-terrorism, Crime and Security Act 2001, ss 37, 125, Sch 8, Pt 4.

Date in force: 14 December 2001 (except in relation to anything done before that date): see the Anti-terrorism, Crime and Security Act 2001, ss 42, 127(2)(a).

Acts intended or likely to stir up racial hatred

18 Use of words or behaviour or display of written material

(1) A person who uses threatening, abusive or insulting words or behaviour, or displays any written material which is threatening, abusive or insulting, is guilty of an offence if—
  (a) he intends thereby to stir up racial hatred, or
  (b) having regard to all the circumstances racial hatred is likely to be stirred up thereby.

(2) An offence under this section may be committed in a public or a private place, except that no offence is committed where the words or behaviour are used, or the written material is displayed, by a person inside a dwelling and are not heard or seen except by other persons in that or another dwelling.

(3) A constable may arrest without warrant anyone he reasonably suspects is committing an offence under this section.

(4) In proceedings for an offence under this section it is a defence for the accused to prove that he was inside a dwelling and had no reason to believe that the words or behaviour used, or the written material displayed, would be heard or seen by a person outside that or any other dwelling.

(5) A person who is not shown to have intended to stir up racial hatred is not guilty of an offence under this section if he did not intend his words or behaviour, or the written material, to be, and was not aware that it might be, threatening, abusive or insulting.

(6) This section does not apply to words or behaviour used, or written material displayed, solely for the purpose of being [included in a programme service].

NOTES

Sub-s (6): words in square brackets substituted by the Broadcasting Act 1990, s 164(2).

19 Publishing or distributing written material

(1) A person who publishes or distributes written material which is threatening, abusive or insulting is guilty of an offence if—
  (a) he intends thereby to stir up racial hatred, or
  (b) having regard to all the circumstances racial hatred is likely to be stirred up thereby.

(2) In proceedings for an offence under this section it is a defence for an accused who is not shown to have intended to stir up racial hatred to prove that he was not aware of the content of the material and did not suspect, and had no reason to suspect, that it was threatening, abusive or insulting.

(3) References in this Part to the publication or distribution of written material are to its publication or distribution to the public or a section of the public.

PART V
MISCELLANEOUS AND GENERAL

41 Commencement

(1) This Act shall come into force on such day as the Secretary of State may appoint by order made by statutory instrument, and different days may be appointed for different provisions or different purposes.

(2) Nothing in a provision of this Act applies in relation to an offence committed or act done before the provision comes into force.

(3) Where a provision of this Act comes into force for certain purposes only, the references in subsection (2) to the provision are references to it so far as it relates to those purposes.

42 Extent

(1) The provisions of this Act extend to England and Wales except so far as they—
  (a) amend or repeal an enactment which does not so extend, or
  (b) relate to the extent of provisions to Scotland or Northern Ireland.

(2) The following provisions of this Act extend to Scotland—
  in Part I, section 9(2) except paragraph (a);
  in Part II, sections 12 and 14 to 16;
  Part III;
  Part V, except sections 38, . . . , 40(4), subsections (1) and (3) of this section and any provision amending or repealing an enactment which does not extend to Scotland.

(3) The following provisions of this Act extend to Northern Ireland—
  sections 38, 41, this subsection, section 43 and paragraph 6 of Schedule 2.

NOTES
  Sub-s (2): word omitted repealed by the Criminal Justice and Public Order Act 1994, s 168(3), Sch 11.

43 Short title

This Act may be cited as the Public Order Act 1986.

Criminal Justice Act 1987

1987 CHAPTER 38

An Act to make further provision for the investigation of and trials for fraud; and for connected purposes

[15th May 1987]

PART I

FRAUD

Conspiracy to defraud

12 Charges of and penalty for conspiracy to defraud

(1) If—
   (a) a person agrees with any other person or persons that a course of conduct shall be pursued; and
   (b) that course of conduct will necessarily amount to or involve the commission of any offence or offences by one or more of the parties to the agreement if the agreement is carried out in accordance with their intentions,

the fact that it will do so shall not preclude a charge of conspiracy to defraud being brought against any of them in respect of the agreement.

(2) . . .

(3) A person guilty of conspiracy to defraud is liable on conviction on indictment to imprisonment for a term not exceeding 10 years or a fine or both.

NOTES

Sub-s (2): amends the Criminal Law Act 1977, s 5(2).

16 Commencement

(1) Subject to subsection (3) below, this Act shall come into force on such day as the Secretary of State may by order made by statutory instrument appoint; and different days may be appointed in pursuance of this subsection for different provisions or different purposes of the same provision.

(2) An order under subsection (1) above may make such transitional provision as appears to the Secretary of State to be necessary or expedient in connection with any provision thereby brought into force.

(3) The following provisions shall come into force on the day this Act is passed—
   section 13;
   this section;
   sections 17 and 18.

17 Extent

(1)   Subject to the following provisions of this section, this Act extends to England and Wales only.

(2)   The following provisions extend also to Scotland—
section 2;
section 11;
[section 11A]
section 16;
this section; and
section 18.

(3)   The following provisions extend also to Northern Ireland—
section 1 (including Schedule 1) and sections 2 and 3;
section 16;
this section; and
section 18.

(4)   Section 13 above extends to Northern Ireland only.

(5)   The extent of any amendment of an enactment in Schedule 2 to this Act is the same as that of the enactment amended.

(6)   Her Majesty may by Order in Council direct that section 2 above shall extend, subject to such modifications as may be specified in the Order, to any of the Channel Islands.

(7)   In subsection (6) above "modifications" includes additions, omissions and amendments.

NOTES

Sub-s (2): words in square brackets inserted by the Criminal Procedure and Investigations Act 1996, s 72, Sch 3, para 7, with effect in accordance with Sch 3, para 8 to that Act.

18 Citation

This Act may be cited as the Criminal Justice Act 1987.

Malicious Communications Act 1988

1988 CHAPTER 27

An Act to make provision for the punishment of persons who send or deliver letters or other articles for the purpose of causing distress or anxiety

[29th July 1988]

1 Offence of sending letters etc with intent to cause distress or anxiety

(1)   Any person who sends to another person—
  (a)   a [letter, electronic communication or article of any description] which conveys—
     (i)   a message which is indecent or grossly offensive;
     (ii)   a threat; or
     (iii) information which is false and known or believed to be false by the sender; or
  (b)   any [article or electronic communication] which is, in whole or part, of an indecent or grossly offensive nature,

is guilty of an offence if his purpose, or one of his purposes, in sending it is that it should, so far as falling within paragraph (a) or (b) above, cause distress or anxiety to the recipient or to any other person to whom he intends that it or its contents or nature should be communicated.

(2)   A person is not guilty of an offence by virtue of subsection (1)(a)(ii) above if he shows—
  (a)   that the threat was used to reinforce a demand [made by him on reasonable grounds]; and
  (b)   that he believed[, and had reasonable grounds for believing,] that the use of the threat was a proper means of reinforcing the demand.

[(2A)   In this section 'electronic communication' includes—
  (a)   any oral or other communication by means of a telecommunication system (within the meaning of the Telecommunications Act 1984 (c 12)); and
  (b)   any communication (however sent) that is in electronic form.]

(3)   In this section references to sending include references to delivering [or transmitting] and to causing to be sent[, delivered or transmitted] and "sender" shall be construed accordingly.

(4)   A person guilty of an offence under this section shall be liable on summary conviction to [imprisonment for a term not exceeding six months or to a fine not exceeding level 5 on the standard scale, or to both].

NOTES

Sub-s (1): words "letter, electronic communication or article of any description" in square brackets substituted by the Criminal Justice and Police Act 2001, s 43(1)(a).

Date in force: this amendment came into force on 11 May 2001 (date of Royal Assent of the Criminal Justice and Police Act 2001) in the absence of any specific commencement provision.

Sub-s (1): in para (b) words "article or electronic communication" in square brackets substituted by the Criminal Justice and Police Act 2001, s 43(1)(b).

Date in force: this amendment came into force on 11 May 2001 (date of Royal Assent of the Criminal Justice and Police Act 2001) in the absence of any specific commencement provision.

Sub-s (2): in para (a) words "made by him on reasonable grounds" in square brackets substituted by the Criminal Justice and Police Act 2001, s 43(2)(a).

Date in force: this amendment came into force on 11 May 2001 (date of Royal Assent of the Criminal Justice and Police Act 2001) in the absence of any specific commencement provision.

Sub-s (2): in para (b) words ", and had reasonable grounds for believing," in square brackets inserted by the Criminal Justice and Police Act 2001, s 43(2)(b).

Date in force: this amendment came into force on 11 May 2001 (date of Royal Assent of the Criminal Justice and Police Act 2001) in the absence of any specific commencement provision.

Sub-s (2A): inserted by the Criminal Justice and Police Act 2001, s 43(3).

Date in force: this amendment came into force on 11 May 2001 (date of Royal Assent of the Criminal Justice and Police Act 2001) in the absence of any specific commencement provision.

Sub-s (3): words "or transmitting" in square brackets inserted by the Criminal Justice and Police Act 2001, s 43(4)(a).

Date in force: this amendment came into force on 11 May 2001 (date of Royal Assent of the Criminal Justice and Police Act 2001) in the absence of any specific commencement provision.

Sub-s (3): words ", delivered or transmitted" in square brackets substituted by the Criminal Justice and Police Act 2001, s 43(4)(b).

Date in force: this amendment came into force on 11 May 2001 (date of Royal Assent of the Criminal Justice and Police Act 2001) in the absence of any specific commencement provision.

Sub-s (4): words from "imprisonment for a" to "or to both" in square brackets substituted by the Criminal Justice and Police Act 2001, s 43(5).

Date in force: in the absence of any specific commencement provision this amendment came into force on 11 May 2001 (date of Royal Assent of the Criminal Justice and Police Act 2001), except in relation to the penalty for an offence committed before that date: see s 43(6) thereof.

3 Short title, commencement and extent

(1)   This Act may be cited as the Malicious Communications Act 1988.

(2)   Section 1 above shall not come into force until the end of the period of two months beginning with the day on which this Act is passed.

(3)   This Act does not extend to Scotland or, except for section 2, to Northern Ireland.

Criminal Justice Act 1988

1988 CHAPTER 33

An Act to make fresh provision for extradition; to amend the rules of evidence in criminal proceedings; to provide for the reference by the Attorney General of certain questions relating to sentencing to the Court of Appeal; to amend the law with regard to the jurisdiction and powers of criminal courts, the collection, enforcement and remission of fines imposed by coroners, juries, supervision orders, the detention of children and young persons, probation and the probation service, criminal appeals, anonymity in cases of rape and similar cases, orders under sections 4 and 11 of the Contempt of Court Act 1981 relating to trials on indictment, orders restricting the access of the public to the whole or any part of a trial on indictment or to any proceedings ancillary to such a trial and orders restricting the publication of any report of the whole or any part of a trial on indictment or any such ancillary proceedings, the alteration of names of petty sessions areas, officers of inner London magistrates' courts and the costs and expenses of prosecution witnesses and certain other persons; to make fresh provision for the payment of compensation by the Criminal Injuries Compensation Board; to make provision for the payment of compensation for a miscarriage of justice which has resulted in a wrongful conviction; to create an offence of torture and an offence of having an article with a blade or point in a public place; to create further offences relating to weapons; to create a summary offence of possession of an indecent photograph of a child; to amend the Police and Criminal Evidence Act 1984 in relation to searches, computer data about fingerprints and bail for persons in customs detention; to make provision in relation to the taking of body samples by the police in Northern Ireland; to amend the Bail Act 1976; to give a justice of the peace power to authorise entry and search of premises for offensive weapons; to provide for the enforcement of the Video Recordings Act 1984 by officers of a weights and measures authority and in Northern Ireland by officers of the Department of Economic Development; to extend to the purchase of easements and other rights over land the power to purchase land conferred on the Secretary of State by section 36 of the Prison Act 1952; and for connected purposes

[29th July 1988]

PART III
OTHER PROVISIONS ABOUT EVIDENCE IN CRIMINAL PROCEEDINGS

[32A Video recordings of testimony from child witnesses]

[(1) This section applies in relation to the following proceedings, namely—

(a) trials on indictment for any offence to which section 32(2) above applies;

(b) appeals to the criminal division of the Court of Appeal and hearings of references under [section 9 of the Criminal Appeal Act 1995] in respect of any such offence; and

(c) proceedings in youth courts for any such offence[, appeals arising our of such proceedings and hearings of references under section 11 of the Criminal Appeal Act 1995 so arising].

(2) In any such proceedings a video recording of an interview which—
  (a) is conducted between an adult and a child who is not the accused or one of the accused ("the child witness"); and
  (b) relates to any matter in issue in the proceedings,

may, with the leave of the court, be given in evidence in so far as it is not excluded by the court under subsection (3) below.

(3) Where a video recording is tendered in evidence under this section, the court shall (subject to the exercise of any power of the court to exclude evidence which is otherwise admissible) give leave under subsection (2) above unless—
  (a) it appears that the child witness will not be available for cross-examination;
  (b) any rules of court requiring disclosure of the circumstances in which the recording was made have not been complied with to the satisfaction of the court; or
  (c) the court is of the opinion, having regard to all the circumstances of the case, that in the interests of justice the recording ought not to be admitted;

and where the court gives such leave it may, if it is of the opinion that in the interests of justice any part of the recording ought not to be admitted, direct that that part shall be excluded.

(4) In considering whether any part of a recording ought to be excluded under subsection (3) above, the court shall consider whether any prejudice to the accused, or one of the accused, which might result from the admission of that part is outweighed by the desirability of showing the whole, or substantially the whole, of the recorded interview.

(5) Where a video recording is admitted under this section—
  (a) the child witness shall be called by the party who tendered it in evidence;
  (b) that witness shall not be examined in chief on any matter which, in the opinion of the court, has been dealt with [adequately] in his recorded testimony.

(6) Where a video recording is given in evidence under this section, any statement made by the child witness which is disclosed by the recording shall be treated as if given by that witness in direct oral testimony; and accordingly—
  (a) any such statement shall be admissible evidence of any fact of which such testimony from him would be admissible;
  (b) no such statement shall be capable of corroborating any other evidence given by him;

and in estimating the weight, if any, to be attached to such a statement, regard shall be had to all the circumstances from which any inference can reasonably be drawn (as to its accuracy or otherwise).

[(6A) Where the court gives leave under subsection (2) above the child witness shall not give relevant evidence (within the meaning given by subsection (6D) *below) otherwise than by means of the video recording; but this is subject to subsection (6B) below.*

(6B)   In a case falling within subsection (6A) above the court may give permission for the child witness to give relevant evidence (within the meaning given by subsection (6D) below) otherwise than by means of the video recording if it appears to the court to be in the interests of justice to give such permission.

(6C)   Permission may be given under subsection (6B) above—
>   *(a)   on an application by a party to the case, or*
>   *(b)   of the court's own motion;*

but no application may be made under paragraph (a) above unless there has been a material change of circumstances since the leave was given under subsection (2) above.

(6D)   For the purposes of subsections (6A) and (6B) above evidence is relevant evidence if—
>   *(a)   it is evidence in chief on behalf of the party who tendered the video recording, and*
>   *(b)   it relates to matter which, in the opinion of the court, is dealt with in the recording and which the court has not directed to be excluded under subsection (3) above.]*

(7)   In this section "child" means a person who—
>   *(a)   in the case of an offence falling within section 32(2)(a) or (b) above, is under fourteen years of age or, if he was under that age when the video recording was made, is under fifteen years of age; or*
>   *(b)   in the case of an offence falling within section 32(2)(c) above, is under seventeen years of age or, if he was under that age when the video recording was made, is under eighteen years of age.*

(8)   Any reference in subsection (7) above to an offence falling within paragraph (a), (b) or (c) of section 32(2) above includes a reference to an offence which consists of attempting or conspiring to commit, or of aiding, abetting, counselling, procuring or inciting the commission of, an offence falling within that paragraph.

(9)   In this section—

"statement" includes any representation of fact, whether made in words or otherwise;

"video recording" means any recording, on any medium, from which a moving image may by any means be produced and includes the accompanying sound-track.

(10)   A magistrates' court inquiring into an offence as examining justices under section 6 of the Magistrates' Courts Act 1980 may consider any video recording as respects which leave under subsection (2) above is to be sought at the trial, < . . . >.

(11)   Without prejudice to the generality of any enactment conferring power to make rules of court, such rules may make such provision as appears to the authority making them to be necessary or expedient for the purposes of this section.

(12) Nothing in this section shall prejudice the admissibility of any video recording which would be admissible apart from this section.]

NOTES

Inserted by the Criminal Justice Act 1991, s 54.

Repealed with savings in relation to a witness in continuing proceedings under this section by the Youth Justice and Criminal Evidence Act 1999, s 67(3), (4), Sch 6, Sch 7, para 3.

Date in force: to be appointed: see the Youth Justice and Criminal Evidence Act 1999, s 68(3).

Sub-s (1): words in square brackets substituted by the Criminal Appeal Act 1995, s 29, Sch 2, para 16(3).

Sub-s (5): in para (b) word in square brackets inserted by the Criminal Justice and Public Order Act 1994, s 50.

Sub-ss (6A)–(6D): inserted, in relation to leave given on or after a day to be appointed, by the Criminal Procedure and Investigations Act 1996, s 62(2), (3).

Sub-s (10): prospectively repealed by the Criminal Justice and Public Order Act 1994, s 168(3), Sch 11, as from a day to be appointed; words omitted repealed, in relation to alleged offences into which no criminal procedure has begun before 1 April 1997, by the Criminal Procedure and Investigations Act 1996, ss 47, 80, Sch 1, para 33, Sch 5.

[33A Evidence given by children]

[(1) A child's evidence in criminal proceedings shall be given unsworn.

(2) A deposition of a child's unsworn evidence may be taken for the purposes of criminal proceedings as if that evidence had been given on oath.

[(2A) A child's evidence shall be received unless it appears to the court that the child is incapable of giving intelligible testimony.]

(3) In this section "child" means a person under fourteen years of age.]

NOTES

Inserted by the Criminal Justice Act 1991, s 52(1).

Repealed by the Youth Justice and Criminal Evidence Act 1999, s 67(3), Sch 6.

Date in force: to be appointed: see the Youth Justice and Criminal Evidence Act 1999, s 68(3).

Sub-s (2A): inserted by the Criminal Justice and Public Order Act 1994, s 168(1), Sch 9, para 33.

PART V
JURISDICTION, IMPRISONMENT, FINES ETC

Jurisdiction

39 Common assault and battery to be summary offences

Common assault and battery shall be summary offences and a person guilty of either of them shall be liable to a fine not exceeding level 5 on the standard scale, to imprisonment for a term not exceeding six months, or to both.

PART XI

MISCELLANEOUS

Articles with blades or points and offensive weapons

139 Offence of having article with blade or point in public place

(1)   Subject to subsections (4) and (5) below, any person who has an article to which this section applies with him in a public place shall be guilty of an offence.

(2)   Subject to subsection (3) below, this section applies to any article which has a blade or is sharply pointed except a folding pocketknife.

(3)   This section applies to a folding pocketknife if the cutting edge of its blade exceeds 3 inches.

(4)   It shall be a defence for a person charged with an offence under this section to prove that he had good reason or lawful authority for having the article with him in a public place.

(5)   Without prejudice to the generality of subsection (4) above, it shall be a defence for a person charged with an offence under this section to prove that he had the article with him—
  (a)   for use at work;
  (b)   for religious reasons; or
  (c)   as part of any national costume.

(6)   A person guilty of an offence under subsection (1) above shall be liable
  [(a)   on summary conviction, to imprisonment for a term not exceeding six months, or a fine not exceeding the statutory maximum, or both;
  (b)   on conviction on indictment, to imprisonment for a term not exceeding two years, or a fine, or both].

(7)   In this section "public place" includes any place to which at the material time the public have or are permitted access, whether on payment or otherwise.

(8)   This section shall not have effect in relation to anything done before it comes into force.

NOTES

Sub-s (6): words in square brackets substituted by the Offensive Weapons Act 1996, s 3.

[139A Offence of having article with blade or point (or offensive weapon) on school premises]

[(1)   Any person who has an article to which section 139 of this Act applies with him on school premises shall be guilty of an offence.

(2)   Any person who has an offensive weapon within the meaning of section 1 of the Prevention of Crime Act 1953 with him on school premises shall be guilty of an offence.

(3) It shall be a defence for a person charged with an offence under subsection (1) or (2) above to prove that he had good reason or lawful authority for having the article or weapon with him on the premises in question.

(4) Without prejudice to the generality of subsection (3) above, it shall be a defence for a person charged with an offence under subsection (1) or (2) above to prove that he had the article or weapon in question with him—
  (a) for use at work,
  (b) for educational purposes,
  (c) for religious reasons, or
  (d) as part of any national costume.

(5) A person guilty of an offence—
  (a) under subsection (1) above shall be liable—
     (i) on summary conviction to imprisonment for a term not exceeding six months, or a fine not exceeding the statutory maximum, or both;
     (ii) on conviction on indictment, to imprisonment for a term not exceeding two years, or a fine, or both;
  (b) under subsection (2) above shall be liable—
     (i) on summary conviction, to imprisonment for a term not exceeding six months, or a fine not exceeding the statutory maximum, or both;
     (ii) on conviction on indictment, to imprisonment for a term not exceeding four years, or a fine, or both.

(6) In this section and section 139B, "school premises" means land used for the purposes of a school excluding any land occupied solely as a dwelling by a person employed at the school; and "school" has the meaning given by [section 4 of the Education Act 1996].

(7) In the application of this section to Northern Ireland—
  (a) the reference in subsection (2) above to section 1 of the Prevention of Crime Act 1953 is to be construed as a reference to Article 22 of the Public Order (Northern Ireland) Order 1987;and
  (b) the reference in subsection (6) above to [section 4 of the Education Act 1996] is to be construed as a reference to Article 2(2) of the Education and Libraries (Northern Ireland) Order 1986.]

NOTES
Inserted by the Offensive Weapons Act 1996, s 4(1).

Sub-ss (6), (7): words in square brackets substituted by the Education Act 1996, s 582(1), Sch 37, para 69.

[139B Power of entry to search for articles with a blade of point and offensive weapons]

[(1) A constable may enter school premises and search those premises and any person on those premises for—
  (a) any article to which section 139 of this Act applies, or
  (b) any offensive weapon within the meaning of section 1 of the Prevention of Crime Act 1953,

if he has reasonable grounds for believing that an offence under section 139A of this Act is being, or has been, committed.

(2)   If in the course of a search under this section a constable discovers an article or weapon which he has reasonable grounds for suspecting to be an article or weapon of a kind described in subsection (1) above, he may seize and retain it.

(3)   The constable may use reasonable force, if necessary, in the exercise of the power of entry conferred by this section.

(4)   In the application of this section to Northern Ireland the reference in subsection (1)(b) above to section 1 of the Prevention of Crime Act 1953 is to be construed as a reference to Article 22 of the Public Order (Northern Ireland) Order 1987.]

NOTES

Inserted by the Offensive Weapons Act 1996, s 4(1).

141 Offensive weapons

(1)   Any person who manufactures, sells or hires or offers for sale or hire, exposes or has in his possession for the purpose of sale or hire, or lends or gives to any other person, a weapon to which this section applies shall be guilty of an offence and liable on summary conviction to imprisonment for a term not exceeding six months or to a fine not exceeding level 5 on the standard scale or both.

(2)   The Secretary of State may by order made by statutory instrument direct that this section shall apply to any description of weapon specified in the order except—
   (a)   any weapon subject to the Firearms Act 1968; and
   (b)   crossbows.

(3)   A statutory instrument containing an order under this section shall not be made unless a draft of the instrument has been laid before Parliament and has been approved by a resolution of each House of Parliament.

(4)   The importation of a weapon to which this section applies is hereby prohibited.

(5)   It shall be a defence for any person charged in respect of any conduct of his relating to a weapon to which this section applies—
   (a)   with an offence under subsection (1) above; or
   (b)   with an offence under section 50(2) or (3) of the Customs and Excise Management Act 1979 (improper importation),

to prove that his conduct was only for the purposes of functions carried out on behalf of the Crown or of a visiting force.

(6)   In this section the reference to the Crown includes the Crown in right of Her Majesty's Government in Northern Ireland; and
   "visiting force" means any body, contingent or detachment of the forces of a country—

   (a) mentioned in subsection (1)(a) of section 1 of the Visiting Forces Act 1952; or

   (b) designated for the purposes of any provision of that Act by Order in Council under subsection (2) of that section,

which is present in the United Kingdom (including United Kingdom territorial waters) or in any place to which subsection (7) below applies on the invitation of Her Majesty's Government in the United Kingdom.

(7) This subsection applies to any place on, under or above an installation in a designated area within the meaning of section 1(7) of the Continental Shelf Act 1964 or any waters within 500 metres of such an installation.

(8) It shall be a defence for any person charged in respect of any conduct of his relating to a weapon to which this section applies—

   (a) with an offence under subsection (1) above; or

   (b) with an offence under section 50(2) or (3) of the Customs and Excise Management Act 1979,

to prove that the conduct in question was only for the purposes of making the weapon available to a museum or gallery to which this subsection applies.

(9) If a person acting on behalf of a museum or gallery to which subsection (8) above applies is charged with hiring or lending a weapon to which this section applies, it shall be a defence for him to prove that he had reasonable grounds for believing that the person to whom he lent or hired it would use it only for cultural, artistic or educational purposes.

(10) Subsection (8) above applies to a museum or gallery only if it does not distribute profits.

(11) In this section "museum or gallery" includes any institution which has as its purpose, or one of its purposes, the preservation, display and interpretation of material of historical, artistic or scientific interest and gives the public access to it.

(12) This section shall not have effect in relation to anything done before it comes into force.

(13) In the application of this section to Northern Ireland the reference in subsection (2) above to the Firearms Act 1968 shall be construed as a reference to the Firearms (Northern Ireland) Order 1981.

[141A Sale of knives and certain articles with blade or point to persons under sixteen]

[(1) Any person who sells to a person under the age of sixteen years an article to which this section applies shall be guilty of an offence and liable on summary 1988 conviction to imprisonment for a term not exceeding six months, or a fine not exceeding level 5 on the standard scale, or both.

(2) Subject to subsection (3) below, this section applies to—

   (a) any knife, knife blade or razor blade,

   (b) any axe, and

(c) any other article which has a blade or which is sharply pointed and which is made or adapted for use for causing injury to the person.

(3)   This section does not apply to any article described in—
  (a) section 1 of the Restriction of Offensive Weapons Act 1959,
  (b) an order made under section 141(2) of this Act, or
  (c) an order made by the Secretary of State under this section.

(4)   It shall be a defence for a person charged with an offence under subsection (1) above to prove that he took all reasonable precautions and exercised all due diligence to avoid the commission of the offence.

(5)   The power to make an order under this section shall be exercisable by statutory instrument which shall be subject to annulment in pursuance of a resolution of either House of Parliament.]

NOTES

Inserted by the Offensive Weapons Act 1996, s 6(1).

Possession of indecent photograph of child

160 [Possession of indecent photograph of child]

(1)   It is an offence for a person to have any indecent photograph [or pseudo-photograph] of a child . . . in his possession.

(2)   Where a person is charged with an offence under subsection (1) above, it shall be a defence for him to prove—
  (a) that he had a legitimate reason for having the photograph [or pseudo-photograph] in his possession; or
  (b) that he had not himself seen the photograph [or pseudo-photograph] and did not know, nor had any cause to suspect, it to be indecent; or
  (c) that the photograph [or pseudo-photograph] was sent to him without any prior request made by him or on his behalf and that he did not keep it for an unreasonable time.

[(2A)   A person shall be liable on conviction on indictment of an offence under this section to imprisonment for a term not exceeding five years or a fine, or both.]

(3)   A person shall be liable on summary conviction of an offence under this section to [imprisonment for a term not exceeding six months or] a fine not exceeding level 5 on the standard scale[, or both].

(4)   Sections 1(3), 2(3), 3 and 7 of the Protection of Children Act 1978 shall have effect as if any reference in them to that Act included a reference to this section.

(5)   . . .

NOTES

Provision heading: substituted by the Criminal Justice and Court Services Act 2000, s 41(3)(b).
Date in force: 11 January 2001: see SI 2000/3302, art 2(a).
Sub-s (1): words in square brackets inserted and words omitted repealed by the Criminal

Justice and Public Order Act 1994, ss 84(4)(a), 168(3), Sch 11.

Sub-ss (2), (3): words in square brackets inserted by the Criminal Justice and Public Order Act 1994, s 84(4)(b), 86(1).

Sub-s (2A): inserted by the Criminal Justice and Court Services Act 2000, s 41(3)(a).

Date in force: 11 January 2001: see SI 2000/3302, art 2(a).

Sub-s (5): repealed by the Criminal Justice and Public Order Act 1994, s 168(3), Sch 11.

PART XII
GENERAL AND SUPPLEMENTARY

171 Commencement

(1)   Subject to the following provisions of this section, this Act shall come into force on such day as the Secretary of State may by order made by statutory instrument appoint and different days may be appointed in pursuance of this subsection for different provisions or different purposes of the same provision.

(2)   An order under this section may make such transitional provision as appears to the Secretary of State to be necessary or expedient in connection with any provision thereby brought into force . . .

(3), (4)   . . .

(5)   The following provisions shall come into force on the day this Act is passed—
section 66;
section 67;
section 103(1), so far as it relates—
    (a) to the addition of two subsections at the end of section 8 of the Drug Trafficking Offences Act 1986;
    (b) to the insertion of a new subsection in section 24 of that Act; and
    (c) to the substitution of two new sections for section 26 of that Act;
section 129;
section 132, so far as it relates to the Local Government Finance Act 1982;
section 141;
section 142;
section 143;
section 144;
section 149;
section 166;
section 167;
section 168;
section 169;
subsection (1) of section 170, so far as relating to the following—
    section 112A(1) of the Land Registration Act 1925;
    the extension of references in the Children and Young Persons Act 1933 to the offences mentioned in Schedule 1 to that Act so as to include offences under Part I of the Child Abduction Act 1984;
    the Visiting Forces Act 1952;
    section 67(6) of the Criminal Justice Act 1967;
    section 29 of the Children and Young Persons Act 1969;

section 6(1) of the Juries Act 1974;

sections 171 and 368 of and Schedule 1 to the Criminal Procedure (Scotland)
    Act 1975;

the Child Care Act 1980;

sections 37 and 133 of the Magistrates' Courts Act 1980;

section 52(7) of the Civic Government (Scotland) Act 1982;

the Criminal Justice Act 1982;

the Police and Criminal Evidence Act 1984;

the Prosecution of Offences Act 1985;

the Criminal Justice Act 1987;

the Criminal Justice (Scotland) Act 1987;

subsection (2) of that section, so far as relating to the following—

    section 49 of the Criminal Justice Act 1967;

    section 29 of the Children and Young Persons Act 1969;

    the Criminal Justice Act 1987;

this section;

sections 172 and 173.

(6)   The following provisions—

section 44;

section 45;

section 46;

section 47;

section 48;

section 58;

section 64;

section 68;

section 69;

section 134;

section 135;

section 136;

section 137;

section 138;

section 139;

section 140;

section 158;

sections 160 and 161;

subsection (1) of section 170, so far as relating to the Sexual Offences (Amendment) Act 1976, the Protection of Children Act 1978 and section 6(5) of the Magistrates' Courts Act 1980;

subsection (2) of that section, so far as relating to the following—

    the Prevention of Corruption Act 1916;

    Schedule 3 to the Criminal Justice Act 1967;

    section 28(3) of the Criminal Justice Act 1972;

    the Sexual Offences (Amendment) Act 1976;

    the Protection of Children Act 1978;

    the Cable and Broadcasting Act 1984;

    section 24(2)(e) of the Police and Criminal Evidence Act 1984, shall come into force at the end of the period of two months beginning with the day this Act is passed.

(7)   Section 162 above shall come into force—

   (a)   on the day appointed under section 23(2) of the Video Recordings Act 1984 for the coming into force of the provisions of that Act not in force at the passing of this Act; or

   (b)   on the passing of this Act,

whichever is the later.

NOTES

   Sub-s (2): words omitted repealed by the Criminal Injuries Compensation Act 1995, s 12(1), (7), Schedule.

   Sub-ss (3), (4): repealed by the Criminal Injuries Compensation Act 1995, s 12(1), (7), Schedule.

172 Extent

(1)   Subject to the following provisions of this section, and to sections 19, 20 and 21 above, this Act extends to England and Wales only.

(2)   The following provisions extend also to Scotland—

   Part I;

   sections 44 to 48;

   section 50;

   section 57;

   section 63;

   section 68;

   section 76(3);

   section 77(10) and (11);

   section 82;

   sections 84 to 88;

   [sections 93A to 93D;

   sections 93F and 93G]

   section 94;

   section 102, so far as relating to other provisions of this Act extending to Scotland;

   . . .

   section 133;

   section 134;

   section 136;

   section 137;

   sections 141 [141A and 142];

   section 143;

   section 145(a) and (b);

   section 162;

   section 170;

   section 171;

this section; and
section 173.

(3)   The following provisions extend also to Northern Ireland—
Part I;
Part IV;
section 50;
section 133;
section 134;
section 135;
section 136;
section 137;
[sections 139 to 139B];
section 141;
section 142;
section 143;
section 152;
section 159;
section 162;
section 166(5);
section 170;
section 171;
this section; and
section 173;

(4)   The following provisions—
section 56;
sections 90 to 93;
[section 93E];
section 103(2);
. . .
section 124;
section 161;

extend to Scotland only.

(5)   Section 95 above extends only to Scotland and Northern Ireland.

(6)   Sections 145(c), 149 and 168 above extend to Northern Ireland only.

(7)   So far as any provision of this Act to which this subsection applies relates to an Act specified in subsection (9) below, it extends to any place to which that Act extends.

(8)   Subsection (7) above applies—
   (a)   to section 50 above;
   (b)   to section 146 above; and
   (c)   to any other provision of this Act so far as it has effect in relation to courts-martial, the Courts-Martial Appeal Court or Standing Civilian Courts.

(9)   The Acts mentioned in subsection (7) above are—
   (a)   the Army Act 1955;

(b)   the Air Force Act 1955;
(c)   the Naval Discipline Act 1957;
(d)   the Courts-Martial (Appeals) Act 1968; and
(e)   the Armed Forces Act 1976.

(10)   Section 158 above extends—
(a)   to Scotland, so far as it relates to courts-martial; and
(b)   to Northern Ireland, so far as it relates to courts-martial and to such a publication or broadcast or inclusion in a cable programme in Northern Ireland as is mentioned in section 4(1) of the Sexual Offences (Amendment) Act 1976 as adapted by section 5(1)(b) of that Act.

(11)   The extent of any amendment of an enactment in Schedule 15 to this Act is the same as that of the enactment amended, except that the amendments of the Offences against the Person Act 1861 do not extend to Northern Ireland.

(12)   The extent of any repeal of an enactment in Schedule 16 to this Act is the same as that of the enactment repealed, subject to the Notes at the end of the Schedule.

NOTES

Sub-s (2): first words in square brackets inserted by the Criminal Justice Act 1993, s 79(13), Sch 5, Part I, para 14(2); words omitted repealed by the Criminal Injuries Compensation Act 1995, s 12(1), Schedule; second words in square brackets substituted by the Offensive Weapons Act 1996, s 6(2).

Sub-s (3): words in square brackets substituted by the Offensive Weapons Act 1996, s 4(2).

Sub-s (4): words in square brackets inserted by the Criminal Justice Act 1993, s 79(13), Sch 5, Part I, para 14(2); words omitted repealed by the Criminal Injuries Compensation Act 1995, s 12(7), Schedule.

173   Citation

This Act may be cited as the Criminal Justice Act 1988.

Firearms (Amendment) Act 1988

1988 CHAPTER 45

An Act to amend the Firearms Act 1968 and to make further provision for regulating the possession of, and transactions relating to, firearms and ammunition.

[15th November 1988]

Shot Guns

5   Restriction on sale of ammunition for smooth-bore guns

(1)   This section applies to ammunition to which section 1 of the principal Act does not apply and which is capable of being used in a shot gun or in a smooth-bore gun to which that section applies.

(2)   It is an offence for a person to sell any such ammunition to another person in the United Kingdom who is neither a registered firearms dealer nor a person who sells such ammunition by way of trade or business unless that other person—

(a)   produces a certificate authorising him to possess a gun of a kind mentioned in subsection (1) above; or

(b)   shows that he is by virtue of that Act or this Act entitled to have possession of such a gun without holding a certificate; or

(c)   produces a certificate authorising another person to possess such a gun, together with that person's written authority to purchase the ammunition on his behalf.

(3)   An offence under this section shall be punishable on summary conviction with imprisonment for a term not exceeding six months or a fine not exceeding level 5 on the standard scale or both.

Converted and De-activated Weapons

6 Shortening of barrels

(1)   Subject to subsection (2) below, it is an offence to shorten to a length less than 24 inches the barrel of any smooth-bore gun to which section 1 of the principal Act applies other than one which has a barrel with a bore exceeding 2 inches in diameter; and that offence shall be punishable—

(a)   on summary conviction, with imprisonment for a term not exceeding six months or a fine not exceeding the statutory maximum or both;

(b)   on indictment, with imprisonment for a term not exceeding five years or a fine or both.

(2)   It is not an offence under this section for a registered firearms dealer to shorten the barrel of a gun for the sole purpose of replacing a defective part of the barrel so as to produce a barrel not less than 24 inches in length.

Firearms Dealers and Other Business

14 Auctioneers, carriers and warehousemen

(1)   It is an offence for an auctioneer, carrier or warehouseman—

(a)   to fail to take reasonable precautions for the safe custody of any firearm or ammunition which, by virtue of section 9(1) of the principal Act, he or any servant of his has in his possession without holding a certificate; or

(b)   to fail to report forthwith to the police the loss or theft of any such firearm or ammunition.

(2)   An offence under this section shall be punishable on summary conviction with imprisonment for a term not exceeding six months or a fine not exceeding level 5 on the standard scale or both.

Exemptions

[15 Approved rifle clubs and muzzle-loading pistol clubs]

[(1)   Subject to subsection (4) below, a member of a rifle club approved by the Secretary of State [or the Scottish Ministers (by virtue of provision made under section 63 of the Scotland Act 1998)] may, without holding a firearm certificate, have in his possession a rifle and ammunition when engaged as a member of the club in connection with target shooting.

(2)   Any rifle club may apply for approval, whether or not it is intended that any club members will, by virtue of subsection (1) above, have rifles or ammunition in their possession without holding firearm certificates.

(3)   The Secretary of State may publish such guidance as he considers appropriate for the purpose of informing those seeking approval for a club of criteria that must be met before any application for such approval will be considered.

(4)   The application of subsection (1) above to members of an approved rifle club may—
  (a)   be excluded in relation to the club, or
  (b)   be restricted to target shooting with specified types of rifle,

by limitations contained in the approval.

(5)   An approval—
  (a)   may be granted subject to such conditions specified in it as the Secretary of State thinks [or, as the case may be, the Scottish Ministers think] fit;
  (b)   may at any time be varied or withdrawn by the Secretary of State [or, as the case may be, the Scottish Ministers]; and
  (c)   shall (unless withdrawn) continue in force for six years from the date on which it is granted or last renewed.

(6)   There shall be payable on the grant or renewal of an approval a fee of £84 but this subsection shall be included in the provisions which may be amended by an order under section 43 of the principal Act.

(7)   A constable or civilian officer authorised in writing in that behalf may, on producing if required his authority, enter any premises occupied or used by an approved rifle club and inspect those premises, and anything on them, for the purpose of ascertaining whether the provisions of this section, and any limitations or conditions in the approval, are being complied with.

(8)   The power of a constable or civilian officer under subsection (7) above to inspect anything on club premises shall include power to require any information which is kept by means of a computer and is accessible from the premises to be made available for inspection in a visible and legible form.

(9)   It is an offence for a person intentionally to obstruct a constable or civilian officer in the exercise of his powers under subsection (7) above; and that offence shall be punishable on summary conviction with a fine not exceeding level 3 on the standard scale.

(10)   In this section and section 15A below—

"approval", means an approval under this section; and "approved" shall be construed accordingly;

"civilian officer" has the same meaning as in the principal Act; and

"rifle club" includes a miniature rifle club.

(11)   This section applies in relation to a muzzle-loading pistol club and its members as it applies to a rifle club and its members with the substitution for any reference to a rifle of a reference to a muzzle-loading pistol.

(12)   In subsection (11) above—

"muzzle-loading pistol club" means a club where muzzle-loading pistols are used for target shooting; and

"muzzle-loading pistol" means a pistol designed to be loaded at the muzzle end of the barrel or chamber with a loose charge and a separate ball (or other missile).]

NOTES

Substituted by the Firearms (Amendment) Act 1997, s 45(1).

Sub-s (1): words "or the Scottish Ministers (by virtue of provision made under section 63 of the Scotland Act 1998)" in square brackets inserted by SI 1999/1750, art 6(1), Sch 5, para 7(1), (2)(a).

Date in force: 1 July 1999: see SI 1999/1750, art 1(1), and SI 1998/3178, art 3.

Sub-s (5): in para (a) words "or, as the case may be, the Scottish Ministers think" in square brackets inserted by SI 1999/1750, art 6(1), Sch 5, para 7(1), (2)(b)(i).

Date in force: 1 July 1999: see SI 1999/1750, art 1(1), and SI 1998/3178, art 3.

Sub-s (5): in para (b) words "or, as the case may be, the Scottish Ministers" in square brackets inserted by SI 1999/1750, art 6(1), Sch 5, para 7(1), (2)(b)(ii).

Date in force: 1 July 1999: see SI 1999/1750, art 1(1), and SI 1998/3178, art 3.

Miscellaneous and Supplementary

27 Short title, citation, commencement and extent

(1)   This Act may be cited as the Firearms (Amendment) Act 1988.

(2)   This Act and the Firearms Acts 1968 and 1982 may be cited together as the Firearms Acts 1968 to 1988.

(3)   Except for section 26 and this section the provisions of this Act shall not come into force until such day as the Secretary of State may appoint by an order made by statutory instrument; and any such order may appoint different days for different provisions or different purposes and contain such transitional provisions as appear to the Secretary of State to be necessary or expedient in connection with any provision brought into force.

(4)   Except for section 26 and this section this Act does not extend to Northern Ireland.

Road Traffic Act 1988

1988 CHAPTER 52

An Act to consolidate certain enactments relating to road traffic with amendments to give effect to recommendations of the Law Commission and the Scottish Law Commission

[15th November 1988]

PART I
PRINCIPAL ROAD SAFETY PROVISIONS

Driving offences

[1 Causing death by dangerous driving]

[A person who causes the death of another person by driving a mechanically propelled vehicle dangerously on a road or other public place is guilty of an offence.]

NOTES

Substituted together with ss 2, 2A, for ss 1, 2 as originally enacted, by the Road Traffic Act 1991, s 1.

[2 Dangerous driving]

[A person who drives a mechanically propelled vehicle dangerously on a road or other public place is guilty of an offence.]

NOTES

Substituted together with ss 1, 2A, for ss 1, 2 as originally enacted, by the Road Traffic Act 1991, s 1.

[2A Meaning of dangerous driving]

[(1) For the purposes of sections 1 and 2 above a person is to be regarded as driving dangerously if (and, subject to subsection (2) below, only if)—

    (a) the way he drives falls far below what would be expected of a competent and careful driver, and

    (b) it would be obvious to a competent and careful driver that driving in that way would be dangerous.

(2) A person is also to be regarded as driving dangerously for the purposes of sections 1 and 2 above if it would be obvious to a competent and careful driver that driving the vehicle in its current state would be dangerous.

(3) In subsections (1) and (2) above "dangerous" refers to danger either of injury to any person or of serious damage to property; and in determining for the purposes of those subsections what would be expected of, or obvious to, a competent and

careful driver in a particular case, regard shall be had not only to the circumstances of which he could be expected to be aware but also to any circumstances shown to have been within the knowledge of the accused.

(4) In determining for the purposes of subsection (2) above the state of a vehicle, regard may be had to anything attached to or carried on or in it and to the manner in which it is attached or carried.]

NOTES

Substituted together with ss 1, 2, for ss 1, 2 as originally enacted, by the Road Traffic Act 1991, s 1.

[3 Careless, and inconsiderate, driving]

[If a person drives a mechanically propelled vehicle on a road or other public place without due care and attention, or without reasonable consideration for other persons using the road or place, he is guilty of an offence.]

NOTES

Substituted by the Road Traffic Act 1991, s 2.

Motor vehicles: drink and drugs

[3A Causing death by careless driving when under influence of drink or drugs]

[(1) If a person causes the death of another person by driving a mechanically propelled vehicle on a road or other public place without due care and attention, or without reasonable consideration for other persons using the road or place, and—
    (a) he is, at the time when he is driving, unfit to drive through drink or drugs, or
    (b) he has consumed so much alcohol that the proportion of it in his breath, blood or urine at that time exceeds the prescribed limit, or
    (c) he is, within 18 hours after that time, required to provide a specimen in pursuance of section 7 of this Act, but without reasonable excuse fails to provide it,

he is guilty of an offence.

(2) For the purposes of this section a person shall be taken to be unfit to drive at any time when his ability to drive properly is impaired.

(3) Subsection (1)(b) and (c) above shall not apply in relation to a person driving a mechanically propelled vehicle other than a motor vehicle.]

NOTES

Inserted by the Road Traffic Act 1991, s 3.

4 Driving, or being in charge, when under influence of drink or drugs

(1)   A person who, when driving or attempting to drive a [mechanically propelled vehicle] on a road or other public place, is unfit to drive through drink or drugs is guilty of an offence.

(2)   Without prejudice to subsection (1) above, a person who, when in charge of a [mechanically propelled vehicle] which is on a road or other public place, is unfit to drive through drink or drugs is guilty of an offence.

(3)   For the purposes of subsection (2) above, a person shall be deemed not to have been in charge of a [mechanically propelled vehicle] if he proves that at the material time the circumstances were such that there was no likelihood of his driving it so long as he remained unfit to drive through drink or drugs.

(4)   The court may, in determining whether there was such a likelihood as is mentioned in subsection (3) above, disregard any injury to him and any damage to the vehicle.

(5)   For the purposes of this section, a person shall be taken to be unfit to drive if his ability to drive properly is for the time being impaired.

(6)   A constable may arrest a person without warrant if he has reasonable cause to suspect that that person is or has been committing an offence under this section.

(7)   For the purpose of arresting a person under the power conferred by subsection (6) above, a constable may enter (if need be by force) any place where that person is or where the constable, with reasonable cause, suspects him to be.

(8)   Subsection (7) above does not extend to Scotland, and nothing in that subsection affects any rule of law in Scotland concerning the right of a constable to enter any premises for any purpose.

NOTES

Sub-ss (1)–(3): words in square brackets substituted by the Road Traffic Act 1991, s 4.

5 Driving or being in charge of a motor vehicle with alcohol concentration above prescribed limit

(1)   If a person—
   (a)   drives or attempts to drive a motor vehicle on a road or other public place, or
   (b)   is in charge of a motor vehicle on a road or other public place,

after consuming so much alcohol that the proportion of it in his breath, blood or urine exceeds the prescribed limit he is guilty of an offence.

(2)   It is a defence for a person charged with an offence under subsection (1)(b) above to prove that at the time he is alleged to have committed the offence the circumstances were such that there was no likelihood of his driving the vehicle whilst the proportion of alcohol in his breath, blood or urine remained likely to exceed the prescribed limit.

(3)   The court may, in determining whether there was such a likelihood as is mentioned in subsection (2) above, disregard any injury to him and any damage to the vehicle.

6 Breath tests

(1)   Where a constable in uniform has reasonable cause to suspect—
- (a)   that a person driving or attempting to drive or in charge of a motor vehicle on a road or other public place has alcohol in his body or has committed a traffic offence whilst the vehicle was in motion, or
- (b)   that a person has been driving or attempting to drive or been in charge of a motor vehicle on a road or other public place with alcohol in his body and that that person still has alcohol in his body, or
- (c)   that a person has been driving or attempting to drive or been in charge of a motor vehicle on a road or other public place and has committed a traffic offence whilst the vehicle was in motion,

he may, subject to section 9 of this Act, require him to provide a specimen of breath for a breath test.

(2)   If an accident occurs owing to the presence of a motor vehicle on a road or other public place, a constable may, subject to section 9 of this Act, require any person who he has reasonable cause to believe was driving or attempting to drive or in charge of the vehicle at the time of the accident to provide a specimen of breath for a breath test.

(3)   A person may be required under subsection (1) or subsection (2) above to provide a specimen either at or near the place where the requirement is made or, if the requirement is made under subsection (2) above and the constable making the requirement thinks fit, at a police station specified by the constable.

(4)   A person who, without reasonable excuse, fails to provide a specimen of breath when required to do so in pursuance of this section is guilty of an offence.

(5)   A constable may arrest a person without warrant if—
- (a)   as a result of a breath test he has reasonable cause to suspect that the proportion of alcohol in that person's breath or blood exceeds the prescribed limit, or
- (b)   that person has failed to provide a specimen of breath for a breath test when required to do so in pursuance of this section and the constable has reasonable cause to suspect that he has alcohol in his body,

but a person shall not be arrested by virtue of this subsection when he is at a hospital as a patient.

(6)   A constable may, for the purpose of requiring a person to provide a specimen of breath under subsection (2) above in a case where he has reasonable cause to suspect that the accident involved injury to another person or of arresting him in such a case under subsection (5) above, enter (if need be by force) any place where that person is or where the constable, with reasonable cause, suspects him to be.

(7) Subsection (6) above does not extend to Scotland, and nothing in that subsection shall affect any rule of law in Scotland concerning the right of a constable to enter any premises for any purpose.

(8) In this section "traffic offence" means an offence under—

(a) any provision of Part II of the Public Passenger Vehicles Act 1981,

(b) any provision of the Road Traffic Regulation Act 1984,

(c) any provision of the Road Traffic Offenders Act 1988 except Part III, or

(d) any provision of this Act except Part V.

7 Provision of specimens for analysis

(1) In the course of an investigation into whether a person has committed an offence under [section 3A, 4] or 5 of this Act a constable may, subject to the following provisions of this section and section 9 of this Act, require him—

(a) to provide two specimens of breath for analysis by means of a device of a type approved by the Secretary of State, or

(b) to provide a specimen of blood or urine for a laboratory test.

(2) A requirement under this section to provide specimens of breath can only be made at a police station.

(3) A requirement under this section to provide a specimen of blood or urine can only be made at a police station or at a hospital; and it cannot be made at a police station unless—

(a) the constable making the requirement has reasonable cause to believe that for medical reasons a specimen of breath cannot be provided or should not be required, or

(b) at the time the requirement is made a device or a reliable device of the type mentioned in subsection (1)(a) above is not available at the police station or it is then for any other reason not practicable to use such a device there, or

[(bb) a device of the type mentioned in subsection (1)(a) above has been used at the police station but the constable who required the specimens of breath has reasonable cause to believe that the device has not produced a reliable indication of the proportion of alcohol in the breath of the person concerned, or]

(c) the suspected offence is one under [section 3A or 4] of this Act and the constable making the requirement has been advised by a medical practitioner that the condition of the person required to provide the specimen might be due to some drug;

but may then be made notwithstanding that the person required to provide the specimen has already provided or been required to provide two specimens of breath.

(4) If the provision of a specimen other than a specimen of breath may be required in pursuance of this section the question whether it is to be a specimen of blood or a specimen of urine shall be decided by the constable making the requirement, but if a medical practitioner is of the opinion that for medical reasons a specimen of blood cannot or should not be taken the specimen shall be a specimen of urine.

(5)   A specimen of urine shall be provided within one hour of the requirement for its provision being made and after the provision of a previous specimen of urine.

(6)   A person who, without reasonable excuse, fails to provide a specimen when required to do so in pursuance of this section is guilty of an offence.

(7)   A constable must, on requiring any person to provide a specimen in pursuance of this section, warn him that a failure to provide it may render him liable to prosecution.

NOTES

Sub-s (1): words in square brackets substituted by the Road Traffic Act 1991, s 48, Sch 4, para 42.

Sub-s (3): para (bb) inserted by the Criminal Procedure and Investigations Act 1996, s 63(1), in relation to a requirement mentioned in sub-s (3) hereof after 1 April 1997; final words in square brackets substituted by the Road Traffic Act 1991, s 48, Sch 4, para 42.

8 Choice of specimens of breath

(1)   Subject to subsection (2) below, of any two specimens of breath provided by any person in pursuance of section 7 of this Act that with the lower proportion of alcohol in the breath shall be used and the other shall be disregarded.

(2)   If the specimen with the lower proportion of alcohol contains no more than 50 microgrammes of alcohol in 100 millilitres of breath, the person who provided it may claim that it should be replaced by such specimen as may be required under section 7(4) of this Act and, if he then provides such a specimen, neither specimen of breath shall be used.

(3)   The Secretary of State may by regulations substitute another proportion of alcohol in the breath for that specified in subsection (2) above.

11 Interpretation of sections 4 to 10

(1)   The following provisions apply for the interpretation of sections [3A] to 10 of this Act.

(2)   In those sections—
"breath test" means a preliminary test for the purpose of obtaining, by means of a device of a type approved by the Secretary of State, an indication whether the proportion of alcohol in a person's breath or blood is likely to exceed the prescribed limit,
"drug" includes any intoxicant other than alcohol,
"fail" includes refuse,
"hospital" means an institution which provides medical or surgical treatment for in-patients or out-patients,
"the prescribed limit" means, as the case may require—
(a)   35 microgrammes of alcohol in 100 millilitres of breath,
(b)   80 milligrammes of alcohol in 100 millilitres of blood, or
(c)   107 milligrammes of alcohol in 100 millilitres of urine,
or such other proportion as may be prescribed by regulations made by the Secretary of State.

(3)   A person does not provide a specimen of breath for a breath test or for analysis unless the specimen—

- (a) is sufficient to enable the test or the analysis to be carried out, and
- (b) is provided in such a way as to enable the objective of the test or analysis to be satisfactorily achieved.

(4)   A person provides a specimen of blood if and only if he consents to its being taken by a medical practitioner and it is so taken.

NOTES

Sub-s (1): figure in square brackets substituted by the Road Traffic Act 1991, s 48, Sch 4, para 44.

Stopping on verges, etc, or in dangerous positions, etc

22 Leaving vehicles in dangerous positions

If a person in charge of a vehicle causes or permits the vehicle or a trailer drawn by it to remain at rest on a road in such a position or in such condition or in such circumstances as to [involve a danger of injury] to other persons using the road, he is guilty of an offence.

NOTES

Words in square brackets substituted by the Road Traffic Act 1991, s 48, Sch 4, para 48.

Other restrictions in interests of safety

[22A Causing danger to road-users]

[(1)   A person is guilty of an offence if he intentionally and without lawful authority or reasonable cause—
- (a)   causes anything to be on or over a road, or
- (b)   interferes with a motor vehicle, trailer or cycle, or
- (c)   interferes (directly or indirectly) with traffic equipment,

in such circumstances that it would be obvious to a reasonable person that to do so would be dangerous.

(2)   In subsection (1) above "dangerous" refers to danger either of injury to any person while on or near a road, or of serious damage to property on or near a road; and in determining for the purposes of that subsection what would be obvious to a reasonable person in a particular case, regard shall be had not only to the circumstances of which he could be expected to be aware but also to any circumstances shown to have been within the knowledge of the accused.

(3)   In subsection (1) above "traffic equipment" means—
- (a)   anything lawfully placed on or near a road by a highway authority;
- (b)   a traffic sign lawfully placed on or near a road by a person other than a highway authority;
- (c)   any fence, barrier or light lawfully placed on or near a road—

     (i) in pursuance of section 174 of the Highways Act 1980, . . . or section 65 of the New Roads and Street Works Act 1991 (which provide for guarding, lighting and signing in streets where works are undertaken), or

    (ii) by a constable or a person acting under the instructions (whether general or specific) of a chief officer of police.

(4)   For the purposes of subsection (3) above anything placed on or near a road shall unless the contrary is proved be deemed to have been lawfully placed there.

(5)   In this section "road" does not include a footpath or bridleway.

(6)   This section does not extend to Scotland.]

NOTES

Inserted by the Road Traffic Act 1991, s 6.

Sub-s (3): words omitted repealed by the New Roads and Street Works Act 1991, s 168(1), (2), Sch 8, para 121(2), Sch 9.

PART II
CONSTRUCTION AND USE OF VEHICLES AND EQUIPMENT

[Using vehicle in dangerous condition]

NOTES

Inserted by the Road Traffic Act 1991, s 8(1).

[40A Using vehicle in dangerous condition etc]

[A person is guilty of an offence if he uses, or causes or permits another to use, a motor vehicle or trailer on a road when—

   (a) the condition of the motor vehicle or trailer, or of its accessories or equipment, or

   (b) the purpose for which it is used, or

   (c) the number of passengers carried by it, or the manner in which they are carried, or

   (d) the weight, position or distribution of its load, or the manner in which it is secured,

is such that the use of the motor vehicle or trailer involves a danger of injury to any person.]

NOTES

Inserted by the Road Traffic Act 1991, s 8(1).

General regulation of construction, use etc

[41A Breach of requirement as to brakes, steering-gear or tyres]

[A person who—

   (a) contravenes or fails to comply with a construction and use requirement as to brakes, steering-gear or tyres, or

(b) uses on a road a motor vehicle or trailer which does not comply with such a requirement, or causes or permits a motor vehicle or trailer to be so used,

is guilty of an offence.]

NOTES
Substituted, together with ss 41B, 42, for s 42 as originally enacted, by the Road Traffic Act 1991, s 8(2).

[41B Breach of requirement as to weight: goods and passenger vehicles]

[(1)   A person who—
  (a) contravenes or fails to comply with a construction and use requirement as to any description of weight applicable to—
     (i) a goods vehicle, or
     (ii) a motor vehicle or trailer adapted to carry more than eight passengers, or
  (b) uses on a road a vehicle which does not comply with such a requirement, or causes or permits a vehicle to be so used,

is guilty of an offence.

(2)   In any proceedings for an offence under this section in which there is alleged a contravention of or failure to comply with a construction and use requirement as to any description of weight applicable to a goods vehicle, it shall be a defence to prove either—
  (a) that at the time when the vehicle was being used on the road—
     (i) it was proceeding to a weighbridge which was the nearest available one to the place where the loading of the vehicle was completed for the purpose of being weighed, or
     (ii) it was proceeding from a weighbridge after being weighed to the nearest point at which it was reasonably practicable to reduce the weight to the relevant limit, without causing an obstruction on any road, or
  (b) in a case where the limit of that weight was not exceeded by more than 5 per cent—
     (i) that that limit was not exceeded at the time when the loading of the vehicle was originally completed, and
     (ii) that since that time no person has made any addition to the load.]

NOTES
Substituted, together with ss 41A, 42, for s 42 as originally enacted, by the Road Traffic Act 1991, s 8(2).

[42 Breach of other construction and use requirements]

[A person who—
  (a) contravenes or fails to comply with any construction or use requirement other than one within section 41A(a) or 41B(1)(a) of this Act, or

(b) uses on a road a motor vehicle or trailer which does not comply with such a requirement, or causes or permits a motor vehicle or trailer to be so used,

is guilty of an offence.]

NOTES
Substituted, together with ss 41A, 41B, for section 42 as originally enacted, by the Road Traffic Act 1991, s 8(2).

Miscellaneous provisions about vehicles and vehicle parts

75 Vehicles not to be sold in unroadworthy condition or altered so as to be unroadworthy

(1) Subject to the provisions of this section no person shall supply a motor vehicle or trailer in an unroadworthy condition.

(2) In this section references to supply include—
(a) sell,
(b) offer to sell or supply, and
(c) expose for sale.

(3) For the purposes of subsection (1) above a motor vehicle or trailer is in an unroadworthy condition if—
(a) it is in such a condition that the use of it on a road in that condition would be unlawful by virtue of any provision made by regulations under section 41 of this Act as respects—
(i) brakes, steering gear or tyres, or
(ii) the construction, weight or equipment of vehicles, or
(iii) . . .
[(b) it is in such a condition that its use on a road would involve a danger of injury to any person].

(4) Subject to the provisions of this section no person shall alter a motor vehicle or trailer so as to render its condition such that the use of it on a road in that condition
[(a)] would be unlawful by virtue of any provision made as respects the construction, weight or equipment of vehicles by regulations under section 41 [or
(b) would involve a danger of injury to any person].

(5) A person who supplies or alters a motor vehicle or trailer in contravention of this section, or causes or permits it to be so supplied or altered, is guilty of an offence.

(6) A person shall not be convicted of an offence under this section in respect of the supply or alteration of a motor vehicle or trailer if he proves—
(a) that it was supplied or altered, as the case may be, for export from Great Britain, or
(b) that he had reasonable cause to believe that the vehicle or trailer would not be used on a road in Great Britain, or would not be so used until it had been put into a condition in which it might lawfully be so used, . . .
(c) . . .

[(6A)   Paragraph (b) of subsection (6) above shall not apply in relation to a person who, in the course of a trade or business—

    (a)   exposes a vehicle or trailer for sale, unless he also proves that he took all reasonable steps to ensure that any prospective purchaser would be aware that its use in its current condition on a road in Great Britain would be unlawful, or

    (b)   offers to sell a vehicle or trailer, unless he also proves that he took all reasonable steps to ensure that the person to whom the offer was made was aware of that fact.]

(7)   Nothing in the preceding provisions of this section shall affect the validity of a contract or any rights arising under a contract.

(8)   . . .

NOTES

Sub-s (3): para (a)(iii) repealed, and para (b) substituted, by the Road Traffic Act 1991, ss 16(2), 83, Sch 8.

Sub-s (4): letter "(a)" and words in square brackets inserted by the Road Traffic Act 1991, s 16(3).

Sub-s (6): para (c) and word immediately preceding it repealed by the Road Traffic Act 1991, ss 16(4), 83, Sch 8.

Sub-s (6A): inserted by the Road Traffic Act 1991, s 16(5).

Sub-s (8): repealed by the Road Traffic Act 1991, s 83, Sch 8.

PART III
LICENSING OF DRIVERS OF VEHICLES

Requirement to hold licence

87 Drivers of a motor vehicles to have driving licences

(1)   It is an offence for a person to drive on a road a motor vehicle of any class [otherwise than in accordance with] a licence authorising him to drive a motor vehicle of that class.

(2)   It is an offence for a person to cause or permit another person to drive on a road a motor vehicle of any class [otherwise than in accordance with a licence authorising that other person] to drive a motor vehicle of that class.

[(3)   . . .]

NOTES

Sub-ss (1), (2): words in square brackets substituted by the Road Traffic Act 1991, s 17(1), (2).

Sub-s (3): inserted by the Road Traffic (Driver Licensing and Information Systems) Act 1989, s 7, Sch 3, para 7, repealed by the Road Traffic (Driver Licensing and Information Systems) Act 1989, s 16, Sch 6.

[Effects of disqualification]

NOTES
Substituted by the Road Traffic Act 1991, s 19.

[103 Obtaining licence, or driving, while disqualified]

[(1)   A person is guilty of an offence if, while disqualified for holding or obtaining a licence, he
  (a)   obtains a licence, or
  (b)   drives a motor vehicle on a road.

(2)   A licence obtained by a person who is disqualified is of no effect (or, where the disqualification relates only to vehicles of a particular class, is of no effect in relation to vehicles of that class).

(3)   A constable in uniform may arrest without warrant any person driving a motor vehicle on a road whom he has reasonable cause to suspect of being disqualified.

(4)   Subsections (1) and (3) above do not apply in relation to disqualification by virtue of section 101 of this Act.

(5)   Subsections (1)(b) and (3) above do not apply in relation to disqualification by virtue of section 102 of this Act.

(6)   In the application of subsections (1) and (3) above to a person whose disqualification is limited to the driving of motor vehicles of a particular class by virtue of—
  (a)   section 102 [117 or 117A] of this Act, or
  (b)   subsection (9) of section 36 of the Road Traffic Offenders Act 1988 (disqualification until test is passed),

the references to disqualification for holding or obtaining a licence and driving motor vehicles are references to disqualification for holding or obtaining a licence to drive and driving motor vehicles of that class.]

NOTES
Substituted by the Road Traffic Act 1991, s 19.
Sub-s (6): words in square brackets substituted by SI 1996/1974, reg 2, Sch 1, para 16.

PART VI
THIRD-PARTY LIABILITIES

Compulsory insurance or security against third-party risks

143 Users of motor vehicles to be insured or secured against third-party risks

(1)   Subject to the provisions of this Part of this Act—
  (a)   a person must not use a motor vehicle on a road [or other public place] unless there is in force in relation to the use of the vehicle by that person

such a policy of insurance or such a security in respect of third party risks as complies with the requirements of this Part of this Act, and

(b) a person must not cause or permit any other person to use a motor vehicle on a road [or other public place] unless there is in force in relation to the use of the vehicle by that other person such a policy of insurance or such a security in respect of third party risks as complies with the requirements of this Part of this Act.

(2) If a person acts in contravention of subsection (1) above he is guilty of an offence.

(3) A person charged with using a motor vehicle in contravention of this section shall not be convicted if he proves—

(a) that the vehicle did not belong to him and was not in his possession under a contract of hiring or of loan,

(b) that he was using the vehicle in the course of his employment, and

(c) that he neither knew nor had reason to believe that there was not in force in relation to the vehicle such a policy of insurance or security as is mentioned in subsection (1) above.

(4) This Part of this Act does not apply to invalid carriages.

NOTES

Sub-s (1): in para (a) words "or other public place" in square brackets inserted by SI 2000/726, reg 2(1), (2)(a).

Date in force: 3 April 2000: see SI 2000/726, reg 1.

Sub-s (1): in para (b) words "or other public place" in square brackets inserted by SI 2000/726, reg 2(1), (2)(b).

Date in force: 3 April 2000: see SI 2000/726, reg 1.

PART VII
MISCELLANEOUS AND GENERAL

Duties in case of accident

170 Duty of driver to stop, report accident and give information or documents

(1) This section applies in a case where, owing to the presence of a [mechanically propelled vehicle] on a road [or other public place], an accident occurs by which—

(a) personal injury is caused to a person other than the driver of that [mechanically propelled vehicle], or

(b) damage is caused—

(i) to a vehicle other than that [mechanically propelled vehicle] or a trailer drawn by that [mechanically propelled vehicle], or

(ii) to an animal other than an animal in or on that [mechanically propelled vehicle] or a trailer drawn by that [mechanically propelled vehicle], or

(iii) to any other property constructed on, fixed to, growing in or otherwise forming part of the land on which the road [or place] in question is situated or land adjacent to such land.

(2) The driver of the [mechanically propelled vehicle] must stop and, if required to do so by any person having reasonable grounds for so requiring, give his name and address and also the name and address of the owner and the identification marks of the vehicle.

(3) If for any reason the driver of the [mechanically propelled vehicle] does not give his name and address under subsection (2) above, he must report the accident.

(4) A person who fails to comply with subsection (2) or (3) above is guilty of an offence.

(5) If, in a case where this section applies by virtue of subsection (1)(a) above, the driver of [a motor vehicle] does not at the time of the accident produce such a certificate of insurance or security, or other evidence, as is mentioned in section 165(2)(a) of this Act—

(a) to a constable, or

(b) to some person who, having reasonable grounds for so doing, has required him to produce it,

the driver must report the accident and produce such a certificate or other evidence.

This subsection does not apply to the driver of an invalid carriage.

(6) To comply with a duty under this section to report an accident or to produce such a certificate of insurance or security, or other evidence, as is mentioned in section 165(2)(a) of this Act, the driver—

(a) must do so at a police station or to a constable, and

(b) must do so as soon as is reasonably practicable and, in any case, within twenty-four hours of the occurrence of the accident.

(7) A person who fails to comply with a duty under subsection (5) above is guilty of an offence, but he shall not be convicted by reason only of a failure to produce a certificate or other evidence if, within [seven] days after the occurrence of the accident, the certificate or other evidence is produced at a police station that was specified by him at the time when the accident was reported.

(8) In this section "animal" means horse, cattle, ass, mule, sheep, pig, goat or dog.

NOTES

Sub-s (1): words "mechanically propelled vehicle" in square brackets in each place they occur substituted by the Road Traffic Act 1991, s 48, Sch 4, para 72(1), (2).

Sub-s (1): words "or other public place" in square brackets inserted by SI 2000/726, reg 2(1), (6)(a).

Date in force: 3 April 2000: see SI 2000/726, reg 1.

Sub-s (1): in para (b)(iii) words "or place" in square brackets inserted by SI 2000/726, reg 2(1), (6)(b).

Date in force: 3 April 2000: see SI 2000/726, reg 1.

Sub-s (2): words "mechanically propelled vehicle" in square brackets substituted by the Road Traffic Act 1991, s 48, Sch 4, para 72(1), (2).

Sub-s (3): words "mechanically propelled vehicle" in square brackets substituted by the Road Traffic Act 1991, s 48, Sch 4, para 72(1), 2).

Sub-s (5): words "a motor vehicle" in square brackets substituted by the Road Traffic Act 1991, s 48, Sch 4, para 72(1), (3).

Sub-s (7): word "seven" in square brackets substituted by the Road Traffic Act 1991, s 48, Sch 4, para 72(1), (4).

Other duties to give information or documents

[172 Duty to give information as to identity of driver etc in certain circumstances]

[(1)   This section applies—
- (a)   to any offence under the preceding provisions of this Act except—
    - (i)   an offence under Part V, or
    - (ii)   an offence under section 13, 16, 51(2), 61(4), 67(9), 68(4), 96 or 120, and to an offence under section 178 of this Act,
- (b)   to any offence under sections 25, 26 or 27 of the Road Traffic Offenders Act 1988,
- (c)   to any offence against any other enactment relating to the use of vehicles on roads, except an offence under paragraph 8 of Schedule 1 to the Road Traffic (Driver Licensing and Information Systems) Act 1989, and
- (d)   to manslaughter, or in Scotland culpable homicide, by the driver of a motor vehicle.

(2)   Where the driver of a vehicle is alleged to be guilty of an offence to which this section applies—
- (a)   the person keeping the vehicle shall give such information as to the identity of the driver as he may be required to give by or on behalf of a chief officer of police, and
- (b)   any other person shall if required as stated above give any information which it is in his power to give and may lead to identification of the driver.

(3)   Subject to the following provisions, a person who fails to comply with a requirement under subsection (2) above shall be guilty of an offence.

(4)   A person shall not be guilty of an offence by virtue of paragraph (a) of subsection (2) above if he shows that he did not know and could not with reasonable diligence have ascertained who the driver of the vehicle was.

(5)   Where a body corporate is guilty of an offence under this section and the offence is proved to have been committed with the consent or connivance of, or to be attributable to neglect on the part of, a director, manager, secretary or other similar officer of the body corporate, or a person who was purporting to act in any such capacity, he, as well as the body corporate, is guilty of that offence and liable to be proceeded against and punished accordingly.

(6)   Where the alleged offender is a body corporate, or in Scotland a partnership or an unincorporated association, or the proceedings are brought against him by virtue

of subsection (5) above or subsection (11) below, subsection (4) above shall not apply unless, in addition to the matters there mentioned, the alleged offender shows that no record was kept of the persons who drove the vehicle and that the failure to keep a record was reasonable.

(7) A requirement under subsection (2) may be made by written notice served by post; and where it is so made—
  (a) it shall have effect as a requirement to give the information within the period of 28 days beginning with the day on which the notice is served, and
  (b) the person on whom the notice is served shall not be guilty of an offence under this section if he shows either that he gave the information as soon as reasonably practicable after the end of that period or that it has not been reasonably practicable for him to give it.

(8) Where the person on whom a notice under subsection (7) above is to be served is a body corporate, the notice is duly served if it is served on the secretary or clerk of that body.

(9) For the purposes of section 7 of the Interpretation Act 1978 as it applies for the purposes of this section the proper address of any person in relation to the service on him of a notice under subsection (7) above is—
  (a) in the case of the secretary or clerk of a body corporate, that of the registered or principal office of that body or (if the body corporate is the registered keeper of the vehicle concerned) the registered address, and
  (b) in any other case, his last known address at the time of service.

(10) In this section—
  "registered address", in relation to the registered keeper of a vehicle, means the address recorded in the record kept under [the Vehicle Excise and Registration Act 1994] with respect to that vehicle as being that person's address, and
  "registered keeper", in relation to a vehicle, means the person in whose name the vehicle is registered under that Act;
and references to the driver of a vehicle include references to the rider of a cycle.

(11) Where, in Scotland, an offence under this section is committed by a partnership or by an unincorporated association other than a partnership and is proved to have been committed with the consent or connivance or in consequence of the negligence of a partner in the partnership or, as the case may be, a person concerned in the management or control of the association, he (as well as the partnership or association) shall be guilty of the offence.]

NOTES
Substituted by the Road Traffic Act 1991, s 21.
Sub-s (10): words in square brackets substituted by the Vehicle Excise and Registration Act 1994, s 63, Sch 3, para 24(10).

Supplementary

197 Short title, commencement and extent

(1) This Act may be cited as the Road Traffic Act 1988.

(2) This Act shall come into force, subject to the transitory provisions in Schedule 5 to the Road Traffic (Consequential Provisions) Act 1988, at the end of the period of six months beginning with the day on which it is passed.

(3) This Act, except section 80 and except as provided by section 184, does not extend to Northern Ireland.

Computer Misuse Act 1990

1990 CHAPTER 18

An Act to make provision for securing computer material against unauthorised access or modification; and for connected purposes

[29th June 1990]

Computer Misuse Offences

1 Unauthorised access to computer material

(1) A person is guilty of an offence if—
  (a) he causes a computer to perform any function with intent to secure access to any program or data held in any computer;
  (b) the access he intends to secure is unauthorised; and
  (c) he knows at the time when he causes the computer to perform the function that that is the case.

(2) The intent a person has to have to commit an offence under this section need not be directed at—
  (a) any particular program or data;
  (b) a program or data of any particular kind; or
  (c) a program or data held in any particular computer.

(3) A person guilty of an offence under this section shall be liable on summary conviction to imprisonment for a term not exceeding six months or to a fine not exceeding level 5 on the standard scale or to both.

2 Unauthorised access with intent to commit or facilitate commission of further offences

(1) A person is guilty of an offence under this section if he commits an offence under section 1 above ("the unauthorised access offence") with intent—
  (a) to commit an offence to which this section applies; or
  (b) to facilitate the commission of such an offence (whether by himself or by any other person);

and the offence he intends to commit or facilitate is referred to below in this section as the further offence.

(2) This section applies to offences—

(a)   for which the sentence is fixed by law; or

(b)   for which a person *of twenty-one years of age or over (not previously convicted)* [who has attained the age of twenty-one years (eighteen in relation to England and Wales) and has no previous convictions] may be sentenced to imprisonment for a term of five years (or, in England and Wales, might be so sentenced but for the restrictions imposed by section 33 of the Magistrates' Courts Act 1980).

(3)   It is immaterial for the purposes of this section whether the further offence is to be committed on the same occasion as the unauthorised access offence or on any future occasion.

(4)   A person may be guilty of an offence under this section even though the facts are such that the commission of the further offence is impossible.

(5)   A person guilty of an offence under this section shall be liable—

(a)   on summary conviction, to imprisonment for a term not exceeding six months or to a fine not exceeding the statutory maximum or to both; and

(b)   on conviction on indictment, to imprisonment for a term not exceeding five years or to a fine or to both.

NOTES

Sub-s (2): in para (b) words "of twenty-one years of age or over (not previously convicted)" in italics repealed and subsequent words in square brackets substituted by the Criminal Justice and Court Services Act 2000, s 74, Sch 7, Pt II, para 98.

Date in force: to be appointed: see the Criminal Justice and Court Services Act 2000, s 80(1).

3 Unauthorised modification of computer material

(1)   A person is guilty of an offence if—

(a)   he does any act which causes an unauthorised modification of the contents of any computer; and

(b)   at the time when he does the act he has the requisite intent and the requisite knowledge.

(2)   For the purposes of subsection (1)(*b*) above the requisite intent is an intent to cause a modification of the contents of any computer and by so doing—

(a)   to impair the operation of any computer;

(b)   to prevent or hinder access to any program or data held in any computer; or

(c)   to impair the operation of any such program or the reliability of any such data.

(3)   The intent need not be directed at—

(a)   any particular computer;

(b)   any particular program or data or a program or data of any particular kind; or

(c)   any particular modification or a modification of any particular kind.

(4)   For the purposes of subsection (1)(*b*) above the requisite knowledge is knowledge that any modification he intends to cause is unauthorised.

(5) It is immaterial for the purposes of this section whether an unauthorised modification or any intended effect of it of a kind mentioned in subsection (2) above is, or is intended to be, permanent or merely temporary.

(6) For the purposes of the Criminal Damage Act 1971 a modification of the contents of a computer shall not regarded as damaging any computer or computer storage medium unless its effect on that computer or computer storage medium impairs its physical condition.

(7) A person guilty of an offence under this section shall be liable—
  (a) on summary conviction, to imprisonment for a term not exceeding six months or to a fine not exceeding the statutory maximum or to both; and
  (b) on conviction on indictment, to imprisonment for a term not exceeding five years or to a fine or to both.

Jurisdiction

4 Territorial scope of offences under this Act

(1) Except as provided below in this section, it is immaterial for the purposes of any offence under section 1 or 3 above—
  (a) whether any act or other event proof of which is required for conviction of the offence occurred in the home country concerned; or
  (b) whether the accused was in the home country concerned at the time of any such act or event.

(2) Subject to subsection (3) below, in the case of such an offence at least one significant link with domestic jurisdiction must exist in the circumstances of the case for the offence to be committed.

(3) There is no need for any such link to exist for the commission of an offence under section 1 above to be established in proof of an allegation to that effect in proceedings for an offence under section 2 above.

(4) Subject to section 8 below, where—
  (a) any such link does in fact exist in the case of an offence under section 1 above; and
  (b) commission of that offence is alleged in proceedings for an offence under section 2 above;

section 2 above shall apply as if anything the accused intended to do or facilitate in any place outside the home country concerned which would be an offence to which section 2 applies if it took place in the home country concerned were the offence in question.

(5) This section is without prejudice to any jurisdiction exercisable by a court in Scotland apart from this section.

(6) References in this Act to the home country concerned are references—
  (a) in the application of this Act to England and Wales, to England and Wales;
  (b) in the application of this Act to Scotland, to Scotland; and
  (c) in the application of this Act to Northern Ireland, to Northern Ireland.

5 Significant links with domestic jurisdiction

(1)   The following provisions of this section apply for the interpretation of section 4 above.

(2)   In relation to an offence under section 1, either of the following is a significant link with domestic jurisdiction—
  (a)   that the accused was in the home country concerned at the time when he did the act which caused the computer to perform the function; or
  (b)   that any computer containing any program or data to which the accused secured or intended to secure unauthorised access by doing that act was in the home country concerned at that time.

(3)   In relation to an offence under section 3, either of the following is a significant link with domestic jurisdiction—
  (a)   that the accused was in the home country concerned at the time when he did the act which caused the unauthorised modification; or
  (b)   that the unauthorised modification took place in the home country concerned.

6 Territorial scope of inchoate offences related to offences under this Act

(1)   On a charge of conspiracy to commit an offence under this Act the following questions are immaterial to the accused's guilt—
  (a)   the question where any person became a party to the conspiracy; and
  (b)   the question whether any act, omission or other event occurred in the home country concerned.

(2)   On a charge of attempting to commit an offence under section 3 above the following questions are immaterial to the accused's guilt—
  (a)   the question where the attempt was made; and
  (b)   the question whether it had an effect in the home country concerned.

(3)   On a charge of incitement to commit an offence under this Act the question where the incitement took place is immaterial to the accused's guilt.

(4)   This section does not extend to Scotland.

7 Territorial scope of inchoate offences related to offences under external law corresponding to offences under this Act

(1)–(3)   . . .

(4)   Subject to section 8 below, if any act done by a person in England and Wales would amount to the offence of incitement to commit an offence under this Act but for the fact that what he had in view would not be an offence triable in England and Wales—
  (a)   what he had in view shall be treated as an offence under this Act for the purposes of any charge of incitement brought in respect of that act; and
  (b)   any such charge shall accordingly be triable in England and Wales.

NOTES
Sub-ss (1), (2): repealed by the Criminal Justice (Terrorism and Conspiracy) Act 1998, s 9(2), Sch 2, Pt II.
Date in force: 4 September 1998: (no specific commencement provision).
Sub-s (3): amends the Criminal Attempts Act 1981, s 1.

8 Relevance of external law

(1)   A person is guilty of an offence triable by virtue of section 4(4) above only if what he intended to do or facilitate would involve the commission of an offence under the law in force where the whole or any part of it was intended to take place.

(2)   . . .

(3)   A person is guilty of an offence triable by virtue of section 1(1A) of the Criminal Attempts Act 1981 or by virtue of section 7(4) above only if what he had in view would involve the commission of an offence under the law in force where the whole or any part of it was intended to take place.

(4)   Conduct punishable under the law in force in any place is an offence under that law for the purposes of this section, however it is described in that law.

(5)   Subject to subsection (7) below, a condition specified in [subsection (1) or (3)] above shall be taken to be satisfied unless not later than rules of court may provide the defence serve on the prosecution a notice—
  (a)   stating that, on the facts as alleged with respect to the relevant conduct, the condition is not in their opinion satisfied;
  (b)   showing their grounds for that opinion; and
  (c)   requiring the prosecution to show that it is satisfied.

(6)   In subsection (5) above "the relevant conduct" means—
  (a)   where the condition in subsection (1) above is in question, what the accused intended to do or facilitate;
  (b)   . . .
  (c)   where the condition in subsection (3) above is in question, what the accused had in view.

(7)   The court, if it thinks fit, may permit the defence to require the prosecution to show that the condition is satisfied without the prior service of a notice under subsection (5) above.

(8)   If by virtue of subsection (7) above a court of solemn jurisdiction in Scotland permits the defence to require the prosecution to show that the condition is satisfied, it shall be competent for the prosecution for that purpose to examine any witness or to put in evidence any production not included in the lists lodged by it.

(9)   In the Crown Court the question whether the condition is satisfied shall be decided by the judge alone.

(10)   In the High Court of Justiciary and in the sheriff court the question whether the condition is satisfied shall be decided by the judge or, as the case may be, the sheriff alone.

Sub-s (2): repealed by the Criminal Justice (Terrorism and Conspiracy) Act 1998, s 9(1), (2), Sch 1, para 6(1)(a), Sch 2, Pt II.

Date in force: 4 September 1998: (no specific commencement provision).

Sub-s (5): words "subsection (1) or (3)" in square brackets substituted by the Criminal Justice (Terrorism and Conspiracy) Act 1998, s 9(1), Sch 1, para 6(1)(b).

Date in force: 4 September 1998: (no specific commencement provision).

Sub-s (6): para (b) repealed by the Criminal Justice (Terrorism and Conspiracy) Act 1998, s 9(1), (2), Sch 1, para 6(1)(c), Sch 2, Pt II.

Date in force: 4 September 1998: (no specific commencement provision).

9 British citizenship immaterial

(1)   In any proceedings brought in England and Wales in respect of any offence to which this section applies it is immaterial to guilt whether or not the accused was a British citizen at the time of any act, omission or other event proof of which is required for conviction of the offence.

(2)   This section applies to the following offences—
  (a)   any offence under this Act;
  (b)   . . .
  (c)   any attempt to commit an offence under section 3 above; and
  (d)   incitement to commit an offence under this Act.

Sub-s (2): para (b) repealed by the Criminal Justice (Terrorism and Conspiracy) Act 1998, s 9(1), (2), Sch 1, para 6(2), Sch 2, Pt II.

Date in force: 4 September 1998: (no specific commencement provision).

Miscellaneous and General

17 Interpretation

(1)   The following provisions of this section apply for the interpretation of this Act.

(2)   A person secures access to any program or data held in a computer if by causing a computer to perform any function he—
  (a)   alters or erases the program or data;
  (b)   copies or moves it to any storage medium other than that in which it is held or to a different location in the storage medium in which it is held;
  (c)   uses it; or
  (d)   has it output from the computer in which it is held (whether by having it displayed or in any other manner);

and references to access to a program or data (and to an intent to secure such access) shall be read accordingly.

(3)   For the purposes of subsection (2)(c) above a person uses a program if the function he causes the computer to perform—
  (a)   causes the program to be executed; or
  (b)   is itself a function of the program.

(4) For the purposes of subsection (2)(d) above—
  (a) a program is output if the instructions of which it consists are output; and
  (b) the form in which any such instructions or any other data is output (and in particular whether or not it represents a form in which, in the case of instructions, they are capable of being executed or, in the case of data, it is capable of being processed by a computer) is immaterial.

(5) Access of any kind by any person to any program or data held in a computer is unauthorised if—
  (a) he is not himself entitled to control access of the kind in question to the program or data; and
  (b) he does not have consent to access by him of the kind in question to the program or data from any person who is so entitled

[but this subsection is subject to section 10].

(6) References to any program or data held in a computer include references to any program or data held in any removable storage medium which is for the time being in the computer; and a computer is to be regarded as containing any program or data held in any such medium.

(7) A modification of the contents of any computer takes place if, by the operation of any function of the computer concerned or any other computer—
  (a) any program or data held in the computer concerned is altered or erased; or
  (b) any program or data is added to its contents;

and any act which contributes towards causing such a modification shall be regarded as causing it.

(8) Such a modification is unauthorised if—
  (a) the person whose act causes it is not himself entitled to determine whether the modification should be made; and
  (b) he does not have consent to the modification from any person who is so entitled.

(9) References to the home country concerned shall be read in accordance with section 4(6) above.

(10) References to a program include references to part of a program.

NOTES

Sub-s (5): words in square brackets inserted by the Criminal Justice and Public Order Act 1994, s 162(2).

18 Citation, commencement etc

(1) This Act may be cited as the Computer Misuse Act 1990.

(2) This Act shall come into force at the end of the period of two months beginning with the day on which it is passed.

(3) An offence is not committed under this Act unless every act or other event proof of which is required for conviction of the offence takes place after this Act comes into force.

Human Fertilisation and Embryology Act 1990

1990 CHAPTER 37

An Act to make provision in connection with human embryos and any subsequent development of such embryos; to prohibit certain practices in connection with embryos and gametes; to establish a Human Fertilisation and Embryology Authority; to make provision about the persons who in certain circumstances are to be treated in law as the parents of a child; and to amend the Surrogacy Arrangements Act 1985

[1st November 1990]

Principal terms used

1 Meaning of "embryo", "gamete" and associated expressions

(1)   In this Act, except where otherwise stated—
  (a)   embryo means a live human embryo where fertilisation is complete, and
  (b)   references to an embryo include an egg in the process of fertilisation,

and, for this purpose, fertilisation is not complete until the appearance of a two cell zygote.

(2)   This Act, so far as it governs bringing about the creation of an embryo, applies only to bringing about the creation of an embryo outside the human body; and in this Act—
  (a)   references to embryos the creation of which was brought about *in vitro* (in their application to those where fertilisation is complete) are to those where fertilisation began outside the human body whether or not it was completed there, and
  (b)   references to embryos taken from a woman do not include embryos whose creation was brought about *in vitro*.

(3)   This Act, so far as it governs the keeping or use of an embryo, applies only to keeping or using an embryo outside the human body.

(4)   References in this Act to gametes, eggs or sperm, except where otherwise stated, are to live human gametes, eggs or sperm but references below in this Act to gametes or eggs do not include eggs in the process of fertilisation.

2 Other terms

(1)   In this Act—
  "the Authority" means the Human Fertilisation and Embryology Authority established under section 5 of this Act,
  "directions" means directions under section 23 of this Act,
  "licence" means a licence under Schedule 2 to this Act and, in relation to a

licence, "the person responsible" has the meaning given by section 17 of this Act, and

"treatment services" means medical, surgical or obstetric services provided to the public or a section of the public for the purpose of assisting women to carry children.

(2)   References in this Act to keeping, in relation to embryos or gametes, include keeping while preserved, whether preserved by cryopreservation or in any other way; and embryos or gametes so kept are referred to in this Act as "stored" (and "store" and "storage" are to be interpreted accordingly).

(3)   For the purposes of this Act, a woman is not to be treated as carrying a child until the embryo has become implanted.

Activities governed by the Act

3 Prohibitions in connection with embryos

(1)   No person shall—
  (a)   bring about the creation of an embryo, or
  (b)   keep or use an embryo,

except in pursuance of a licence.

(2)   No person shall place in a woman—
  (a)   a live embryo other than a human embryo, or
  (b)   any live gametes other than human gametes.

(3)   A licence cannot authorise—
  (a)   keeping or using an embryo after the appearance of the primitive streak,
  (b)   placing an embryo in any animal,
  (c)   keeping or using an embryo in any circumstances in which regulations prohibit its keeping or use, or
  (d)   replacing a nucleus of a cell of an embryo with a nucleus taken from a cell of any person, embryo or subsequent development of an embryo.

(4)   For the purposes of subsection (3)(*a*) above, the primitive streak is to be taken to have appeared in an embryo not later than the end of the period of 14 days beginning with the day when the gametes are mixed, not counting any time during which the embryo is stored.

[3A Prohibition in connection with germ cells]

[(1)   No person shall, for the purpose of providing fertility services for any woman, use female germ cells taken or derived from an embryo or a foetus or use embryos created by using such cells.

(2)   In this section—
  "female germ cells" means cells of the female germ line and includes such cells at any stage of maturity and accordingly includes eggs; and
  "fertility services" means medical, surgical or obstetric services provided for the purpose of assisting women to carry children.]

Inserted by the Criminal Justice and Public Order Act 1994, s 156(1).

4 Prohibitions in connection with gametes

(1)   No person shall—
-   (a)   store any gametes, or
-   (b)   in the course of providing treatment services for any woman, use the sperm of any man unless the services are being provided for the woman and the man together or use the eggs of any other woman, or
-   (c)   mix gametes with the live gametes of any animal,

except in pursuance of a licence.

(2)   A licence cannot authorise storing or using gametes in any circumstances in which regulations prohibit their storage or use.

(3)   No person shall place sperm and eggs in a woman in any circumstances specified in regulations except in pursuance of a licence.

(4)   Regulations made by virtue of subsection (3) above may provide that, in relation to licences only to place sperm and eggs in a woman in such circumstances, sections 12 to 22 of this Act shall have effect with such modifications as may be specified in the regulations.

(5)   Activities regulated by this section or section 3 of this Act are referred to in this Act as "activities governed by this Act".

Offences

41 Offences

(1)   A person who—
-   (a)   contravenes section 3(2)[, 3A] or 4(1)(c) of this Act, or
-   (b)   does anything which, by virtue of section 3(3) of this Act, cannot be authorised by a licence,

is guilty of an offence and liable on conviction on indictment to imprisonment for a term not exceeding ten years or a fine or both.

(2)   A person who—
-   (a)   contravenes section 3(1) of this Act, otherwise than by doing something which, by virtue of section 3(3) of this Act, cannot be authorised by a licence,
-   (b)   keeps or uses any gametes in contravention of section 4(1)(a) or (b) of this Act,
-   (c)   contravenes section 4(3) of this Act, or
-   (d)   fails to comply with any directions given by virtue of section 24(7)(a) of this Act,

is guilty of an offence.

(3)   If a person—

(a) provides any information for the purposes of the grant of a licence, being information which is false or misleading in a material particular, and

(b) either he knows the information to be false or misleading in a material particular or he provides the information recklessly,

he is guilty of an offence.

(4) A person guilty of an offence under subsection (2) or (3) above is liable—

(a) on conviction on indictment, to imprisonment for a term not exceeding two years or a fine or both, and

(b) on summary conviction, to imprisonment for a term not exceeding six months or a fine not exceeding the statutory maximum or both.

(5) A person who discloses any information in contravention of section 33 of this Act is guilty of an offence and liable—

(a) on conviction on indictment, to imprisonment for a term not exceeding two years or a fine or both, and

(b) on summary conviction, to imprisonment for a term not exceeding six months or a fine not exceeding the statutory maximum or both.

(6) A person who—

(a) fails to comply with a requirement made by virtue of section 39(1)(b) or (2)(b) or 40(2)(b)(ii) or (5)(b) of this Act, or

(b) intentionally obstructs the exercise of any rights conferred by a warrant issued under section 40 of this Act,

is guilty of an offence.

(7) A person who without reasonable excuse fails to comply with a requirement imposed by regulations made by virtue of section 10(2)(a) of this Act is guilty of an offence.

(8) Where a person to whom a licence applies or the nominal licensee gives or receives any money or other benefit, not authorised by directions, in respect of any supply of gametes or embryos, he is guilty of an offence.

(9) A person guilty of an offence under subsection (6), (7) or (8) above is liable on summary conviction to imprisonment for a term not exceeding six months or a fine not exceeding level five on the standard scale or both.

(10) It is a defence for a person ("the defendant") charged with an offence of doing anything which, under section 3(1) or 4(1) of this Act, cannot be done except in pursuance of a licence to prove—

(a) that the defendant was acting under the direction of another, and

(b) that the defendant believed on reasonable grounds—

(i) that the other person was at the material time the person responsible under a licence, a person designated by virtue of section 17(2)(b) of this Act as a person to whom a licence applied, or a person to whom directions had been given by virtue of section 24(9) of this Act, and

(ii) that the defendant was authorised by virtue of the licence or directions to do the thing in question.

(11)   It is a defence for a person charged with an offence under this Act to prove—

   (a)   that at the material time he was a person to whom a licence applied or to whom directions had been given, and

   (b)   that he took all such steps as were reasonable and exercised all due diligence to avoid committing the offence.

NOTES

Sub-s (1): in para (a) number in square brackets inserted by the Criminal Justice and Public Order Act 1994, s 156(2).

Miscellaneous and General

49 Short title, commencement, etc

(1)   This Act may be cited as the Human Fertilisation and Embryology Act 1990.

(2)   This Act shall come into force on such day as the Secretary of State may by order made by statutory instrument appoint and different days may be appointed for different provisions and for different purposes.

(3)   Sections 27 to 29 of this Act shall have effect only in relation to children carried by women as a result of the placing in them of embryos or of sperm and eggs, or of their artificial insemination (as the case may be), after the commencement of those sections.

(4)   Section 27 of the Family Law Reform Act 1987 (artificial insemination) does not have effect in relation to children carried by women as the result of their artificial insemination after the commencement of sections 27 to 29 of this Act.

(5)   Schedule 4 to this Act (which makes minor and consequential amendments) shall have effect.

(6)   An order under this section may make such transitional provision as the Secretary of State considers necessary or desirable and, in particular, may provide that where activities are carried on under the supervision of a particular individual, being activities which are carried on under the supervision of that individual at the commencement of sections 3 and 4 of this Act, those activities are to be treated, during such period as may be specified in or determined in accordance with the order, as authorised by a licence (having, in addition to the conditions required by this Act, such conditions as may be so specified or determined) under which that individual is the person responsible.

(7)   Her Majesty may by Order in Council direct that any of the provisions of this Act shall extend, with such exceptions, adaptations and modifications (if any) as may be specified in the Order, to any of the Channel Islands.

Criminal Procedure (Insanity and Unfitness to Plead) Act 1991

1991 CHAPTER 25

An Act to amend the law relating to the special verdict and unfitness to plead; to increase the powers of courts in the event of defendants being found to be insane or unfit to plead; and to provide for a trial of the facts in the cases of defendants found to be unfit to plead

[27th June 1991]

1 Acquittals on grounds of insanity

(1)   A jury shall not return a special verdict under section 2 of the Trial of Lunatics Act 1883 (acquittal on ground of insanity) except on the written or oral evidence of two or more registered medical practitioners at least one of whom is duly approved.

(2)   Subsections (2) and (3) of section 54 of the Mental Health Act 1983 ("the 1983 Act") shall have effect with respect to proof of the accused's mental condition for the purposes of the said section 2 as they have effect with respect to proof of an offender's mental condition for the purposes of section 37(2)(a) of that Act.

5 Orders under 1964 and 1968 Acts

(1)   The provisions of Schedule 1 to this Act shall apply in relation to the following orders, namely—
   (a)   any order made by the Crown Court under section 5 of the 1964 Act that the accused be admitted to hospital; and
   (b)   any order made by the Court of Appeal under section 6, 14 or 14A of the 1968 Act that the appellant be so admitted.

(2)   The 1983 Act shall have effect, in its application to guardianship orders within the meaning of that Act, as if the reference in section 37(1) to a person being convicted before the Crown Court of such an offence as is there mentioned included references—
   (a)   to a special verdict being returned that the accused is not guilty by reason of insanity, or to findings being recorded that the accused is under a disability and that he did the act or made the omission charged against him; and
   (b)   to the Court of Appeal being, on an appeal against conviction or under section 12 of the 1968 Act, of such opinion as is mentioned in section 6(1) or 14(1) of that Act;

and in relation to guardianship orders made by virtue of this subsection, references in the 1983 Act to the offender shall be construed accordingly.

(3)   The power to make a supervision and treatment order within the meaning given by Part I of Schedule 2 to this Act shall be exercisable, subject to and in accordance with Part II of that Schedule—

(a)   by the Crown Court in cases to which section 5 of the 1964 Act applies; and

(b)   by the Court of Appeal in cases to which section 6 or 14 of the 1968 Act applies;

and Part III of that Schedule shall have effect with respect to the revocation and amendment of such orders.

(4)   [Section 12(1) of the Powers of Criminal Courts (Sentencing) Act 2000] shall have effect, in its application to orders for absolute discharge, as if—

(a)   the reference to a person being convicted by or before a court of such an offence as is there mentioned included such references as are mentioned in subsection (2)(a) and (b) above; and

(b)   the reference to the court being of opinion that it is inexpedient to inflict punishment included a reference to it thinking that an order for absolute discharge would be most suitable in all the circumstances of the case.

NOTES

Sub-s (4): words "Section 12(1) of the Powers of Criminal Courts (Sentencing) Act 2000" in square brackets substituted by the Powers of Criminal Courts (Sentencing) Act 2000, s 165(1), Sch 9, para 133.

Date in force: 25 August 2000: see the Powers of Criminal Courts (Sentencing) Act 2000, s 168(1).

6 Interpretation etc

(1)   In this Act—

"the 1964 Act" means the Criminal Procedure (Insanity) Act 1964;

"the 1968 Act" means the Criminal Appeal Act 1968;

"the 1983 Act" means the Mental Health Act 1983;

"duly approved", in relation to a registered medical practitioner, means approved for the purposes of section 12 of the 1983 Act by the Secretary of State as having special experience in the diagnosis or treatment of mental disorder;

["local probation board" means a local probation board established under section 4 of the Criminal Justice and Court Services Act 2000].

(2)   Other expressions used in this Act which are also used in the 1983 Act have the same meanings as in Part III of that Act; and references to that Act in sections 137 to 139 of that Act shall include references to Schedule 1 to this Act.

NOTES

Sub-s (1): definition "local probation board" inserted by the Criminal Justice and Court Services Act 2000, s 74, Sch 7, Pt II, paras 99, 100.

Date in force: 1 April 2001: see SI 2001/919, art 2(f)(ii).

9 Short title, commencement and extent

(1)   This Act may be cited as the Criminal Procedure (Insanity and Unfitness to Plead) Act 1991.

(2)   This Act shall come into force on such day as the Secretary of State may by order made by statutory instrument appoint.

(3)   This Act extends to England and Wales only.

Water Resources Act 1991

1991 CHAPTER 57

An Act to consolidate enactments relating to the National Rivers Authority and the matters in relation to which it exercises functions, with amendments to give effect to recommendations of the Law Commission

[25th July 1991]

Chapter II
Pollution Offences

Principal offences

85 Offences of polluting controlled waters

(1)   A person contravenes this section if he causes or knowingly permits any poisonous, noxious or polluting matter or any solid waste matter to enter any controlled waters.

(2)   A person contravenes this section if he causes or knowingly permits any matter, other than trade effluent or sewage effluent, to enter controlled waters by being discharged from a drain or sewer in contravention of a prohibition imposed under section 86 below.

(3)   A person contravenes this section if he causes or knowingly permits any trade effluent or sewage effluent to be discharged—
  (a)   into any controlled waters; or
  (b)   from land in England and Wales, through a pipe, into the sea outside the seaward limits of controlled waters.

(4)   A person contravenes this section if he causes or knowingly permits any trade effluent or sewage effluent to be discharged, in contravention of any prohibition imposed under section 86 below, from a building or from any fixed plant—
  (a)   on to or into any land; or
  (b)   into any waters of a lake or pond which are not inland freshwaters.

(5)   A person contravenes this section if he causes or knowingly permits any matter whatever to enter any inland freshwaters so as to tend (either directly or in combination with other matter which he or another person causes or permits to enter those waters) to impede the proper flow of the waters in a manner leading, or likely to lead, to a substantial aggravation of—
  (a)   pollution due to other causes; or
  (b)   the consequences of such pollution.

(6) Subject to the following provisions of this Chapter, a person who contravenes this section or the conditions of any consent given under this Chapter for the purposes of this section shall be guilty of an offence and liable—

    (a) on summary conviction, to imprisonment for a term not exceeding three months or to a fine not exceeding £20,000 or to both;

    (b) on conviction on indictment, to imprisonment for a term not exceeding two years or to a fine or to both.

86 Prohibition of certain discharges by notice or regulations

(1) For the purposes of section 85 above a discharge of any effluent or other matter is, in relation to any person, in contravention of a prohibition imposed under this section if, subject to the following provisions of this section—

    (a) the [Agency] has given that person notice prohibiting him from making or, as the case may be, continuing the discharge; or

    (b) the [Agency] has given that person notice prohibiting him from making or, as the case may be, continuing the discharge unless specified conditions are observed, and those conditions are not observed.

(2) For the purposes of section 85 above a discharge of any effluent or other matter is also in contravention of a prohibition imposed under this section if the effluent or matter discharged—

    (a) contains a prescribed substance or a prescribed concentration of such a substance; or

    (b) derives from a prescribed process or from a process involving the use of prescribed substances or the use of such substances in quantities which exceed the prescribed amounts.

(3) Nothing in subsection (1) above shall authorise the giving of a notice for the purposes of that subsection in respect of discharges from a vessel; and nothing in any regulations made by virtue of subsection (2) above shall require any discharge from a vessel to be treated as a discharge in contravention of a prohibition imposed under this section.

(4) A notice given for the purposes of subsection (1) above shall expire at such time as may be specified in the notice.

(5) The time specified for the purposes of subsection (4) above shall not be before the end of the period of three months beginning with the day on which the notice is given, except in a case where the [Agency] is satisfied that there is an emergency which requires the prohibition in question to come into force at such time before the end of that period as may be so specified.

(6) Where, in the case of such a notice for the purposes of subsection (1) above as (but for this subsection) would expire at a time at or after the end of the said period of three months, an application is made before that time for a consent under this Chapter in respect of the discharge to which the notice relates, that notice shall be deemed not to expire until the result of the application becomes final—

    (a) on the grant or withdrawal of the application;

(b) on the expiration, without the bringing of an appeal with respect to the decision on the application, of any period prescribed as the period within which any such appeal must be brought; or

(c) on the withdrawal or determination of any such appeal.

NOTES

Sub-ss (1), (5): words in square brackets substituted by the Environment Act 1995, s 120, Sch 22, para 128.

87 Discharges into and from public sewers etc

[(1) This section applies for the purpose of determining liability where sewage effluent is discharged as mentioned in subsection (3) or (4) of section 85 above from any sewer or works ("the discharging sewer") vested in a sewerage undertaker ("the discharging undertaker").

(1A) If the discharging undertaker did not cause, or knowingly permit, the discharge it shall nevertheless be deemed to have caused the discharge if—

(a) matter included in the discharge was received by it into the discharging sewer or any other sewer or works vested in it;

(b) it was bound (either unconditionally or subject to conditions which were observed) to receive that matter into that sewer or works; and

(c) subsection (1B) below does not apply.

(1B) This subsection applies where the sewage effluent was, before being discharged from the discharging sewer, discharged through a main connection into that sewer or into any other sewer or works vested in the discharging undertaker by another sewerage undertaker ("the sending undertaker") under an agreement having effect between the discharging undertaker and the sending undertaker under section 110A of the Water Industry Act 1991.

(1C) Where subsection (1B) above applies, the sending undertaker shall be deemed to have caused the discharge if, although it did not cause, or knowingly permit, the sewage effluent to be discharged into the discharging sewer, or into any other sewer or works of the discharging undertaker—

(a) matter included in the discharge was received by it into a sewer or works vested in it; and

(b) it was bound (either unconditionally or subject to conditions which were observed) to receive that matter into that sewer or works.]

(2) A sewerage undertaker shall not be guilty of an offence under section 85 above by reason only of the fact that a discharge from a sewer or works vested in the undertaker contravenes conditions of a consent relating to the discharge if—

(a) the contravention is attributable to a discharge which another person caused or permitted to be made into the sewer or works;

(b) the undertaker either was not bound to receive the discharge into the sewer or works or was bound to receive it there subject to conditions which were not observed; and

(c) the undertaker could not reasonably have been expected to prevent the discharge into the sewer or works.

(3)   A person shall not be guilty of an offence under section 85 above in respect of a discharge which he caused or permitted to be made into a sewer or works vested in a sewerage undertaker if the undertaker was bound to receive the discharge there either unconditionally or subject to conditions which were observed.

[(4)   In this section "main connection" has the same meaning as in section 110A of the Water Industry Act 1991.]

NOTES

Sub-ss (1), (1A)–(1C): substituted for sub-s (1) as originally enacted, by the Competition and Service (Utilities) Act 1992, s 46(1).

Sub-s (4): inserted by the Competition and Service (Utilities) Act 1992, s 46(2).

88 Defence to principal offences in respect of authorised discharges

(1)   Subject to the following provisions of this section, a person shall not be guilty of an offence under section 85 above in respect of the entry of any matter into any waters or any discharge if the entry occurs or the discharge is made under and in accordance with, or as a result of any act or omission under and in accordance with—

  (a)   a consent given under this Chapter or under Part II of the Control of Pollution Act 1974 (which makes corresponding provision for Scotland);

  [(aa) a permit granted, under regulations under section 2 of the Pollution Prevention and Control Act 1999, by an authority exercising functions under the regulations that are exercisable for the purpose of preventing or reducing emissions in to the air, water and land;]

  (b)   *an authorisation for a prescribed process designated for central control granted under Part I of the Environmental Protection Act 1990;*

  (c)   a waste management or disposal licence;

  (d)   a licence granted under Part II of the Food and Environment Protection Act 1985;

  (e)   section 163 below or section 165 of the Water Industry Act 1991 (discharges for works purposes);

  (f)   any local statutory provision or statutory order which expressly confers power to discharge effluent into water; or

  (g)   any prescribed enactment.

(2)   Schedule 10 to this Act shall have effect, subject to section 91 below, with respect to the making of applications for consents under this Chapter for the purposes of subsection (1)(a) above and with respect to the giving, revocation and modification of such consents.

(3)   Nothing in any disposal licence shall be treated for the purposes of subsection (1) above as authorising—

  (a)   any entry or discharge as is mentioned in subsections (2) to (4) of section 85 above; or

  (b)   any act or omission so far as it results in any such entry or discharge.

(4)   In this section—

  "disposal licence" means a licence issued in pursuance of section 5 of the Control of Pollution Act 1974;

"statutory order" means—

    (a) any order under section 168 below or section 167 of the Water Industry Act 1991 (compulsory works orders); or

    (b) any order, byelaw, scheme or award made under any other enactment, including an order or scheme confirmed by Parliament or brought into operation in accordance with special parliamentary procedure;

and

"waste management licence" means such a licence granted under Part II of the Environmental Protection Act 1990.

NOTES

Sub-s (1): para (aa) inserted by SI 2000/1973, reg 39, Sch 10, Pt 1, para 9.

Date in force: 1 August 2000: see SI 2000/1973, reg 1(1).

Sub-s (1): para (b) repealed by the Pollution Prevention and Control Act 1999, s 6(2), Sch 3.

Date in force: to be appointed: see the Pollution Prevention and Control Act 1999, s 7(3).

89 Other defences to principal offences

(1) A person shall not be guilty of an offence under section 85 above in respect of the entry of any matter into any waters or any discharge if—

    (a) the entry is caused or permitted, or the discharge is made, in an emergency in order to avoid danger to life or health;

    (b) that person takes all such steps as are reasonably practicable in the circumstances for minimising the extent of the entry or discharge and of its polluting effects; and

    (c) particulars of the entry or discharge are furnished to the [Agency] as soon as reasonably practicable after the entry occurs.

(2) A person shall not be guilty of an offence under section 85 above by reason of his causing or permitting any discharge of trade or sewage effluent from a vessel.

(3) A person shall not be guilty of an offence under section 85 above by reason only of his permitting water from an abandoned mine [or an abandoned part of a mine] to enter controlled waters.

[(3A) Subsection (3) above shall not apply to the owner or former operator of any mine or part of a mine if the mine or part in question became abandoned after 31st December 1999.

(3B) In determining for the purposes of subsection (3A) above whether a mine or part of a mine became abandoned before, on or after 31st December 1999 in a case where the mine or part has become abandoned on two or more occasions, of which—

    (a) at least one falls on or before that date, and

    (b) at least one falls after that date,

the mine or part shall be regarded as becoming abandoned after that date (but without prejudice to the operation of subsection (3) above in relation to that mine or part at, or in relation to, any time before the first of those occasions which falls after that date).

(3C)   Where, immediately before a part of a mine becomes abandoned, that part is the only part of the mine not falling to be regarded as abandoned for the time being, the abandonment of that part shall not be regarded for the purposes of subsection (3A) or (3B) above as constituting the abandonment of the mine, but only of that part of it.]

(4)   A person shall not, otherwise than in respect of the entry of any poisonous, noxious or polluting matter into any controlled waters, be guilty of an offence under section 85 above by reason of his depositing the solid refuse of a mine or quarry on any land so that it falls or is carried into inland freshwaters if—

(a)   he deposits the refuse on the land with the consent of the [Agency];

(b)   no other site for the deposit is reasonably practicable; and

(c)   he takes all reasonably practicable steps to prevent the refuse from entering those inland freshwaters.

(5)   A highway authority or other person entitled to keep open a drain by virtue of section 100 of the Highways Act 1980 shall not be guilty of an offence under section 85 above by reason of his causing or permitting any discharge to be made from a drain kept open by virtue of that section unless the discharge is made in contravention of a prohibition imposed under section 86 above.

(6)   In this section "mine" and "quarry" have the same meanings as in the Mines and Quarries Act 1954.

NOTES

Sub-ss (1), (4): words in square brackets substituted by the Environment Act 1995, s 120, Sch 22, para 128.

Sub-s (3): words "or an abandoned part of a mine" in square brackets inserted by the Environment Act 1995, s 60(1).

Date in force: 1 July 1998: see SI 1998/604, art 3.

Sub-ss (3A)–(3C): inserted by the Environment Act 1995, s 60(2).

Date in force: 1 July 1998: see SI 1998/604, art 3.

PART IX
MISCELLANEOUS AND SUPPLEMENTAL

Other supplemental provisions

225 Short title, commencement and extent

(1)   This Act may be cited as the Water Resources Act 1991.

(2)   This Act shall come into force on 1st December 1991.

(3)   Subject to subsections (4) to (6) of section 2 and to section 224 above, to the extension of section 166(3) above to Scotland and to the extension, by virtue of any other enactment, of any provision of this Act to the territorial sea, this Act extends to England and Wales only.

(4)   Nothing in this Act, so far as it extends to Scotland, shall authorise the [Agency] to acquire any land in Scotland compulsorily.

NOTES

Sub-s (4): word in square brackets substituted by the Environment Act 1995, s 120, Sch 22, para 128.

Sexual Offences Act 1993

1993 CHAPTER 30

An Act to abolish the presumption of criminal law that a boy under the age of fourteen is incapable of sexual intercourse

[20th July 1993]

1 Abolition of presumption of sexual incapacity

The presumption of criminal law that a boy under the age of fourteen is incapable of sexual intercourse (whether natural or unnatural) is hereby abolished.

2 Short title, commencement and extent

(1) This Act may be cited as the Sexual Offences Act 1993.

(2) This Act shall come into force at the end of the period of two months beginning with the day on which it is passed.

(3) This Act does not apply to acts done before its commencement.

(4) This Act extends to England and Wales only.

Criminal Justice Act 1993

1993 CHAPTER 36

An Act to make provision about the jurisdiction of courts in England and Wales in relation to certain offences of dishonesty and blackmail; to amend the law about drug trafficking offences and to implement provisions of the Community Council Directive No 91/308/EEC; to amend Part VI of the Criminal Justice Act 1988; to make provision with respect to the financing of terrorism, the proceeds of terrorist-related activities and the investigation of terrorist activities; to amend Part I of the Criminal Justice Act 1991; to implement provisions of the Community Council Directive No 89/592/EEC and to amend and restate the law about insider dealing in securities; to provide for certain offences created by the Banking Coordination (Second Council Directive) Regulations 1992 to be punishable in the same way as offences under sections 39, 40 and 41 of the Banking Act 1987 and to enable regulations implementing Article 15 of the Community Council Directive No 89/646/EEC and Articles 3, 6 and 7 of the Community Council Directive No 92/30/EEC to create offences punishable in that way; to make provision with respect to the penalty for causing death by dangerous driving or causing death by careless driving while under the influence of drink or drugs; to make it an offence to assist in or induce certain conduct which for the purposes of, or in connection with, the provisions of Community law is unlawful in another member State; to provide for the introduction of safeguards in connection with the return of persons under backing of warrants arrangements; to amend the Criminal Procedure (Scotland) Act 1975 and Part I of the Prisoners and Criminal Proceedings (Scotland) Act 1993; and for connected purposes

[27 July 1993]

PART I
JURISDICTION

1 Offences to which this Part applies

(1)   This Part applies to two groups of offences—
   (a)   any offence mentioned in subsection (2) (a "Group A offence"); and
   (b)   any offence mentioned in subsection (3) (a "Group B offence").

(2)   The Group A offences are—
   (a)   an offence under any of the following provisions of the Theft Act 1968—
      section 1 (theft);
      section 15 (obtaining property by deception);
      [section 15A (obtaining a money transfer by deception);]
      section 16 (obtaining pecuniary advantage by deception);
      section 17 (false accounting);
      section 19 (false statements by company directors, etc);
      section 20(2) (procuring execution of valuable security by deception);

        section 21 (blackmail);
        section 22 (handling stolen goods);
        [section 24A (retaining credits from dishonest sources, etc);]

(b)   an offence under either of the following provisions of the Theft Act 1978—
        section 1 (obtaining services by deception);
        section 2 (avoiding liability by deception);

(c)   an offence under any of the following provisions of the Forgery and Counterfeiting Act 1981—
        section 1 (forgery);
        section 2 (copying a false instrument);
        section 3 (using a false instrument);
        section 4 (using a copy of a false instrument);
        section 5 (offences which relate to money orders, share certificates, passports, etc);
        [section 14 (offences of counterfeiting notes and coins);
        section 15 (offences of passing etc counterfeit notes and coins);
        section 16 (offences involving the custody or control of counterfeit notes and coins);
        section 17 (offences involving the making or custody or control of counterfeiting materials and implements);
        section 20 (prohibition of importation of counterfeit notes and coins);
        section 21 (prohibition of exportation of counterfeit notes and coins);]

(d)   the common law offence of cheating in relation to the public revenue.

(3)   The Group B offences are—

(a)   conspiracy to commit a Group A offence;
(b)   conspiracy to defraud;
(c)   attempting to commit a Group A offence;
(d)   incitement to commit a Group A offence.

(4)   The Secretary of State may by order amend subsection (2) or (3) by adding or removing any offence.

(5)   The power to make such an order shall be exercisable by statutory instrument.

(6)   No order shall be made under subsection (4) unless a draft of it has been laid before and approved by a resolution of each House of Parliament.

NOTES

Sub-s (2): in para (a) words "section 15A (obtaining a money transfer by deception);" and "section 24A (retaining credit cards from dishonest sources, etc);" in square brackets inserted by the Theft (Amendment) Act 1996, s 3(2), (3).

Sub-s (2): in para (c) words from "section 14 (offences of counterfeiting notes and coins);" to "section 21 (prohibition of exportation of counterfeit notes and coins);" inserted by SI 2000/1878, art 2.

Date in force: 1 August 2000: see SI 2000/1878, art 1.

2 Jurisdiction in respect of Group A offences

(1)   For the purposes of this Part, "relevant event", in relation to any Group A offence, means any act or omission or other event (including any result of one or more acts or omissions) proof of which is required for conviction of the offence.

(2)   For the purpose of determining whether or not a particular event is a relevant event in relation to a Group A offence, any question as to where it occurred is to be disregarded.

(3)   A person may be guilty of a Group A offence if any of the events which are relevant events in relation to the offence occurred in England and Wales.

3 Questions immaterial to jurisdiction in the case of certain offences

(1)   A person may be guilty of a Group A or Group B offence whether or not—
  (a)   he was a British citizen at any material time;
  (b)   he was in England and Wales at any such time.

(2)   On a charge of conspiracy to commit a Group A offence, or on a charge of conspiracy to defraud in England and Wales, the defendant may be guilty of the offence whether or not—
  (a)   he became a party to the conspiracy in England and Wales;
  (b)   any act or omission or other event in relation to the conspiracy occurred in England and Wales.

(3)   On a charge of attempting to commit a Group A offence, the defendant may be guilty of the offence whether or not—
  (a)   the attempt was made in England and Wales;
  (b)   it had an effect in England and Wales.

(4)   Subsection (1)(a) does not apply where jurisdiction is given to try the offence in question by an enactment which makes provision by reference to the nationality of the person charged.

(5)   Subsection (2) does not apply in relation to any charge under the Criminal Law Act 1977 brought by virtue of section 1A of that Act.

(6)   Subsection (3) does not apply in relation to any charge under the Criminal Attempts Act 1981 brought by virtue of section 1A of that Act.

4 Rules for determining certain jurisdictional questions relating to the location of events

In relation to a Group A or Group B offence—
  (a)   there is an obtaining of property in England and Wales if the property is either despatched from or received at a place in England and Wales; and
  (b)   there is a communication in England and Wales of any information, instruction, request, demand or other matter if it is sent by any means—

(i)   from a place in England and Wales to a place elsewhere; or

(ii) from a place elsewhere to a place in England and Wales.

5 Conspiracy, attempt and incitement

(1), (2)   . . .

(3)   A person may be guilty of conspiracy to defraud if—

(a)   a party to the agreement constituting the conspiracy, or a party's agent, did anything in England and Wales in relation to the agreement before its formation, or

(b)   a party to it became a party in England and Wales (by joining it either in person or through an agent), or

(c)   a party to it, or a party's agent, did or omitted anything in England and Wales in pursuance of it,

and the conspiracy would be triable in England and Wales but for the fraud which the parties to it had in view not being intended to take place in England and Wales.

(4)   A person may be guilty of incitement to commit a Group A offence if the incitement—

(a)   takes place in England and Wales; and

(b)   would be triable in England and Wales but for what the person charged had in view not being an offence triable in England and Wales.

(5)   Subsections (3) and (4) are subject to section 6.

NOTES

Sub-s (1): repealed by the Criminal Justice (Terrorism and Conspiracy) Act 1998, s 9(1), (2), Sch 1, para 7(1), Sch 2, Pt II.

Date in force: 4 September 1998: (no specific commencement provision).

Sub-s (2): inserts the Criminal Attempts Act 1981, s 1A.

6 Relevance of external law

(1)   A person is guilty of an offence triable . . . by virtue of section 5(3), only if the pursuit of the agreed course of conduct would at some stage involve—

(a)   an act or omission by one or more of the parties, or

(b)   the happening of some other event,

constituting an offence under the law in force where the act, omission or other event was intended to take place.

(2)   A person is guilty of an offence triable by virtue of section 1A of the Criminal Attempts Act 1981, or by virtue of section 5(4), only if what he had in view would involve the commission of an offence under the law in force where the whole or any part of it was intended to take place.

(3)   Conduct punishable under the law in force in any place is an offence under that law for the purposes of this section, however it is described in that law.

(4)   Subject to subsection (6), a condition specified in subsection (1) or (2) shall be taken to be satisfied unless, not later than rules of court may provide, the defence serve on the prosecution a notice—

   (a)   stating that, on the facts as alleged with respect to the relevant conduct, the condition is not in their opinion satisfied;
   (b)   showing their grounds for that opinion; and
   (c)   requiring the prosecution to show that it is satisfied.

(5)   In subsection (4) "the relevant conduct" means—

   (a)   where the condition in subsection (1) is in question, the agreed course of conduct; and
   (b)   where the condition in subsection (2) is in question, what the defendant had in view.

(6)   The court, if it thinks fit, may permit the defence to require the prosecution to show that the condition is satisfied without the prior service of a notice under subsection (4).

(7)   In the Crown Court, the question whether the condition is satisfied shall be decided by the judge alone.

(8)   . . .

NOTES

Sub-s (1): words omitted repealed by the Criminal Justice (Terrorism and Conspiracy) Act 1998, s 9(1), (2), Sch 1, para 7(2), Sch 2, Pt II.

Date in force: 4 September 1998: (no specific commencement provision).

Sub-s (8): amends the Criminal Justice Act 1987, s 9(3).

PART VII
SUPPLEMENTARY

78 Commencement etc

(1)   Sections 70 and 71 shall come into force at the end of the period of two months beginning with the day on which this Act is passed.

(2)   Sections 68, 69, 75, 76 and 79(1) to (12), paragraph 2 of Schedule 5 and, in so far as relating to the Criminal Procedure (Scotland) Act 1975 and the Prisoners and Criminal Proceedings (Scotland) Act 1993, Schedule 6, shall come into force on the passing of this Act.

(3)   The other provisions of this Act shall come into force on such day as may be appointed by the Secretary of State by an order made by statutory instrument.

(4)   Different days may be appointed under subsection (3) for different provisions and different purposes.

(5)   Nothing in any provision in Part I applies to any act, omission or other event occurring before the coming into force of that provision.

(6)   Where a person is charged with a relevant offence which was committed before the coming into force of a provision of Part II, Part III, or (as the case may

be) Part IV, that provision shall not affect the question whether or not that person is guilty of the offence [and, where it confers a power on the court, shall not apply in proceedings instituted before the coming into force of that provision].

(7), (8)   . . .

(9)   In subsection (6) "relevant offence" means an offence in relation to which provision is made by Part II, Part III or Part IV, other than an offence created by that Part.

(10)   An order under subsection (3) may contain such transitional provisions and savings as the Secretary of State considers appropriate.

(11)   . . .

(12)   . . .

NOTES

Sub-s (6): words in square brackets substituted, with retrospective effect, by the Criminal Justice and Public Order Act 1994, s 168(1), Sch 9, para 53.

Sub-s (7): repealed by the Drug Trafficking Act 1994, s 67, Sch 3.

Sub-ss (8), (12): repealed by the Northern Ireland (Emergency Provisions) Act 1996, s 63(7), Sch 7, Part I.

Sub-s (11): repealed by the Terrorism Act 2000, s 125(2), Sch 16, Pt I.

Date in force: 19 February 2001: see SI 2001/421, art 2.

79 Short title, extent etc

(1)   This Act may be cited as the Criminal Justice Act 1993.

(2)   The following provisions of this Act extend to the United Kingdom—
Part V;
sections 21(1) and (3)(h), 23, . . . 45 to 51, 70 to 72, 77, 78 and this section;
Schedules 1 and 2; and
paragraphs 4 . . . and 6 of Schedule 4.

(3)   The following provisions of this Act extend only to Great Britain—
sections . . . 21(3)(e), . . . 29 to 32, 34(1), 35, 67(1) and 73; and
paragraph 3 of Schedule 4.

(4)   The following provisions of this Act extend only to Scotland—
sections 17, 19, 20(2), 21(3)(c) and (d), 22(2), 24(12) to (15), 26(2), 33, 68, 69, 75 and 76; and
paragraph 2 of Schedule 4.

(5)   Sections 21(3)(f) and 34(2) [and paragraph 5 of Schedule 4] extend to Scotland and Northern Ireland only.

(6)   . . .

(7)   Section 72 also extends to the Channel Islands and the Isle of Man.

(8)   The provisions of Schedules 5 and 6 have the same extent as the provisions on which they operate.

(9)   Otherwise, this Act extends to England and Wales only.

(10)   Her Majesty may by Order in Council direct that such provisions of this Act as may be specified in the Order shall extend, with such exceptions and modifications as appear to Her Majesty to be appropriate, to any colony.

(11)   . . .

(12)   An Order in Council under paragraph 1(1)(b) of Schedule 1 to the Northern Ireland Act 1974 (legislation for Northern Ireland in the interim period) which contains a statement that it is made only for purposes corresponding to purposes of any of sections 16, 18 and 29 to 32—
   (a)   shall not be subject to paragraph 1(4) and (5) of that Schedule (affirmative resolution of both Houses of Parliament); but
   (b)   shall be subject to annulment in pursuance of a resolution of either House of Parliament.

(13)   Schedule 5 (consequential amendments) shall have effect.

(14)   The repeals and revocations set out in Schedule 6 (which include the repeal of two enactments which are spent) shall have effect.

NOTES

Sub-ss (2), (3): words omitted repealed by the Drug Trafficking Act 1994, ss 65, 67, Sch 1, para 30(2), (3), Sch 3.

Sub-s (5): words in square brackets inserted by the Drug Trafficking Act 1994, s 65, Sch 1, para 30(4).

Sub-s (6): repealed by the Northern Ireland (Emergency Provisions) Act 1996, s 63(7), Sch 7, Part I.

Sub-s (11): repealed by the Northern Ireland Act 1998, s 100(2), Sch 15.

Date in force: 2 December 1999: see SI 1999/3209, art 2, Schedule.

Criminal Justice and Public Order Act 1994

1994 CHAPTER 33

An Act to make further provision n relation to criminal justice (including employment in the prison service); to amend or extend the criminal law and powers for preventing crime and enforcing that law; to amend the Video Recordings Act 1984; and for purposes connected with those purposes

[3 November 1994]

PART III
COURSE OF JUSTICE: EVIDENCE, PROCEDURE, ETC

Intimidation, etc, of witnesses, jurors and others

51 Intimidation, etc, of witnesses, jurors and others

[(1) A person commits an offence if—
  (a) he does an act which intimidates, and is intended to intimidate, another person ("the victim"),
  (b) he does the act knowing or believing that the victim is assisting in the investigation of an offence or is a witness or potential witness or a juror or potential juror in proceedings for an offence, and
  (c) he does it intending thereby to cause the investigation or the course of justice to be obstructed, perverted or interfered with.

(2) A person commits an offence if—
  (a) he does an act which harms, and is intended to harm, another person or, intending to cause another person to fear harm, he threatens to do an act which would harm that other person,
  (b) he does or threatens to do the act knowing or believing that the person harmed or threatened to be harmed ("the victim"), or some other person, has assisted in an investigation into an offence or has given evidence or particular evidence in proceedings for an offence, or has acted as a juror or concurred in a particular verdict in proceedings for an offence, and
  (c) he does or threatens to do it because of that knowledge or belief.

(3) For the purposes of subsections (1) and (2) it is immaterial that the act is or would be done, or that the threat is made—
  (a) otherwise than in the presence of the victim, or
  (b) to a person other than the victim.]

(4) The harm that may be done or threatened may be financial as well as physical (whether to the person or a person's property) and similarly as respects an intimidatory act which consists of threats.

(5) The intention required by subsection (1)(c) and the motive required by subsection (2)(c) above need not be the only or the predominating intention or motive with which the act is done or, in the case of subsection (2), threatened.

(6) A person guilty of an offence under this section shall be liable—
    (a) on conviction on indictment, to imprisonment for a term not exceeding five years or a fine or both;
    (b) on summary conviction, to imprisonment for a term not exceeding six months or a fine not exceeding the statutory maximum or both.

(7) If, in proceedings against a person for an offence under subsection (1) above, it is proved that he did an act falling within paragraph (a) with the knowledge or belief required by paragraph (b), he shall be presumed, unless the contrary is proved, to have done the act with the intention required by paragraph (c) of that subsection.

(8) If, in proceedings against a person for an offence under subsection (2) above, it is proved that [within the relevant period—
    (a) he did an act which harmed, and was intended to harm, another person, or
    (b) intending to cause another person fear of harm, he threatened to do an act which would harm that other person,

and that he did the act, or (as the case may be) threatened to do the act,] with the knowledge or belief required by paragraph (b), he shall be presumed, unless the contrary is proved, to have done the act [or (as the case may be) threatened to do the act] with the motive required by paragraph (c) of that subsection.

(9) In this section—
    "investigation into an offence" means such an investigation by the police or other person charged with the duty of investigating offences or charging offenders;
    "offence" includes an alleged or suspected offence;
    "potential", in relation to a juror, means a person who has been summoned for jury service at the court at which proceedings for the offence are pending; and
    "the relevant period"—

    (a) in relation to a witness or juror in any proceedings for an offence, means the period beginning with the institution of the proceedings and ending with the first anniversary of the conclusion of the trial or, if there is an appeal or [a reference under section 9 or 11 of the Criminal Appeal Act 1995], of the conclusion of the appeal;

    (b) in relation to a person who has, or is believed by the accused to have, assisted in an investigation into an offence, but was not also a witness in proceedings for an offence, means the period of one year beginning with any act of his, or any act believed by the accused to be an act of his, assisting in the investigation; and

    (c) in relation to a person who both has, or is believed by the accused to have, assisted in the investigation into an offence and was a witness in proceedings for the offence, means the period beginning with any act of his, or any act believed by the accused to be an act of his, assisting in the investigation and ending with the anniversary mentioned in paragraph (a) above.

(10) For the purposes of the definition of the relevant period in subsection (9) above—

    (a) proceedings for an offence are instituted at the earliest of the following times—

        (i) when a justice of the peace issues a summons or warrant under section 1 of the Magistrates' Courts Act 1980 in respect of the offence;

        (ii) when a person is charged with the offence after being taken into custody without a warrant;

        (iii) when a bill of indictment is preferred by virtue of section 2(2)(b) of the Administration of Justice (Miscellaneous Provisions) Act 1933;

    (b) proceedings at a trial of an offence are concluded with the occurrence of any of the following, the discontinuance of the prosecution, the discharge of the jury without a finding, the acquittal of the accused or the sentencing of or other dealing with the accused for the offence of which he was convicted; and

    (c) proceedings on an appeal are concluded on the determination of the appeal or the abandonment of the appeal.

(11) This section is in addition to, and not in derogation of, any offence subsisting at common law.

NOTES

Sub-ss (1)–(3): substituted by the Youth Justice and Criminal Evidence Act 1999, s 67(1), Sch 4, paras 21, 22(1), (2).

Date in force: 14 April 2000: see SI 2000/1034, art 2(b).

Sub-s (8): words from "within the relevant" to "do the act," in square brackets substituted by the Youth Justice and Criminal Evidence Act 1999, s 67(1), Sch 4, paras 21, 22(1), (3)(a).

Date in force: 14 April 2000: see SI 2000/1034, art 2(b).

Sub-s (8): words "or (as the case may be) threatened to do the act" in square brackets inserted by the Youth Justice and Criminal Evidence Act 1999, s 67(1), Sch 4, paras 21, 22(1), (3)(b).

Date in force: 14 April 2000: see SI 2000/1034, art 2(b).

Sub-s (9): in definition "the relevant period" words in square brackets substituted by the Criminal Appeal Act 1995, s 29, Sch 2, para 19.

PART XII
MISCELLANEOUS AND GENERAL

General

172 Short title, commencement and extent

(1) This Act may be cited as the Criminal Justice and Public Order Act 1994.

(2) With the exception of section 82 and subject to subsection (4) below, this Act shall come into force on such day as the Secretary of State or, in the case of sections 52 and 53, the Lord Chancellor may appoint by order made by statutory instrument, and different days may be appointed for different provisions or different purposes.

(3) Any order under subsection (2) above may make such transitional provisions and savings as appear to the authority making the order necessary or expedient in connection with any provision brought into force by the order.

(4) The following provisions and their related amendments, repeals and revocations shall come into force on the passing of this Act, namely sections 5 to 15 (and Schedules 1 and 2), 61, 63, 65, 68 to 71, 77 to 80, 81, 83, 90, Chapters I and IV of Part VIII, sections 142 to 148, 150, 158(1), (3) and (4), 166, 167, 171, paragraph 46 of Schedule 9 and this section.

(5) No order shall be made under subsection (6) of section 166 above unless a draft of the order has been laid before, and approved by a resolution of, each House of Parliament.

(6) For the purposes of subsection (4) above—
   (a) the following are the amendments related to the provisions specified in that subsection, namely, in Schedule 10, paragraphs 26, 35, 36, 59, 60 and 63(1), (3), (4) and (5);
   (b) the repeals and revocations related to the provisions specified in that subsection are those specified in the Note at the end of Schedule 11.

(7) Except as regards any provisions applied under section 39 and subject to the following provisions, this Act extends to England and Wales only.

(8) Sections 47(3), 49, [60 to 67], 70, 71, 81, 82, 146(4), 157(1), 163, 169 and 170 also extend to Scotland.

(9) Section 83(1) extends to England and Wales and Northern Ireland.

(10) This section, sections 68, 69, 83(3) to (5), 88 to 92, 136 to 141, 156, 157(2), (3), (4), (5) and (9), 158, 159, 161, 162, 164, 165, 168, 171 and Chapter IV of Part VIII extend to the United Kingdom and sections 158 and 159 also extend to the Channel Islands and the Isle of Man.

(11) Sections 93, 95 and 101(8), so far as relating to the delivery of prisoners to or from premises situated in a part of the British Islands outside England and Wales, extend to that part of those Islands.

(12) Sections 102(1) to (3), 104, 105 and 117, so far as relating to the transfer of prisoners to or from premises situated in a part of the British Islands outside Scotland, extend to that part of those Islands, but otherwise Chapter II of Part VIII extends to Scotland only.

(13) Sections 47(4), 83(2), 84(5) to (7), 87, Part IX, sections 145(2), 146(2), 148, 151(2), 152(2), 153, 157(7) and 160(2) extend to Scotland only.

(14) Sections 118, 120, 121 and 125, so far as relating to the delivery of prisoners to or from premises situated in a part of the British Islands outside Northern Ireland, extend to that part of those islands, but otherwise Chapter III of Part VIII extends to Northern Ireland only.

(15) Sections 53, 84(8) to (11), 85(4) to (6), 86(2), 145(3), 147 and 157(8) extend to Northern Ireland only.

(16) Where any enactment is amended, repealed or revoked by Schedule 9, 10 or 11 to this Act the amendment, repeal or revocation has the same extent as that enactment; except that Schedules 9 and 11 do not extend to Scotland in so far as they relate to section 17(1) of the Video Recordings Act 1984.

NOTES

Sub-s (8): words "60 to 67" in square brackets substituted by the Knives Act 1997, s 8(1), (11).

Date in force: 1 March 1999: see SI 1999/5, art 2.

Drug Trafficking Act 1994

1994 CHAPTER 37

An Act to consolidate the Drug Trafficking Offences Act 1986 and certain other provisions of the Criminal Justice (International Co-operation) Act 1990 relating to drug trafficking

[3 November 1994]

PART III
OFFENCES IN CONNECTION WITH PROCEEDS OF DRUG TRAFFICKING

50 Assisting another person to retain the benefit of drug trafficking

(1) Subject to subsection (3) below, a person is guilty of an offence if he enters into or is otherwise concerned in an arrangement whereby—

  (a) the retention or control by or on behalf of another person (call him "A") of A's proceeds of drug trafficking is facilitated (whether by concealment, removal from the jurisdiction, transfer to nominees or otherwise), or

  (b) A's proceeds of drug trafficking—

(i)   are used to secure that funds are placed at A's disposal, or

(ii) are used for A's benefit to acquire property by way of investment,

and he knows or suspects that A is a person who carries on or has carried on drug trafficking or has benefited from drug trafficking.

(2)   In this section, references to any person's proceeds of drug trafficking include a reference to any property which in whole or in part directly or indirectly represented in his hands his proceeds of drug trafficking.

(3)   Where a person discloses to a constable a suspicion or belief that any funds or investments are derived from or used in connection with drug trafficking, or discloses to a constable any matter on which such a suspicion or belief is based—

(a) the disclosure shall not be treated as a breach of any restriction upon the disclosure of information imposed by statute or otherwise; and

(b) if he does any act in contravention of subsection (1) above and the disclosure relates to the arrangement concerned, he does not commit an offence under this section if—

    (i)   the disclosure is made before he does the act concerned and the act is done with the consent of the constable; or

    (ii) the disclosure is made after he does the act, but is made on his initiative and as soon as it is reasonable for him to make it.

(4)   In proceedings against a person for an offence under this section, it is a defence to prove—

(a) that he did not know or suspect that the arrangement related to any person's proceeds of drug trafficking;

(b) that he did not know or suspect that by the arrangement the retention or control by or on behalf of A of any property was facilitated or, as the case may be, that by the arrangement any property was used as mentioned in subsection (1)(b) above; or

(c) that—

    (i)   he intended to disclose to a constable such a suspicion, belief or matter as is mentioned in subsection (3) above in relation to the arrangement, but

    (ii) there is reasonable excuse for his failure to make any such disclosure in the manner mentioned in paragraph (b)(i) or (ii) of that subsection.

(5)   In the case of a person who was in employment at the time in question, subsections (3) and (4) above shall have effect in relation to disclosures, and intended disclosures, to the appropriate person in accordance with the procedure established by his employer for the making of such disclosures as they have effect in relation to disclosures, and intended disclosures, to a constable.

PART IV
MISCELLANEOUS AND SUPPLEMENTAL

Supplemental

68 Extent

(1) Subject to the following provisions of this section, this Act extends to England and Wales only.

(2) The following provisions of this Act also extend to Scotland—
  (a) section 11(11);
  (b) sections 32 to 35 and 36(1);
  (c) Part II;
  (d) section 59(10) to (13);
  (e) this section;
  (f) section 69;
  (g) sections 1, 41, 62, 63, 64, 65(1), 66 and 67(1), so far as they relate to provisions which extend to Scotland; and
  (h) Schedule 2.

(3) The following provisions of this Act also extend to Northern Ireland—
  (a) Part II;
  (b) this section;
  (c) section 69;
  (d) sections 63, 64, 65(1), 66 and 67(1), so far as they relate to provisions which extend to Northern Ireland; and
  (e) Schedule 2.

(4) Section 67(2) of this Act extends to Northern Ireland only.

(5) The modifications of other enactments specified in section 65(2) to (4) of this Act, and the amendments specified in Schedule 1 to this Act, have the same extent as the enactments to which they relate.

(6) Subject to subsection (7) below, the repeals contained in Schedule 3 to this Act have the same extent as the provisions to which they relate.

(7) The repeals of—
  (a) sections 14 and 23A of the Criminal Justice (International Co-operation) Act 1990, and
  (b) paragraph 5 of Schedule 4 to the Criminal Justice Act 1993,

extend to England and Wales only.

69 Short title and commencement

(1) This Act may be cited as the Drug Trafficking Act 1994.

(2) This Act comes into force at the end of the period of three months beginning with the day on which it is passed.

Police Act 1996

1996 CHAPTER 16

An Act to consolidate the Police Act 1964, Part IX of the Police and Criminal Evidence Act 1984, Chapter I of Part I of the Police and Magistrates' Courts Act 1994 and certain other enactments relating to the police

[22 May 1996]

PART V
MISCELLANEOUS AND GENERAL

Offences

89 Assaults on constables

(1)   Any person who assaults a constable in the execution of his duty, or a person assisting a constable in the execution of his duty, shall be guilty of an offence and liable on summary conviction to imprisonment for a term not exceeding six months or to a fine not exceeding level 5 on the standard scale, or to both.

(2)   Any person who resists or wilfully obstructs a constable in the execution of his duty, or a person assisting a constable in the execution of his duty, shall be guilty of an offence and liable on summary conviction to imprisonment for a term not exceeding one month or to a fine not exceeding level 3 on the standard scale, or to both.

(3)   This section also applies to a constable who is a member of a police force maintained in Scotland or Northern Ireland when he is executing a warrant, or otherwise acting in England or Wales, by virtue of any enactment conferring powers on him in England and Wales.

Supplemental

105 Extent

(1)   Except as provided by subsections (2) to (5), this Act extends to England and Wales only.

(2)   The following provisions of this Act extend to Scotland (and in the case of section 99(1) to Scotland only)—

section 21;
[section 25(1A);]
Part III;
paragraph 8 of Schedule 5 (and section 66 so far as it relates to that paragraph);
sections 98, 99(1), 101(2), 102 and 104 to 106 and paragraphs 1 to 5, 7 and 11(1), (2) and (4) of Schedule 8 (and section 103 so far as it relates to those paragraphs).

(3)   The following provisions of this Act extend to Northern Ireland (and in the case of section 99(2) to Northern Ireland only)—

sections 61 and 62;

sections 98, 99(2), 102 and 104 to 106 and paragraphs 1 to 4 of Schedule 8 (and section 103 so far as it relates to those paragraphs).

(4)   Subject to subsection (5), the amendments in Schedule 7 and the repeals and revocations in Schedule 9 have the same extent as the enactments to which they refer and section 103 extends accordingly.

(5)   Paragraphs 2 to 6 of Schedule 7 extend to England, Wales and Scotland only.

NOTES

Sub-s (2): entry relating to "section 25(1A);" inserted by the Anti-terrorism, Crime and Security Act 2001, s 101, Sch 7, paras 20, 28.

Date in force: 14 December 2001: see the Anti-terrorism, Crime and Security Act 2001, s 127(2)(f).

106 Short title

This Act may be cited as the Police Act 1996.

Law Reform (Year and a Day Rule) Act 1996

1996 CHAPTER 19

An Act to abolish the "year and a day rule" and, in consequence of its abolition, to impose a restriction on the institution in certain circumstances of proceedings for a fatal offence.

[17th June 1996]

1 Abolition of "year and a day rule"

The rule known as the "year and a day rule" (that is, the rule that, for the purposes of offences involving death and of suicide, an act or omission is conclusively presumed not to have caused a person's death if more than a year and a day elapsed before he died) is abolished for all purposes.

2 Restriction on institution of proceedings for a fatal offence

(1)   Proceedings to which this section applies may only be instituted by or with the consent of the Attorney General.

(2)   This section applies to proceedings against a person for a fatal offence if—
  (a)   the injury alleged to have caused the death was sustained more than three years before the death occurred, or

(b) the person has previously been convicted of an offence committed in circumstances alleged to be connected with the death.

(3) In subsection (2) "fatal offence" means—

(a) murder, manslaughter, infanticide or any other offence of which one of the elements is causing a person's death, or

(b) the offence of aiding, abetting, counselling or procuring a person's suicide.

(4) No provision that proceedings may be instituted only by or with the consent of the Director of Public Prosecutions shall apply to proceedings to which this section applies.

(5) In the application of this section to Northern Ireland—

(a) the reference in subsection (1) to the Attorney General is to the Attorney General for Northern Ireland, and

(b) the reference in subsection (4) to the Director of Public Prosecutions is to the Director of Public Prosecutions for Northern Ireland.

3 Short title, commencement and extent

(1) This Act may be cited as the Law Reform (Year and a Day Rule) Act 1996.

(2) Section 1 does not affect the continued application of the rule referred to in that section to a case where the act or omission (or the last of the acts or omissions) which caused the death occurred before the day on which this Act is passed.

(3) Section 2 does not come into force until the end of the period of two months beginning with the day on which this Act is passed; but that section applies to the institution of proceedings after the end of that period in any case where the death occurred during that period (as well as in any case where the death occurred after the end of that period).

(4) This Act extends to England and Wales and Northern Ireland.

Education Act 1996

1996 CHAPTER 56

An Act to consolidate the Education Act 1944 and certain other enactments relating to education, with amendments to give effect to recommendations of the Law Commission [24 July 1996]

Part X
Miscellaneous and General

Chapter II
[Punishment and Restraint of Pupils]

NOTES

Words "Punishment and Restraint of Pupils" in square brackets substituted by the Education Act 1997, s 57(1), Sch 7, para 38.

Date in force: 1 September 1998: see SI 1998/386, art 2(4), Sch 1, Pt IV.

[Power to restrain pupils]

NOTES

Inserted by the Education Act 1997, s 4.
Date in force: 1 September 1998: see SI 1998/386, art 2(4), Sch 1, Pt IV.

[550A Power of members of staff to restrain pupils]

[(1) A member of the staff of a school may use, in relation to any pupil at the school, such force as is reasonable in the circumstances for the purpose of preventing the pupil from doing (or continuing to do) any of the following, namely—

(a) committing any offence,
(b) causing personal injury to, or damage to the property of, any person (including the pupil himself), or
(c) engaging in any behaviour prejudicial to the maintenance of good order and discipline at the school or among any of its pupils, whether that behaviour occurs during a teaching session or otherwise.

(2) Subsection (1) applies where a member of the staff of a school is—

(a) on the premises of the school, or
(b) elsewhere at a time when, as a member of its staff, he has lawful control or charge of the pupil concerned;

but it does not authorise anything to be done in relation to a pupil which constitutes the giving of corporal punishment within the meaning of section 548.

(3) Subsection (1) shall not be taken to prevent any person from relying on any defence available to him otherwise than by virtue of this section.

(4) In this section—

"member of the staff", in relation to a school, means any teacher who works at the school and any other person who, with the authority of the head teacher, has lawful control or charge of pupils at the school;

"offence" includes anything that would be an offence but for the operation of any presumption that a person under a particular age is incapable of committing an offence.]

NOTES

Inserted by the Education Act 1997, s 4.
Date in force: 1 September 1998: see SI 1998/386, art 2(4), Sch 1, Pt IV.

[Detention]

NOTES

Inserted by the Education Act 1997, s 5.
Date in force: 1 September 1998: see SI 1998/386, art 2(4), Sch 1, Pt IV.

[550B Detention outside school hours lawful despite absence of parental consent]

[(1)   Where a pupil to whom this section applies is required on disciplinary grounds to spend a period of time in detention at his school after the end of any school session, his detention shall not be rendered unlawful by virtue of the absence of his parent's consent to it if the conditions set out in subsection (3) are satisfied.

(2)   This section applies to any pupil who has not attained the age of 18 and is attending—
  (a)   a school maintained by a local education authority;
  (b)   . . .or
  (c)   a city technology college[, city college for the technology of the arts or city academy].

(3)   The conditions referred to in subsection (1) are as follows—
  (a)   the head teacher of the school must have previously determined, and have—
    (i)   made generally known within the school, and
    (ii)   taken steps to bring to the attention of the parent of every person who is for the time being a registered pupil there,
    that the detention of pupils after the end of a school session is one of the measures that may be taken with a view to regulating the conduct of pupils;
  (b)   the detention must be imposed by the head teacher or by another teacher at the school specifically or generally authorised by him for the purpose;
  (c)   the detention must be reasonable in all the circumstances; and
  (d)   the pupil's parent must have been given at least 24 hours' notice in writing that the detention was due to take place.

(4)   In determining for the purposes of subsection (3)(c) whether a pupil's detention is reasonable, the following matters in particular shall be taken into account—
  (a)   whether the detention constitutes a proportionate punishment in the circumstances of the case; and
  (b)   any special circumstances relevant to its imposition on the pupil which are known to the person imposing it (or of which he ought reasonably to be aware) including in particular—
    (i)   the pupil's age,
    (ii)   any special educational needs he may have,
    (iii)   any religious requirements affecting him, and
    (iv)   where arrangements have to be made for him to travel from the school to his home, whether suitable alternative arrangements can reasonably be made by his parent.

(5)   Section 572, which provides for the methods by which notices may be served under this Act, does not preclude a notice from being given to a pupil's parent under this section by any other effective method.]

Inserted by the Education Act 1997, s 5.

Date in force: 1 September 1998: see SI 1998/386, art 2(4), Sch 1, Pt IV.

Sub-s (2): para (b) repealed by the School Standards and Framework Act 1998, s 140(1), (3), Sch 30, para 165, Sch 31.

Date in force: 1 September 1999: see SI 1999/2323, art 2(1), Sch 1.

Sub-s (2): in para (c) words ", city college for the technology of the arts or city academy" in square brackets substituted by the Learning and Skills Act 2000, s 149, Sch 9, paras 1, 62.

Date in force: 28 July 2000: see the Learning and Skills Act 2000, s 154(5)(d).

Final provisions

583 Short title, commencement and extent

(1)   This Act may be cited as the Education Act 1996.

(2)   Subject to subsection (3), this Act shall come into force on 1st November 1996 (and references to the commencement of this Act are to its coming into force on that date).

(3)   The following provisions—
   section 8,
   section 317(6),
   section 348,
   section 528,
   Part II of Schedule 37 and section 582(1) so far as relating thereto, and
   Part II of Schedule 38 and section 582(2) so far as relating thereto,

shall come into force on such day as the Secretary of State may by order appoint; and different days may be appointed for different provisions and for different purposes.

(4)   The Secretary of State may by order make such incidental, supplemental, saving or transitional provision as he thinks fit in connection with the coming into force in accordance with subsection (2) of any provision of this Act reproducing the effect of a provision of the Education Act 1993 which has not previously been brought into force by an order under section 308(3) of that Act (commencement).

(5)   Where an order under subsection (3) brings into force any provision of section 317(6) or 528, then in relation to the coming into force of that provision—
   (a)   section 568(5) and (6) shall not apply to the order, but
   (b)   the order may make such provision as is authorised to be made, by virtue of section 67(2) and (3) of the Disability Discrimination Act 1995 (regulations and orders), by an order under section 70(3) of that Act (commencement).

(6)   Subject to subsections (7) and (8), this Act extends to England and Wales only.

(7)   This section, section 493 and section 569 so far as relating to regulations under section 493 extend also to Scotland; and this section extends also to Northern Ireland.

(8)   Section 582 and Schedules 37 to 40 have the same extent as the enactments to which they relate.

Theft (Amendment) Act 1996

1996 CHAPTER 62

An Act to amend the Theft Act 1968 and the Theft Act 1978; and for connected purposes

[18th December 1996]

1 Obtaining a money transfer by deception

(1)   . . .

(2)   Nothing in this section has effect in relation to anything done before the day on which this Act is passed.

NOTES

Sub-s (1): adds the Theft Act 1968, ss 15A, 15B.

3 The new offences: jurisdiction

(1)   In section 1(2) of the Criminal Justice Act 1993 (Group A offences for the purposes of the jurisdictional provisions) paragraph (a) (list of offences under the Theft Act 1968) shall be amended as follows.

(2), (3)   . . .

NOTES

Sub-ss (2), (3): amend the Criminal Justice Act 1993, s 1(2).

4 Application to loans of offence of obtaining services by deception

(1)   . . .

(2)   Nothing in this section has effect in relation to anything done before the day on which this Act is passed.

NOTES

Sub-s (1): adds the Theft Act 1978, s 1(3).

5 Short title and extent

(1)   This Act may be cited as the Theft (Amendment) Act 1996.

(2)   Subject to subsection (3), this Act extends to England and Wales only.

(3) An Order in Council under paragraph 1(1)(b) of Schedule 1 to the Northern Ireland Act 1974 (legislation for Northern Ireland in the interim period) which contains a statement that it is made only for purposes corresponding to the purposes of this Act—

(a) shall not be subject to paragraph 1(4) and (5) of that Schedule (affirmative resolution of both Houses of Parliament); but

(b) shall be subject to annulment by resolution of either House.

Firearms (Amendment) Act 1997

1997 CHAPTER 5

An Act to amend the Firearms Acts 1968 to 1992; to make provision in relation to the licensing and regulation of pistol clubs; to make further provision for regulating the possession of, and transactions relating to, firearms and ammunition; and for connected purposes

[27th February 1997]

PART I
PROHIBITION OF WEAPONS AND AMMUNITION AND CONTROL OF SMALL-CALIBRE PISTOLS

Special exemptions from prohibition of small firearms

2 Slaughtering instruments

The authority of the Secretary of State [or the Scottish Ministers (by virtue of provision made under section 63 of the Scotland Act 1998)] is not required by virtue of subsection (1)(aba) of section 5 of the 1968 Act—

(a) for a person to have in his possession, or to purchase or acquire, or to sell or transfer, a slaughtering instrument if he is authorised by a firearm certificate to have the instrument in his possession, or to purchase or acquire it;

(b) for a person to have a slaughtering instrument in his possession if he is entitled, under section 10 of the 1968 Act, to have it in his possession without a firearm certificate.

NOTES

Words "or the Scottish Ministers (by virtue of provision made under section 63 of the Scotland Act 1998)" in square brackets inserted by SI 1999/1750, art 6(1), Sch 5, para 18(1), (2).

Date in force: 1 July 1999: see SI 1999/1750, art 1(1), and SI 1998/3178, art 3.

3 Firearms used for humane killing of animals

The authority of the Secretary of State [or the Scottish Ministers (by virtue of provision made under section 63 of the Scotland Act 1998)] is not required by virtue of subsection (1)(aba) of section 5 of the 1968 Act for a person to have in his possession, or to purchase or acquire, or to sell or transfer, a firearm if he is authorised by a firearm certificate to have the firearm in his possession, or to purchase or acquire it, subject to a condition that it is only for use in connection with the humane killing of animals.

NOTES

Words "or the Scottish Ministers (by virtue of provision made under section 63 of the Scotland Act 1998)" in square brackets inserted by SI 1999/1750, art 6(1), Sch 5, para 18(1), (3).

Date in force: 1 July 1999: see SI 1999/1750, art 1(1), and SI 1998/3178, art 3.

4 Shot pistols used for shooting vermin

(1)   The authority of the Secretary of State [or the Scottish Ministers (by virtue of provision made under section 63 of the Scotland Act 1998)] is not required by virtue of subsection (1)(aba) of section 5 of the 1968 Act for a person to have in his possession, or to purchase or acquire, or to sell or transfer, a shot pistol if he is authorised by a firearm certificate to have the shot pistol in his possession, or to purchase or acquire it, subject to a condition that it is only for use in connection with the shooting of vermin.

(2)   For the purposes of this section, "shot pistol" means a smoothbored gun which is chambered for .410 cartridges or 9mm rim-fire cartridges.

NOTES

Sub-s (1): words "or the Scottish Ministers (by virtue of provision made under section 63 of the Scotland Act 1998)" in square brackets inserted by SI 1999/1750, art 6(1), Sch 5, para 18(1), (4).

Date in force: 1 July 1999: see SI 1999/1750, art 1(1), and SI 1998/3178, art 3.

5 Races at athletic meetings

The authority of the Secretary of State [or the Scottish Ministers (by virtue of provision made under section 63 of the Scotland Act 1998)] is not required by virtue of subsection (1)(aba) of section 5 of the 1968 Act—

(a)   for a person to have a firearm in his possession at an athletic meeting for the purpose of starting races at that meeting; or

(b)   for a person to have in his possession, or to purchase or acquire, or to sell or transfer, a firearm if he is authorised by a firearm certificate to have the firearm in his possession, or to purchase or acquire it, subject to a condition that it is only for use in connection with starting races at athletic meetings.

NOTES

Words "or the Scottish Ministers (by virtue of provision made under section 63 of the Scotland Act 1998)" in square brackets inserted by SI 1999/1750, art 6(1), Sch 5, para 18(1), (5).

Date in force: 1 July 1999: see SI 1999/1750, art 1(1), and SI 1998/3178, art 3.

6 Trophies of war

The authority of the Secretary of State [or the Scottish Ministers (by virtue of provision made under section 63 of the Scotland Act 1998)] is not required by virtue of subsection (1)(aba) of section 5 of the 1968 Act for a person to have in his possession a firearm which was acquired as a trophy of war before 1st January 1946 if he is authorised by a firearm certificate to have it in his possession.

NOTES

Words "or the Scottish Ministers (by virtue of provision made under section 63 of the Scotland Act 1998)" in square brackets inserted by SI 1999/1750, art 6(1), Sch 5, para 18(1), (6).

Date in force: 1 July 1999: see SI 1999/1750, art 1(1), and SI 1998/3178, art 3.

7 Firearms of historic interest

(1)   The authority of the Secretary of State [or the Scottish Ministers (by virtue of provision made under section 63 of the Scotland Act 1998)] is not required by virtue of subsection (1)(aba) of section 5 of the 1968 Act for a person to have in his possession, or to purchase or acquire, or to sell or transfer, a firearm which—

(a)   was manufactured before 1st January 1919; and
(b)   is of a description specified under subsection (2) below,

if he is authorised by a firearm certificate to have the firearm in his possession, or to purchase or acquire it, subject to a condition that he does so only for the purpose of its being kept or exhibited as part of a collection.

(2)   The Secretary of State may by order made by statutory instrument specify a description of firearm for the purposes of subsection (1) above if it appears to him that—

(a)   firearms of that description were manufactured before 1st January 1919; and
(b)   ammunition for firearms of that type is not readily available.

(3)   The authority of the Secretary of State [or the Scottish Ministers (by virtue of provision made under section 63 of the Scotland Act 1998)] is not required by virtue of subsection (1)(aba) of section 5 of the 1968 Act for a person to have in his possession, or to purchase or acquire, or to sell or transfer, a firearm which—

(a)   is of particular rarity, aesthetic quality or technical interest, or
(b)   is of historical importance,

if he is authorised by a firearm certificate to have the firearm in his possession subject to a condition requiring it to be kept and used only at a place designated for the purposes of this subsection by the Secretary of State [or the Scottish Ministers (by virtue of provision made under section 63 of the Scotland Act 1998)].

(4)   This section has effect without prejudice to section 58(2) of the 1968 Act (antique firearms).

NOTES

Sub-s (1): words "or the Scottish Ministers (by virtue of provision made under section 63 of the Scotland Act 1998)" in square brackets inserted by SI 1999/1750, art 6(1), Sch 5, para 18(1), (7)(a).

Date in force: 1 July 1999: see SI 1999/1750, art 1(1), and SI 1998/3178, art 3.

Sub-s (3): words "or the Scottish Ministers (by virtue of provision made under section 63 of the Scotland Act 1998)" in square brackets in both places they occur inserted by SI 1999/1750, art 6(1), Sch 5, para 18(1), (7)(b).

Date in force: 1 July 1999: see SI 1999/1750, art 1(1), and SI 1998/3178, art 3.

Weapons and ammunition used for treating animals

8 Weapons and ammunition used for treating animals

The authority of the Secretary of State [or the Scottish Ministers (by virtue of provision made under section 63 of the Scotland Act 1998)] is not required by virtue of subsection (1)(aba), (b) or (c) of section 5 of the 1968 Act for a person to have in his possession, or to purchase or acquire, or to sell or transfer, any firearm, weapon or ammunition designed or adapted for the purpose of tranquillising or otherwise treating any animal, if he is authorised by a firearm certificate to possess, or to purchase or acquire, the firearm, weapon or ammunition subject to a condition restricting its use to use in connection with the treatment of animals.

NOTES

Words "or the Scottish Ministers (by virtue of provision made under section 63 of the Scotland Act 1998)" in square brackets inserted by SI 1999/1750, art 6(1), Sch 5, para 18(1), (8).

Date in force: 1 July 1999: see SI 1999/1750, art 1(1), and SI 1998/3178, art 3.

PART III
REGULATION OF FIREARMS AND AMMUNITION

Miscellaneous

48 Firearms powered by compressed carbon dioxide

Any reference to an air rifle, air pistol or air gun—
  (a) in the Firearms Acts 1968 to 1997; or
  (b) in the Firearms (Dangerous Air Weapons) Rules 1969 or the Firearms (Dangerous Air Weapons) (Scotland) Rules 1969,

shall include a reference to a rifle, pistol or gun powered by compressed carbon dioxide.

PART IV
FINAL PROVISIONS

53 Short title, commencement and extent

(1) This Act may be cited as the Firearms (Amendment) Act 1997.

(2) This Act and the Firearms Acts 1968 to 1992 may be cited together as the Firearms Acts 1968 to 1997.

(3)   This Act shall come into force on such day as the Secretary of State may by order made by statutory instrument appoint; and different days may be appointed for different purposes and different areas.

(4)   An order under subsection (3) above may contain such transitional provision and savings (whether or not involving the modification of any statutory provision) as appear to the Secretary of State to be necessary or expedient in connection with any provisions brought into force.

Protection from Harassment Act 1997

1997 CHAPTER 40

An Act to make provision for protecting persons from harassment and similar conduct

[21st March 1997]

England and Wales

1 Prohibition of harassment

(1)   A person must not pursue a course of conduct—
  (a)   which amounts to harassment of another, and
  (b)   which he knows or ought to know amounts to harassment of the other.

(2)   For the purposes of this section, the person whose course of conduct is in question ought to know that it amounts to harassment of another if a reasonable person in possession of the same information would think the course of conduct amounted to harassment of the other.

(3)   Subsection (1) does not apply to a course of conduct if the person who pursued it shows—
  (a)   that it was pursued for the purpose of preventing or detecting crime,
  (b)   that it was pursued under any enactment or rule of law or to comply with any condition or requirement imposed by any person under any enactment, or
  (c)   that in the particular circumstances the pursuit of the course of conduct was reasonable.

2 Offence of harassment

(1)   A person who pursues a course of conduct in breach of section 1 is guilty of an offence.

(2)   A person guilty of an offence under this section is liable on summary conviction to imprisonment for a term not exceeding six months, or a fine not exceeding level 5 on the standard scale, or both.

(3)   In section 24(2) of the Police and Criminal Evidence Act 1984 (arrestable offences), after paragraph (m) there is inserted—

"(n) an offence under section 2 of the Protection from Harassment Act 1997 (harassment).".

4 Putting people in fear of violence

(1)   A person whose course of conduct causes another to fear, on at least two occasions, that violence will be used against him is guilty of an offence if he knows or ought to know that his course of conduct will cause the other so to fear on each of those occasions.

(2)   For the purposes of this section, the person whose course of conduct is in question ought to know that it will cause another to fear that violence will be used against him on any occasion if a reasonable person in possession of the same information would think the course of conduct would cause the other so to fear on that occasion.

(3)   It is a defence for a person charged with an offence under this section to show that—

(a)   his course of conduct was pursued for the purpose of preventing or detecting crime,

(b)   his course of conduct was pursued under any enactment or rule of law or to comply with any condition or requirement imposed by any person under any enactment, or

(c)   the pursuit of his course of conduct was reasonable for the protection of himself or another or for the protection of his or another's property.

(4)   A person guilty of an offence under this section is liable—

(a)   on conviction on indictment, to imprisonment for a term not exceeding five years, or a fine, or both, or

(b)   on summary conviction, to imprisonment for a term not exceeding six months, or a fine not exceeding the statutory maximum, or both.

(5)   If on the trial on indictment of a person charged with an offence under this section the jury find him not guilty of the offence charged, they may find him guilty of an offence under section 2.

(6)   The Crown Court has the same powers and duties in relation to a person who is by virtue of subsection (5) convicted before it of an offence under section 2 as a magistrates' court would have on convicting him of the offence.

5 Restraining orders

(1)   A court sentencing or otherwise dealing with a person ("the defendant") convicted of an offence under section 2 or 4 may (as well as sentencing him or dealing with him in any other way) make an order under this section.

(2)   The order may, for the purpose of protecting the victim of the offence, or any other person mentioned in the order, from further conduct which—

(a)   amounts to harassment, or

(b)   will cause a fear of violence,

prohibit the defendant from doing anything described in the order.

(3)   The order may have effect for a specified period or until further order.

(4)   The prosecutor, the defendant or any other person mentioned in the order may apply to the court which made the order for it to be varied or discharged by a further order.

(5)   If without reasonable excuse the defendant does anything which he is prohibited from doing by an order under this section, he is guilty of an offence.

(6)   A person guilty of an offence under this section is liable—
   (a)   on conviction on indictment, to imprisonment for a term not exceeding five years, or a fine, or both, or
   (b)   on summary conviction, to imprisonment for a term not exceeding six months, or a fine not exceeding the statutory maximum, or both.

7 Interpretation of this group of sections

(1)   This section applies for the interpretation of sections 1 to 5.

(2)   References to harassing a person include alarming the person or causing the person distress.

(3)   A "course of conduct" must involve conduct on at least two occasions.

[(3A)   A person's conduct on any occasion shall be taken, if aided, abetted, counselled or procured by another—
   (a)   to be conduct on that occasion of the other (as well as conduct of the person whose conduct it is); and
   (b)   to be conduct in relation to which the other's knowledge and purpose, and what he ought to have known, are the same as they were in relation to what was contemplated or reasonably foreseeable at the time of the aiding, abetting, counselling or procuring.]

(4)   "Conduct" includes speech.

NOTES
   Sub-s (3A): inserted by the Criminal Justice and Police Act 2001, s 44(1).
   Date in force: 1 August 2001 (in relation to any aiding, abetting, counselling or procuring that takes place after that date): see the Criminal Justice and Police Act 2001, ss 44(2), 138(2) and SI 2001/2223, art 3(b).

General

12 National security, etc

(1)   If the Secretary of State certifies that in his opinion anything done by a specified person on a specified occasion related to—
   (a)   national security,
   (b)   the economic well-being of the United Kingdom, or
   (c)   the prevention or detection of serious crime,

and was done on behalf of the Crown, the certificate is conclusive evidence that this Act does not apply to any conduct of that person on that occasion.

(2)   In subsection (1), "specified" means specified in the certificate in question.

(3)   A document purporting to be a certificate under subsection (1) is to be received in evidence and, unless the contrary is proved, be treated as being such a certificate.

14 Extent

(1)   Sections 1 to 7 extend to England and Wales only.

(2)   Sections 8 to 11 extend to Scotland only.

(3)   This Act (except section 13) does not extend to Northern Ireland.

15 Commencement

(1)   Sections 1, 2, 4, 5 and 7 to 12 are to come into force on such day as the Secretary of State may by order made by statutory instrument appoint.

(2)   Sections 3 and 6 are to come into force on such day as the Lord Chancellor may by order made by statutory instrument appoint.

(3)   Different days may be appointed under this section for different purposes.

16 Short title

This Act may be cited as the Protection from Harassment Act 1997.

Sex Offenders Act 1997

1997 CHAPTER 51

An Act to require the notification of information to the police by persons who have committed certain sexual offences; to make provisions with respect to the commission of certain sexual acts outside the United Kingdom; and for connected purposes

[21 March 1997]

PART II
SEXUAL OFFENCES COMMITTED OUTSIDE THE UNITED KINGDOM

7 Extension of jurisdiction: England and Wales and Northern Ireland

(1)   Subject to subsection (2) below, any act done by a person in a country or territory outside the United Kingdom which—
    (a)   constituted an offence under the law in force in that country or territory; and

(b)   would constitute a sexual offence to which this section applies if it had been done in England and Wales, or in Northern Ireland,

shall constitute that sexual offence under the law of that part of the United Kingdom.

(2)   No proceedings shall by virtue of this section be brought against any person unless he was at the commencement of this section, or has subsequently become, a British citizen or resident in the United Kingdom.

(3)   An act punishable under the law in force in any country or territory constitutes an offence under that law for the purposes of this section, however it is described in that law.

(4)   Subject to subsection (5) below, the condition in subsection (1)(a) above shall be taken to be satisfied unless, not later than rules of court may provide, the defence serve on the prosecution a notice—

(a)   stating that, on the facts as alleged with respect to the act in question, the condition is not in their opinion satisfied;

(b)   showing their grounds for that opinion; and

(c)   requiring the prosecution to show that it is satisfied.

(5)   The court, if it thinks fit, may permit the defence to require the prosecution to show that the condition is satisfied without the prior service of a notice under subsection (4) above.

(6)   In the Crown Court the question whether the condition is satisfied is to be decided by the judge alone.

(7)   Schedule 2 to this Act (which lists the sexual offences to which this section applies) shall have effect.

PART III
SUPPLEMENTAL

10 Short title, commencement and extent

(1)   This Act may be cited as the Sex Offenders Act 1997.

(2)   This Act shall come into force on such day as the Secretary of State may by order made by statutory instrument appoint, and different days may be appointed for different purposes and for different areas.

(3)   Nothing in section 7 or 8 above applies to any act done before the commencement of that section.

[(3A)   The Secretary of State may by order make any modifications of section 5A above which he considers necessary or expedient for the purpose of enabling courts in Northern Ireland to exercise the powers conferred by that section.

The power to make an order under this subsection is exercisable by statutory instrument, which shall be subject to annulment in pursuance of a resolution of either House of Parliament.]

(4)   This Act, except section 8 above, extends to England and Wales and Northern Ireland.

(5) Part I of this Act, section 8 above and this section extend to Scotland.

[(6) Any power to make regulations or an order under this Act may be exercised so as to make different provision for different purposes.]

NOTES

Sub-s (3A): inserted by the Criminal Justice and Court Services Act 2000, s 66, Sch 5, paras 1(1), 6(3).

Date in force (in relation to England and Wales and Northern Ireland): 2 May 2001: see SI 2001/1651, art 2(a).

Date in force (in relation to Scotland): 31 May 2001: see SSI 2001/166, art 3.

Sub-s (6): inserted by the Criminal Justice and Court Services Act 2000, s 66, Sch 5, paras 1(1), 9.

Date in force (in relation to England and Wales and Northern Ireland): 2 May 2001: see SI 2001/1651, art 2(a).

Date in force (in relation to Scotland): 31 May 2001: see SSI 2001/166, art 3.

Crime and Disorder Act 1998

1998 CHAPTER 37

An Act to make provision for preventing crime and disorder; to create certain racially-aggravated offences; to abolish the rebuttable presumption that a child is doli incapax and to make provision as to the effect of a child's failure to give evidence at his trial; to abolish the death penalty for treason and piracy; to make changes to the criminal justice system; to make further provision for dealing with offenders; to make further provision with respect to remands and committals for trial and the release and recall of prisoners; to amend Chapter I of Part II of the Crime (Sentences) Act 1997 and to repeal Chapter I of Part III of the Crime and Punishment (Scotland) Act 1997; to make amendments designed to facilitate, or otherwise desirable in connection with, the consolidation of certain enactments; and for connected purposes.

[31st July 1998]

PART II
CRIMINAL LAW

[Racially or religiously aggravated] offences: England and Wales

NOTES

Cross-heading: words "Racially or religiously aggravated" in square brackets substituted by the Anti-terrorism, Crime and Security Act 2001, s 39(1), (2).

Date in force: 14 December 2001 (except in relation to anything done before that date): see the Anti-terrorism, Crime and Security Act 2001, ss 42, 127(2)(a).

28 Meaning of "[racially or religiously aggravated]"

(1)   An offence is [racially or religiously aggravated] for the purposes of sections 29 to 32 below if—

   (a)   at the time of committing the offence, or immediately before or after doing so, the offender demonstrates towards the victim of the offence hostility based on the victim's membership (or presumed membership) of a [racial or religious group]; or

   (b)   the offence is motivated (wholly or partly) by hostility towards members of a [racial or religious group] based on their membership of that group.

(2)   In subsection (1)(a) above—

   "membership", in relation to a [racial or religious group], includes association with members of that group;

   "presumed" means presumed by the offender.

(3)   It is immaterial for the purposes of paragraph (a) or (b) of subsection (1) above whether or not the offender's hostility is also based, to any extent, [on any other factor not mentioned in that paragraph].

(4)   In this section "racial group" means a group of persons defined by reference to race, colour, nationality (including citizenship) or ethnic or national origins.

[(5)   In this section "religious group" means a group of persons defined by reference to religious belief or lack of religious belief.]

NOTES

   Section heading: words "racially or religiously aggravated" in square brackets substituted by the Anti-terrorism, Crime and Security Act 2001, s 39(1), (3)(a).

   Date in force: 14 December 2001 (except in relation to anything done before that date): see the Anti-terrorism, Crime and Security Act 2001, ss 42, 127(2)(a).

   Sub-s (1): words "racially or religiously aggravated" in square brackets substituted by the Anti-terrorism, Crime and Security Act 2001, s 39(1), (3)(a).

   Date in force: 14 December 2001 (except in relation to anything done before that date): see the Anti-terrorism, Crime and Security Act 2001, ss 42, 127(2)(a).

   Sub-s (1): in paras (a), (b) words "racial or religious group" in square brackets substituted by the Anti-terrorism, Crime and Security Act 2001, s 39(1), (3)(b).

   Date in force: 14 December 2001 (except in relation to anything done before that date): see the Anti-terrorism, Crime and Security Act 2001, ss 42, 127(2)(a).

   Sub-s (2): in definition "membership" words "racial or religious group" in square brackets substituted by the Anti-terrorism, Crime and Security Act 2001, s 39(1), (3)(b).

   Date in force: 14 December 2001 (except in relation to anything done before that date): see the Anti-terrorism, Crime and Security Act 2001, ss 42, 127(2)(a).

   Sub-s (3): words "on any other factor not mentioned in that paragraph" in square brackets substituted by the Anti-terrorism, Crime and Security Act 2001, s 39(1), (3)(c).

   Date in force: 14 December 2001 (except in relation to anything done before that date): see the Anti-terrorism, Crime and Security Act 2001, ss 42, 127(2)(a).

   Sub-s (5): inserted by the Anti-terrorism, Crime and Security Act 2001, s 39(1), (4).

   Date in force: 14 December 2001 (except in relation to anything done before that date): see the Anti-terrorism, Crime and Security Act 2001, ss 42, 127(2)(a).

29 [Racially or religiously aggravated] assaults

(1) A person is guilty of an offence under this section if he commits—
  (a) an offence under section 20 of the Offences Against the Person Act 1861 (malicious wounding or grievous bodily harm);
  (b) an offence under section 47 of that Act (actual bodily harm); or
  (c) common assault,

which is [racially or religiously aggravated] for the purposes of this section.

(2) A person guilty of an offence falling within subsection (1)(a) or (b) above shall be liable—
  (a) on summary conviction, to imprisonment for a term not exceeding six months or to a fine not exceeding the statutory maximum, or to both;
  (b) on conviction on indictment, to imprisonment for a term not exceeding seven years or to a fine, or to both.

(3) A person guilty of an offence falling within subsection (1)(c) above shall be liable—
  (a) on summary conviction, to imprisonment for a term not exceeding six months or to a fine not exceeding the statutory maximum, or to both;
  (b) on conviction on indictment, to imprisonment for a term not exceeding two years or to a fine, or to both.

NOTES

Section heading: words "Racially or religiously aggravated" in square brackets substituted by the Anti-terrorism, Crime and Security Act 2001, s 39(1), (5)(a), (6)(a).

Date in force: 14 December 2001 (except in relation to anything done before that date): see the Anti-terrorism, Crime and Security Act 2001, ss 42, 127(2)(a).

Sub-s (1): words "racially or religiously aggravated" in square brackets substituted by the Anti-terrorism, Crime and Security Act 2001, s 39(1), (5)(b), (6)(a).

Date in force: 14 December 2001 (except in relation to anything done before that date): see the Anti-terrorism, Crime and Security Act 2001, ss 42, 127(2)(a).

30 [Racially or religiously aggravated] criminal damage

(1) A person is guilty of an offence under this section if he commits an offence under section 1(1) of the Criminal Damage Act 1971 (destroying or damaging property belonging to another) which is [racially or religiously aggravated] for the purposes of this section.

(2) A person guilty of an offence under this section shall be liable—
  (a) on summary conviction, to imprisonment for a term not exceeding six months or to a fine not exceeding the statutory maximum, or to both;
  (b) on conviction on indictment, to imprisonment for a term not exceeding fourteen years or to a fine, or to both.

(3) For the purposes of this section, section 28(1)(a) above shall have effect as if the person to whom the property belongs or is treated as belonging for the purposes of that Act were the victim of the offence.

NOTES

Section heading: words "Racially or religiously aggravated" in square brackest substituted by the Anti-terrorism, Crime and Security Act 2001, s 39(1), (5)(a), (6)(b).

Date in force: 14 December 2001 (except in relation to anything done before that date): see the Anti-terrorism, Crime and Security Act 2001, ss 42, 127(2)(a).

Sub-s (1): words "racially or religiously aggravated" in square brackets substituted by the Anti-terrorism, Crime and Security Act 2001, s 39(1), (5)(b), (6)(b).

Date in force: 14 December 2001 (except in relation to anything done before that date): see the Anti-terrorism, Crime and Security Act 2001, ss 42, 127(2)(a).

31 [Racially or religiously aggravated] public order offences

(1)   A person is guilty of an offence under this section if he commits—

(a)   an offence under section 4 of the Public Order Act 1986 (fear or provocation of violence);

(b)   an offence under section 4A of that Act (intentional harassment, alarm or distress); or

(c)   an offence under section 5 of that Act (harassment, alarm or distress),

which is [racially or religiously aggravated] for the purposes of this section.

(2)   A constable may arrest without warrant anyone whom he reasonably suspects to be committing an offence falling within subsection (1)(a) or (b) above.

(3)   A constable may arrest a person without warrant if—

(a)   he engages in conduct which a constable reasonably suspects to constitute an offence falling within subsection (1)(c) above;

(b)   he is warned by that constable to stop; and

(c)   he engages in further such conduct immediately or shortly after the warning.

The conduct mentioned in paragraph (a) above and the further conduct need not be of the same nature.

(4)   A person guilty of an offence falling within subsection (1)(a) or (b) above shall be liable—

(a)   on summary conviction, to imprisonment for a term not exceeding six months or to a fine not exceeding the statutory maximum, or to both;

(b)   on conviction on indictment, to imprisonment for a term not exceeding two years or to a fine, or to both.

(5)   A person guilty of an offence falling within subsection (1)(c) above shall be liable on summary conviction to a fine not exceeding level 4 on the standard scale.

(6)   If, on the trial on indictment of a person charged with an offence falling within subsection (1)(a) or (b) above, the jury find him not guilty of the offence charged, they may find him guilty of the basic offence mentioned in that provision.

(7)   For the purposes of subsection (1)(c) above, section 28(1)(a) above shall have effect as if the person likely to be caused harassment, alarm or distress were the victim of the offence.

NOTES
Section heading: words "Racially or religiously aggravated" in square brackets substituted by the Anti-terrorism, Crime and Security Act 2001, s 39(1), (5)(a), (6)(c).
Date in force: 14 December 2001 (except in relation to anything done before that date): see the Anti-terrorism, Crime and Security Act 2001, ss 42, 127(2)(a).
Sub-s (1): words "racially or religiously aggravated" in square brackets substituted by the Anti-terrorism, Crime and Security Act 2001, s 39(1), (5)(b), (6)(c).
Date in force: 14 December 2001 (except in relation to anything done before that date): see the Anti-terrorism, Crime and Security Act 2001, ss 42, 127(2)(a).

32 [Racially or religiously aggravated] harassment etc

(1)   A person is guilty of an offence under this section if he commits—
   (a)   an offence under section 2 of the Protection from Harassment Act 1997 (offence of harassment); or
   (b)   an offence under section 4 of that Act (putting people in fear of violence),

which is [racially or religiously aggravated] for the purposes of this section.

(2)   In section 24(2) of the 1984 Act (arrestable offences), after paragraph (o) there shall be inserted—
    "(p) an offence falling within section 32(1)(a) of the Crime and Disorder Act 1998 (racially-aggravated harassment);".

(3)   A person guilty of an offence falling within subsection (1)(a) above shall be liable—
   (a)   on summary conviction, to imprisonment for a term not exceeding six months or to a fine not exceeding the statutory maximum, or to both;
   (b)   on conviction on indictment, to imprisonment for a term not exceeding two years or to a fine, or to both.

(4)   A person guilty of an offence falling within subsection (1)(b) above shall be liable—
   (a)   on summary conviction, to imprisonment for a term not exceeding six months or to a fine not exceeding the statutory maximum, or to both;
   (b)   on conviction on indictment, to imprisonment for a term not exceeding seven years or to a fine, or to both.

(5)   If, on the trial on indictment of a person charged with an offence falling within subsection (1)(a) above, the jury find him not guilty of the offence charged, they may find him guilty of the basic offence mentioned in that provision.

(6)   If, on the trial on indictment of a person charged with an offence falling within subsection (1)(b) above, the jury find him not guilty of the offence charged, they may find him guilty of an offence falling within subsection (1)(a) above.

(7)   Section 5 of the Protection from Harassment Act 1997 (restraining orders) shall have effect in relation to a person convicted of an offence under this section as if the reference in subsection (1) of that section to an offence under section 2 or 4 included a reference to an offence under this section.

NOTES
Section heading: words "Racially or religiously aggravated" in square brackets substituted by the Anti-terrorism, Crime and Security Act 2001, s 39(1), (5)(a), (6)(d).

Date in force: 14 December 2001 (except in relation to anything done before that date): see the Anti-terrorism, Crime and Security Act 2001, ss 42, 127(2)(a).

Sub-s (1): words "racially or religiously aggravated" in square brackets substituted by the Anti-terrorism, Crime and Security Act 2001, s 39(1), (5)(b), (6)(d).

Date in force: 14 December 2001 (except in relation to anything done before that date): see the Anti-terrorism, Crime and Security Act 2001, ss 42, 127(2)(a).

PART V
MISCELLANEOUS AND SUPPLEMENTAL

Supplemental

121 Short title, commencement and extent

(1)   This Act may be cited as the Crime and Disorder Act 1998.

(2)   This Act, except this section, sections 109 and 111(8) above and paragraphs 55, 99 and 117 of Schedule 8 to this Act, shall come into force on such day as the Secretary of State may by order appoint; and different days may be appointed for different purposes or different areas.

(3)   Without prejudice to the provisions of Schedule 9 to this Act, an order under subsection (2) above may make such transitional provisions and savings as appear to the Secretary of State necessary or expedient in connection with any provision brought into force by the order.

(4)   Subject to subsections (5) to (12) below, this Act extends to England and Wales only.

(5)   The following provisions extend to Scotland only, namely—
  (a)   Chapter II of Part I;
  (b)   section 33;
  (c)   Chapter II of Part IV;
  (d)   sections 108 to 112 and 117(2); and
  (e)   paragraphs 55, 70, 71, 98 to 108, 115 to 124 and 140 to 143 of Schedule 8 and section 119 above so far as relating to those paragraphs.

(6)   The following provisions also extend to Scotland, namely—
  (a)   Chapter III of Part I;
  (b)   section 36(3) to (5);
  (c)   section 65(9);
  (d)   section 115;
  (e)   paragraph 3 of Schedule 3 to this Act and section 52(6) above so far as relating to that paragraph;
  (f)   . . .

    (g)   paragraphs 1, 7(1) and (3), 14(1) and (2), 35, 36, 45, 135, 136 and 138 of Schedule 8 to this Act and section 119 above so far as relating to those paragraphs; and

    (h)   this section.

(7)   Sections 36(1), (2)(a), (b) and (d) and (6)(b) and section 118 above extend to Northern Ireland only.

(8)   Section 36(3)(b), (4) and (5) above, paragraphs 7(1) and (3), 45, 135 and 138 of Schedule 8 to this Act, section 119 above so far as relating to those paragraphs and this section also extend to Northern Ireland.

(9)   Section 36(5) above, paragraphs 7(1) and (3), 45 and 134 of Schedule 8 to this Act, section 119 above so far as relating to those paragraphs and this section also extend to the Isle of Man.

(10)   Section 36(5) above, paragraphs 7(1) and (3), 45 and 135 of Schedule 8 to this Act, section 119 above so far as relating to those paragraphs and this section also extend to the Channel Islands.

(11)   The repeals in Schedule 10 to this Act, and section 120(2) above so far as relating to those repeals, have the same extent as the enactments on which the repeals operate.

(12)   Section 9(4) of the Repatriation of Prisoners Act 1984 (power to extend Act to Channel Islands and Isle of Man) applies to the amendments of that Act made by paragraphs 56 to 60 of Schedule 8 to this Act; and in Schedule 1 to the 1997 Act—

    (a)   paragraph 14 (restricted transfers between the United Kingdom and the Channel Islands) as applied in relation to the Isle of Man; and

    (b)   paragraph 19 (application of Schedule in relation to the Isle of Man),

apply to the amendments of that Schedule made by paragraph 135 of Schedule 8 to this Act.

NOTES

Sub-s (6): para (f) repealed by the Powers of Criminal Courts (Sentencing) Act 2000, s 165(4), Sch 12, Pt I.

Date in force: 25 August 2000: see the Powers of Criminal Courts (Sentencing) Act 2000, s 168(1).

Human Rights Act 1998

1998 CHAPTER 42

An Act to give further effect to rights and freedoms guaranteed under the European Convention on Human Rights; to make provision with respect to holders of certain judicial offices who become judges of the European Court of Human Rights; and for connected purposes.

[9th November 1998]

Introduction

1 The Convention Rights

(1) In this Act "the Convention rights" means the rights and fundamental freedoms set out in—

    (a) Articles 2 to 12 and 14 of the Convention,

    (b) Articles 1 to 3 of the First Protocol, and

    (c) Articles 1 and 2 of the Sixth Protocol,

as read with Articles 16 to 18 of the Convention.

(2) Those Articles are to have effect for the purposes of this Act subject to any designated derogation or reservation (as to which see sections 14 and 15).

(3) The Articles are set out in Schedule 1.

(4) The [Lord Chancellor] may by order make such amendments to this Act as he considers appropriate to reflect the effect, in relation to the United Kingdom, of a protocol.

(5) In subsection (4) "protocol" means a protocol to the Convention—

    (a) which the United Kingdom has ratified; or

    (b) which the United Kingdom has signed with a view to ratification.

(6) No amendment may be made by an order under subsection (4) so as to come into force before the protocol concerned is in force in relation to the United Kingdom.

NOTES

Sub-s (4): words "Lord Chancellor" in square brackets substituted by SI 2001/3500, art 8, Sch 2, Pt I, para 7(a).

Date in force: 26 November 2001: see SI 2001/3500, art 1(2).

3 Interpretation of legislation

(1) So far as it is possible to do so, primary legislation and subordinate legislation must be read and given effect in a way which is compatible with the Convention rights.

(2) This section—

    (a) applies to primary legislation and subordinate legislation whenever enacted;

(b) does not affect the validity, continuing operation or enforcement of any incompatible primary legislation; and

(c) does not affect the validity, continuing operation or enforcement of any incompatible subordinate legislation if (disregarding any possibility of revocation) primary legislation prevents removal of the incompatibility.

4 Declaration of incompatibility

(1) Subsection (2) applies in any proceedings in which a court determines whether a provision of primary legislation is compatible with a Convention right.

(2) If the court is satisfied that the provision is incompatible with a Convention right, it may make a declaration of that incompatibility.

(3) Subsection (4) applies in any proceedings in which a court determines whether a provision of subordinate legislation, made in the exercise of a power conferred by primary legislation, is compatible with a Convention right.

(4) If the court is satisfied—
   (a) that the provision is incompatible with a Convention right, and
   (b) that (disregarding any possibility of revocation) the primary legislation concerned prevents removal of the incompatibility,

it may make a declaration of that incompatibility.

(5) In this section "court" means—
   (a) the House of Lords;
   (b) the Judicial Committee of the Privy Council;
   (c) the Courts-Martial Appeal Court;
   (d) in Scotland, the High Court of Justiciary sitting otherwise than as a trial court or the Court of Session;
   (e) in England and Wales or Northern Ireland, the High Court or the Court of Appeal.

(6) A declaration under this section ("a declaration of incompatibility")—
   (a) does not affect the validity, continuing operation or enforcement of the provision in respect of which it is given; and
   (b) is not binding on the parties to the proceedings in which it is made.

SCHEDULE 1
THE ARTICLES

Section 1(3)

PART I
THE CONVENTION

Rights and Freedoms

Article 2
Right to life

1 Everyone's right to life shall be protected by law. No one shall be deprived of his life intentionally save in the execution of a sentence of a court following his conviction of a crime for which this penalty is provided by law.

2   Deprivation of life shall not be regarded as inflicted in contravention of this Article when it results from the use of force which is no more than absolutely necessary:

(a)   in defence of any person from unlawful violence;

(b)   in order to effect a lawful arrest or to prevent the escape of a person lawfully detained;

(c)   in action lawfully taken for the purpose of quelling a riot or insurrection.

Article 3
Prohibition of torture

No one shall be subjected to torture or to inhuman or degrading treatment or punishment.

Article 4
Prohibition of slavery and forced labour

1   No one shall be held in slavery or servitude.

2   No one shall be required to perform forced or compulsory labour.

3   For the purpose of this Article the term "forced or compulsory labour" shall not include:

(a)   any work required to be done in the ordinary course of detention imposed according to the provisions of Article 5 of this Convention or during conditional release from such detention;

(b)   any service of a military character or, in case of conscientious objectors in countries where they are recognised, service exacted instead of compulsory military service;

(c)   any service exacted in case of an emergency or calamity threatening the life or well-being of the community;

(d)   any work or service which forms part of normal civic obligations.

Article 5
Right to liberty and security

1   Everyone has the right to liberty and security of person. No one shall be deprived of his liberty save in the following cases and in accordance with a procedure prescribed by law:

(a)   the lawful detention of a person after conviction by a competent court;

(b)   the lawful arrest or detention of a person for non-compliance with the lawful order of a court or in order to secure the fulfilment of any obligation prescribed by law;

(c)   the lawful arrest or detention of a person effected for the purpose of bringing him before the competent legal authority on reasonable suspicion of having committed an offence or when it is reasonably considered necessary to prevent his committing an offence or fleeing after having done so;

(d)   the detention of a minor by lawful order for the purpose of educational supervision or his lawful detention for the purpose of bringing him before the competent legal authority;

(e)   the lawful detention of persons for the prevention of the spreading of infectious diseases, of persons of unsound mind, alcoholics or drug addicts or vagrants;

(f)   the lawful arrest or detention of a person to prevent his effecting an unauthorised entry into the country or of a person against whom action is being taken with a view to deportation or extradition.

2   Everyone who is arrested shall be informed promptly, in a language which he understands, of the reasons for his arrest and of any charge against him.

3   Everyone arrested or detained in accordance with the provisions of paragraph 1(c) of this Article shall be brought promptly before a judge or other officer authorised by law to exercise judicial power and shall be entitled to trial within a reasonable time or to release pending trial. Release may be conditioned by guarantees to appear for trial.

4   Everyone who is deprived of his liberty by arrest or detention shall be entitled to take proceedings by which the lawfulness of his detention shall be decided speedily by a court and his release ordered if the detention is not lawful.

5   Everyone who has been the victim of arrest or detention in contravention of the provisions of this Article shall have an enforceable right to compensation.

Article 6
Right to a fair trial

1   In the determination of his civil rights and obligations or of any criminal charge against him, everyone is entitled to a fair and public hearing within a reasonable time by an independent and impartial tribunal established by law. Judgment shall be pronounced publicly but the press and public may be excluded from all or part of the trial in the interest of morals, public order or national security in a democratic society, where the interests of juveniles or the protection of the private life of the parties so require, or to the extent strictly necessary in the opinion of the court in special circumstances where publicity would prejudice the interests of justice.

2   Everyone charged with a criminal offence shall be presumed innocent until proved guilty according to law.

3   Everyone charged with a criminal offence has the following minimum rights:
  (a)   to be informed promptly, in a language which he understands and in detail, of the nature and cause of the accusation against him;
  (b)   to have adequate time and facilities for the preparation of his defence;
  (c)   to defend himself in person or through legal assistance of his own choosing or, if he has not sufficient means to pay for legal assistance, to be given it free when the interests of justice so require;
  (d)   to examine or have examined witnesses against him and to obtain the attendance and examination of witnesses on his behalf under the same conditions as witnesses against him;
  (e)   to have the free assistance of an interpreter if he cannot understand or speak the language used in court.

Article 7
No punishment without law

1   No one shall be held guilty of any criminal offence on account of any act or omission which did not constitute a criminal offence under national or international law at the time when it was committed. Nor shall a heavier penalty be imposed than the one that was applicable at the time the criminal offence was committed.

2   This Article shall not prejudice the trial and punishment of any person for any act or omission which, at the time when it was committed, was criminal according to the general principles of law recognised by civilised nations.

Article 8
Right to respect for private and family life

1 Everyone has the right to respect for his private and family life, his home and his correspondence.

2 There shall be no interference by a public authority with the exercise of this right except such as is in accordance with the law and is necessary in a democratic society in the interests of national security, public safety or the economic well-being of the country, for the prevention of disorder or crime, for the protection of health or morals, or for the protection of the rights and freedoms of others.

Article 9
Freedom of thought, conscience and religion

1 Everyone has the right to freedom of thought, conscience and religion; this right includes freedom to change his religion or belief and freedom, either alone or in community with others and in public or private, to manifest his religion or belief, in worship, teaching, practice and observance.

2 Freedom to manifest one's religion or beliefs shall be subject only to such limitations as are prescribed by law and are necessary in a democratic society in the interests of public safety, for the protection of public order, health or morals, or for the protection of the rights and freedoms of others.

Article 10
Freedom of expression

1 Everyone has the right to freedom of expression. This right shall include freedom to hold opinions and to receive and impart information and ideas without interference by public authority and regardless of frontiers. This Article shall not prevent States from requiring the licensing of broadcasting, television or cinema enterprises.

2 The exercise of these freedoms, since it carries with it duties and responsibilities, may be subject to such formalities, conditions, restrictions or penalties as are prescribed by law and are necessary in a democratic society, in the interests of national security, territorial integrity or public safety, for the prevention of disorder or crime, for the protection of health or morals, for the protection of the reputation or rights of others, for preventing the disclosure of information received in confidence, or for maintaining the authority and impartiality of the judiciary.

Article 11
Freedom of assembly and association

1 Everyone has the right to freedom of peaceful assembly and to freedom of association with others, including the right to form and to join trade unions for the protection of his interests.

2 No restrictions shall be placed on the exercise of these rights other than such as are prescribed by law and are necessary in a democratic society in the interests of national security or public safety, for the prevention of disorder or crime, for the protection of health or morals or for the protection of the rights and freedoms of others. This Article shall not prevent the imposition of lawful restrictions on the exercise of these rights by members of the armed forces, of the police or of the administration of the State.

Article 12
Right to marry

Men and women of marriageable age have the right to marry and to found a family, according to the national laws governing the exercise of this right.

Article 14
Prohibition of discrimination

The enjoyment of the rights and freedoms set forth in this Convention shall be secured without discrimination on any ground such as sex, race, colour, language, religion, political or other opinion, national or social origin, association with a national minority, property, birth or other status.

Article 16
Restrictions on political activity of aliens

Nothing in Articles 10, 11 and 14 shall be regarded as preventing the High Contracting Parties from imposing restrictions on the political activity of aliens.

Article 17
Prohibition of abuse of rights

Nothing in this Convention may be interpreted as implying for any State, group or person any right to engage in any activity or perform any act aimed at the destruction of any of the rights and freedoms set forth herein or at their limitation to a greater extent than is provided for in the Convention.

Article 18
Limitation on use of restrictions on rights

The restrictions permitted under this Convention to the said rights and freedoms shall not be applied for any purpose other than those for which they have been prescribed.

PART II
THE FIRST PROTOCOL

Article 1
Protection of property

Every natural or legal person is entitled to the peaceful enjoyment of his possessions. No one shall be deprived of his possessions except in the public interest and subject to the conditions provided for by law and by the general principles of international law.

The preceding provisions shall not, however, in any way impair the right of a State to enforce such laws as it deems necessary to control the use of property in accordance with the general interest or to secure the payment of taxes or other contributions or penalties.

Article 2
Right to education

No person shall be denied the right to education. In the exercise of any functions which it assumes in relation to education and to teaching, the State shall respect the right of parents to ensure such education and teaching in conformity with their own religious and philosophical convictions.

Article 3
Right to free elections

The High Contracting Parties undertake to hold free elections at reasonable intervals by secret ballot, under conditions which will ensure the free expression of the opinion of the people in the choice of the legislature.

PART III
THE SIXTH PROTOCOL

Article 1
Abolition of the death penalty

The death penalty shall be abolished. No one shall be condemned to such penalty or executed.

Article 2
Death penalty in time of war

A State may make provision in its law for the death penalty in respect of acts committed in time of war or of imminent threat of war; such penalty shall be applied only in the instances laid down in the law and in accordance with its provisions. The State shall communicate to the Secretary General of the Council of Europe the relevant provisions of that law.

Terrorism Act 2000

2000 CHAPTER 11

An Act to make provision about terrorism; and to make temporary provision for Northern Ireland about the prosecution and punishment of certain offences, the preservation of peace and the maintenance of order.

[20th July 2000]

PART I
INTRODUCTORY

1 Terrorism: interpretation

(1)   In this Act "terrorism" means the use or threat of action where—
 (a)   the action falls within subsection (2),

(b) the use or threat is designed to influence the government or to intimidate the public or a section of the public, and

(c) the use or threat is made for the purpose of advancing a political, religious or ideological cause.

(2) Action falls within this subsection if it—

(a) involves serious violence against a person,

(b) involves serious damage to property,

(c) endangers a person's life, other than that of the person committing the action,

(d) creates a serious risk to the health or safety of the public or a section of the public, or

(e) is designed seriously to interfere with or seriously to disrupt an electronic system.

(3) The use or threat of action falling within subsection (2) which involves the use of firearms or explosives is terrorism whether or not subsection (1)(b) is satisfied.

(4) In this section—

(a) "action" includes action outside the United Kingdom,

(b) a reference to any person or to property is a reference to any person, or to property, wherever situated,

(c) a reference to the public includes a reference to the public of a country other than the United Kingdom, and

(d) "the government" means the government of the United Kingdom, of a Part of the United Kingdom or of a country other than the United Kingdom.

(5) In this Act a reference to action taken for the purposes of terrorism includes a reference to action taken for the benefit of a proscribed organisation.

2 Temporary legislation

(1) The following shall cease to have effect—

(a) the Prevention of Terrorism (Temporary Provisions) Act 1989, and

(b) the Northern Ireland (Emergency Provisions) Act 1996.

(2) Schedule 1 (which preserves certain provisions of the 1996 Act, in some cases with amendment, for a transitional period) shall have effect.

PART II

PROSCRIBED ORGANISATIONS

Procedure

3 Proscription

(1) For the purposes of this Act an organisation is proscribed if—

(a) it is listed in Schedule 2, or

(b) it operates under the same name as an organisation listed in that Schedule.

(2) Subsection (1)(b) shall not apply in relation to an organisation listed in Schedule 2 if its entry is the subject of a note in that Schedule.

(3)   The Secretary of State may by order—
  (a)   add an organisation to Schedule 2;
  (b)   remove an organisation from that Schedule;
  (c)   amend that Schedule in some other way.

(4)   The Secretary of State may exercise his power under subsection (3)(a) in respect of an organisation only if he believes that it is concerned in terrorism.

(5)   For the purposes of subsection (4) an organisation is concerned in terrorism if it—
  (a)   commits or participates in acts of terrorism,
  (b)   prepares for terrorism,
  (c)   promotes or encourages terrorism, or
  (d)   is otherwise concerned in terrorism.

Offences

11 Membership

(1)   A person commits an offence if he belongs or professes to belong to a proscribed organisation.

(2)   It is a defence for a person charged with an offence under subsection (1) to prove—
  (a)   that the organisation was not proscribed on the last (or only) occasion on which he became a member or began to profess to be a member, and
  (b)   that he has not taken part in the activities of the organisation at any time while it was proscribed.

(3)   A person guilty of an offence under this section shall be liable—
  (a)   on conviction on indictment, to imprisonment for a term not exceeding ten years, to a fine or to both, or
  (b)   on summary conviction, to imprisonment for a term not exceeding six months, to a fine not exceeding the statutory maximum or to both.

(4)   In subsection (2) "proscribed" means proscribed for the purposes of any of the following—
  (a)   this Act;
  (b)   the Northern Ireland (Emergency Provisions) Act 1996;
  (c)   the Northern Ireland (Emergency Provisions) Act 1991;
  (d)   the Prevention of Terrorism (Temporary Provisions) Act 1989;
  (e)   the Prevention of Terrorism (Temporary Provisions) Act 1984;
  (f)   the Northern Ireland (Emergency Provisions) Act 1978;
  (g)   the Prevention of Terrorism (Temporary Provisions) Act 1976;
  (h)   the Prevention of Terrorism (Temporary Provisions) Act 1974;
  (i)   the Northern Ireland (Emergency Provisions) Act 1973.

12 Support

(1)   A person commits an offence if—
  (a)   he invites support for a proscribed organisation, and

(b) the support is not, or is not restricted to, the provision of money or other property (within the meaning of section 15).

(2) A person commits an offence if he arranges, manages or assists in arranging or managing a meeting which he knows is—
(a) to support a proscribed organisation,
(b) to further the activities of a proscribed organisation, or
(c) to be addressed by a person who belongs or professes to belong to a proscribed organisation.

(3) A person commits an offence if he addresses a meeting and the purpose of his address is to encourage support for a proscribed organisation or to further its activities.

(4) Where a person is charged with an offence under subsection (2)(c) in respect of a private meeting it is a defence for him to prove that he had no reasonable cause to believe that the address mentioned in subsection (2)(c) would support a proscribed organisation or further its activities.

(5) In subsections (2) to (4)—
(a) "meeting" means a meeting of three or more persons, whether or not the public are admitted, and
(b) a meeting is private if the public are not admitted.

(6) A person guilty of an offence under this section shall be liable—
(a) on conviction on indictment, to imprisonment for a term not exceeding ten years, to a fine or to both, or
(b) on summary conviction, to imprisonment for a term not exceeding six months, to a fine not exceeding the statutory maximum or to both.

13 Uniform

(1) A person in a public place commits an offence if he—
(a) wears an item of clothing, or
(b) wears, carries or displays an article,

in such a way or in such circumstances as to arouse reasonable suspicion that he is a member or supporter of a proscribed organisation.

(2) A constable in Scotland may arrest a person without a warrant if he has reasonable grounds to suspect that the person is guilty of an offence under this section.

(3) A person guilty of an offence under this section shall be liable on summary conviction to—
(a) imprisonment for a term not exceeding six months,
(b) a fine not exceeding level 5 on the standard scale, or
(c) both.

PART III
TERRORIST PROPERTY

Interpretation

14 Terrorist property

(1)   In this Act "terrorist property" means—
    (a)   money or other property which is likely to be used for the purposes of terrorism (including any resources of a proscribed organisation),
    (b)   proceeds of the commission of acts of terrorism, and
    (c)   proceeds of acts carried out for the purposes of terrorism.

(2)   In subsection (1)—
    (a)   a reference to proceeds of an act includes a reference to any property which wholly or partly, and directly or indirectly, represents the proceeds of the act (including payments or other rewards in connection with its commission), and
    (b)   the reference to an organisation's resources includes a reference to any money or other property which is applied or made available, or is to be applied or made available, for use by the organisation.

Offences

15 Fund-raising

(1)   A person commits an offence if he—
    (a)   invites another to provide money or other property, and
    (b)   intends that it should be used, or has reasonable cause to suspect that it may be used, for the purposes of terrorism.

(2)   A person commits an offence if he—
    (a)   receives money or other property, and
    (b)   intends that it should be used, or has reasonable cause to suspect that it may be used, for the purposes of terrorism.

(3)   A person commits an offence if he—
    (a)   provides money or other property, and
    (b)   knows or has reasonable cause to suspect that it will or may be used for the purposes of terrorism.

(4)   In this section a reference to the provision of money or other property is a reference to its being given, lent or otherwise made available, whether or not for consideration.

16 Use and possession

(1)   A person commits an offence if he uses money or other property for the purposes of terrorism.

(2)   A person commits an offence if he—

(a) possesses money or other property, and

(b) intends that it should be used, or has reasonable cause to suspect that it may be used, for the purposes of terrorism.

17 Funding arrangements

A person commits an offence if—

(a) he enters into or becomes concerned in an arrangement as a result of which money or other property is made available or is to be made available to another, and

(b) he knows or has reasonable cause to suspect that it will or may be used for the purposes of terrorism.

18 Money laundering

(1) A person commits an offence if he enters into or becomes concerned in an arrangement which facilitates the retention or control by or on behalf of another person of terrorist property—

(a) by concealment,

(b) by removal from the jurisdiction,

(c) by transfer to nominees, or

(d) in any other way.

(2) It is a defence for a person charged with an offence under subsection (1) to prove that he did not know and had no reasonable cause to suspect that the arrangement related to terrorist property.

19 Disclosure of information: duty

(1) This section applies where a person—

(a) believes or suspects that another person has committed an offence under any of sections 15 to 18, and

(b) bases his belief or suspicion on information which comes to his attention in the course of a trade, profession, business or employment.

[(1A) But this section does not apply if the information came to the person in the course of a business in the regulated sector.]

(2) The person commits an offence if he does not disclose to a constable as soon as is reasonably practicable—

(a) his belief or suspicion, and

(b) the information on which it is based.

(3) It is a defence for a person charged with an offence under subsection (2) to prove that he had a reasonable excuse for not making the disclosure.

(4) Where—

(a) a person is in employment,

(b) his employer has established a procedure for the making of disclosures of the matters specified in subsection (2), and

(c) he is charged with an offence under that subsection,

it is a defence for him to prove that he disclosed the matters specified in that subsection in accordance with the procedure.

(5)   Subsection (2) does not require disclosure by a professional legal adviser of—
  (a)   information which he obtains in privileged circumstances, or
  (b)   a belief or suspicion based on information which he obtains in privileged circumstances.

(6)   For the purpose of subsection (5) information is obtained by an adviser in privileged circumstances if it comes to him, otherwise than with a view to furthering a criminal purpose—
  (a)   from a client or a client's representative, in connection with the provision of legal advice by the adviser to the client,
  (b)   from a person seeking legal advice from the adviser, or from the person's representative, or
  (c)   from any person, for the purpose of actual or contemplated legal proceedings.

(7)   For the purposes of subsection (1)(a) a person shall be treated as having committed an offence under one of sections 15 to 18 if—
  (a)   he has taken an action or been in possession of a thing, and
  (b)   he would have committed an offence under one of those sections if he had been in the United Kingdom at the time when he took the action or was in possession of the thing.

[(7A)   The reference to a business in the regulated sector must be construed in accordance with Schedule 3A.

(7B)   The reference to a constable includes a reference to a person authorised for the purposes of this section by the Director General of the National Criminal Intelligence Service.]

(8)   A person guilty of an offence under this section shall be liable—
  (a)   on conviction on indictment, to imprisonment for a term not exceeding five years, to a fine or to both, or
  (b)   on summary conviction, to imprisonment for a term not exceeding six months, or to a fine not exceeding the statutory maximum or to both.

NOTES

Sub-s (1A): inserted by the Anti-terrorism, Crime and Security Act 2001, s 3, Sch 2, Pt 3, para 5(1), (3).

Date in force: 20 December 2001: see SI 2001/4019, art 2(1)(c).

Sub-ss (7A), (7B): inserted by the Anti-terrorism, Crime and Security Act 2001, s 3, Sch 2, Pt 3, para 5(1), (4).

Date in force: 20 December 2001: see SI 2001/4019, art 2(1)(c).

21 Cooperation with police

(1)   A person does not commit an offence under any of sections 15 to 18 if he is acting with the express consent of a constable.

(2)   Subject to subsections (3) and (4), a person does not commit an offence under any of sections 15 to 18 by involvement in a transaction or arrangement relating to money or other property if he discloses to a constable—
  (a)   his suspicion or belief that the money or other property is terrorist property, and
  (b)   the information on which his suspicion or belief is based.

(3)   Subsection (2) applies only where a person makes a disclosure—
  (a)   after he becomes concerned in the transaction concerned,
  (b)   on his own initiative, and
  (c)   as soon as is reasonably practicable.

(4)   Subsection (2) does not apply to a person if—
  (a)   a constable forbids him to continue his involvement in the transaction or arrangement to which the disclosure relates, and
  (b)   he continues his involvement.

(5)   It is a defence for a person charged with an offence under any of sections 15(2) and (3) and 16 to 18 to prove that—
  (a)   he intended to make a disclosure of the kind mentioned in subsections (2) and (3), and
  (b)   there is reasonable excuse for his failure to do so.

(6)   Where—
  (a)   a person is in employment, and
  (b)   his employer has established a procedure for the making of disclosures of the same kind as may be made to a constable under subsection (2),

this section shall have effect in relation to that person as if any reference to disclosure to a constable included a reference to disclosure in accordance with the procedure.

(7)   A reference in this section to a transaction or arrangement relating to money or other property includes a reference to use or possession.

PART IV
TERRORIST INVESTIGATIONS

Information and evidence

39 Disclosure of information, &c

(1)   Subsection (2) applies where a person knows or has reasonable cause to suspect that a constable is conducting or proposes to conduct a terrorist investigation.

(2)   The person commits an offence if he—
  (a)   discloses to another anything which is likely to prejudice the investigation, or
  (b)   interferes with material which is likely to be relevant to the investigation.

(3)   Subsection (4) applies where a person knows or has reasonable cause to suspect that a disclosure has been or will be made under any of sections 19 to 21 [or 38B].

(4)   The person commits an offence if he—
  (a)   discloses to another anything which is likely to prejudice an investigation resulting from the disclosure under that section, or
  (b)   interferes with material which is likely to be relevant to an investigation resulting from the disclosure under that section.

(5)   It is a defence for a person charged with an offence under subsection (2) or (4) to prove—
  (a)   that he did not know and had no reasonable cause to suspect that the disclosure or interference was likely to affect a terrorist investigation, or
  (b)   that he had a reasonable excuse for the disclosure or interference.

(6)   Subsections (2) and (4) do not apply to a disclosure which is made by a professional legal adviser—
  (a)   to his client or to his client's representative in connection with the provision of legal advice by the adviser to the client and not with a view to furthering a criminal purpose, or
  (b)   to any person for the purpose of actual or contemplated legal proceedings and not with a view to furthering a criminal purpose.

(7)   A person guilty of an offence under this section shall be liable—
  (a)   on conviction on indictment, to imprisonment for a term not exceeding five years, to a fine or to both, or
  (b)   on summary conviction, to imprisonment for a term not exceeding six months, to a fine not exceeding the statutory maximum or to both.

(8)   For the purposes of this section—
  (a)   a reference to conducting a terrorist investigation includes a reference to taking part in the conduct of, or assisting, a terrorist investigation, and
  (b)   a person interferes with material if he falsifies it, conceals it, destroys it or disposes of it, or if he causes or permits another to do any of those things.

NOTES

Sub-s (3): words "or 38B" in square brackets inserted by the Anti-terrorism, Crime and Security Act 2001, s 117(1), (3).
   Date in force: 14 December 2001: see the Anti-terrorism, Crime and Security Act 2001, s 127(2)(h).

PART V
COUNTER-TERRORIST POWERS

Parking

48 Authorisations

(1)   An authorisation under this section authorises any constable in uniform to prohibit or restrict the parking of vehicles on a road specified in the authorisation.

(2)   An authorisation may be given only if the person giving it considers it expedient for the prevention of acts of terrorism.

(3)   An authorisation may be given—
   (a)   where the road specified is outside Northern Ireland and is wholly or partly within a police area other than one mentioned in paragraphs (b) or (c), by a police officer for the area who is of at least the rank of assistant chief constable;
   (b)   where the road specified is wholly or partly in the metropolitan police district, by a police officer for the district who is of at least the rank of commander of the metropolitan police;
   (c)   where the road specified is wholly or partly in the City of London, by a police officer for the City who is of at least the rank of commander in the City of London police force;
   (d)   where the road specified is in Northern Ireland, by a [member of the Police Service of Northern Ireland] who is of at least the rank of assistant chief constable.

(4)   If an authorisation is given orally, the person giving it shall confirm it in writing as soon as is reasonably practicable.

NOTES

Sub-s (3): in para (d) words "member of the Police Service of Northern Ireland" in square brackets substituted by the Police (Northern Ireland) Act 2000, s 78(2)(c).

Date in force: 4 November 2001: see the Police (Northern Ireland) Act 2000 (Commencement No 3 and Transitional Provisions) Order 2001, SR 2001/396, art 2, Schedule.

51 Offences

(1)   A person commits an offence if he parks a vehicle in contravention of a prohibition or restriction imposed by virtue of section 48.

(2)   A person commits an offence if—
   (a)   he is the driver or other person in charge of a vehicle which has been permitted to remain at rest in contravention of any prohibition or restriction imposed by virtue of section 48, and
   (b)   he fails to move the vehicle when ordered to do so by a constable in uniform.

(3)   It is a defence for a person charged with an offence under this section to prove that he had a reasonable excuse for the act or omission in question.

(4)   Possession of a current disabled person's badge shall not itself constitute a reasonable excuse for the purposes of subsection (3).

(5)   A person guilty of an offence under subsection (1) shall be liable on summary conviction to a fine not exceeding level 4 on the standard scale.

(6)   A person guilty of an offence under subsection (2) shall be liable on summary conviction to—
   (a)   imprisonment for a term not exceeding three months,
   (b)   a fine not exceeding level 4 on the standard scale, or
   (c)   both.

52 Interpretation

In sections 48 to 51—

"disabled person's badge" means a badge issued, or having effect as if issued, under any regulations for the time being in force under section 21 of the Chronically Sick and Disabled Persons Act 1970 (in relation to England and Wales and Scotland) or section 14 of the Chronically Sick and Disabled Persons (Northern Ireland) Act 1978 (in relation to Northern Ireland);

"driver" means, in relation to a vehicle which has been left on any road, the person who was driving it when it was left there;

"parking" means leaving a vehicle or permitting it to remain at rest;

"traffic sign" has the meaning given in section 142(1) of the Road Traffic Regulation Act 1984 (in relation to England and Wales and Scotland) and in Article 28 of the Road Traffic Regulation (Northern Ireland) Order 1997 (in relation to Northern Ireland);

"vehicle" has the same meaning as in section 99(5) of the Road Traffic Regulation Act 1984 (in relation to England and Wales and Scotland) and Article 47(4) of the Road Traffic Regulation (Northern Ireland) Order 1997 (in relation to Northern Ireland).

PART VI
MISCELLANEOUS

Terrorist offences

54 Weapons training

(1)   A person commits an offence if he provides instruction or training in the making or use of
   (a)   firearms,
   [(aa) radioactive material or weapons designed or adapted for the discharge of any radioactive material,]
   (b)   explosives, or
   (c)   chemical, biological or nuclear weapons.

(2)   A person commits an offence if he receives instruction or training in the making or use of—
   (a)   firearms,
   [(aa) radioactive material or weapons designed or adapted for the discharge of any radioactive material,]
   (b)   explosives, or
   (c)   chemical, biological or nuclear weapons.

(3)   A person commits an offence if he invites another to receive instruction or training and the receipt—
   (a)   would constitute an offence under subsection (2), or
   (b)   would constitute an offence under subsection (2) but for the fact that it is to take place outside the United Kingdom.

(4)   For the purpose of subsections (1) and (3)—

(a) a reference to the provision of instruction includes a reference to making it available either generally or to one or more specific persons, and

(b) an invitation to receive instruction or training may be either general or addressed to one or more specific persons.

(5) It is a defence for a person charged with an offence under this section in relation to instruction or training to prove that his action or involvement was wholly for a purpose other than assisting, preparing for or participating in terrorism.

(6) A person guilty of an offence under this section shall be liable—

(a) on conviction on indictment, to imprisonment for a term not exceeding ten years, to a fine or to both, or

(b) on summary conviction, to imprisonment for a term not exceeding six months, to a fine not exceeding the statutory maximum or to both.

(7) A court by or before which a person is convicted of an offence under this section may order the forfeiture of anything which the court considers to have been in the person's possession for purposes connected with the offence.

(8) Before making an order under subsection (7) a court must give an opportunity to be heard to any person, other than the convicted person, who claims to be the owner of or otherwise interested in anything which can be forfeited under that subsection.

(9) An order under subsection (7) shall not come into force until there is no further possibility of it being varied, or set aside, on appeal (disregarding any power of a court to grant leave to appeal out of time).

NOTES

Sub-s (1): para (aa) inserted by the Anti-terrorism, Crime and Security Act 2001, s 120(1).
Date in force: 14 December 2001: see the Anti-terrorism, Crime and Security Act 2001, s 127(2)(h).
Sub-s (2): para (aa) inserted by the Anti-terrorism, Crime and Security Act 2001, s 120(1).
Date in force: 14 December 2001: see the Anti-terrorism, Crime and Security Act 2001, s 127(2)(h).

55 Weapons training: interpretation

In section 54—

["biological weapon" means a biological agent or toxin (within the meaning of the Biological Weapons Act 1974) in a form capable of use for hostile purposes or anything to which section 1(1)(b) of that Act applies,]

"chemical weapon" has the meaning given by section 1 of the Chemical Weapons Act 1996, and

["radioactive material" means radioactive material capable of endangering life or causing harm to human health]

. . ..

NOTES

Definition "biological weapon" substituted by the Anti-terrorism, Crime and Security Act 2001, s 120(2)(a).

Date in force: 14 December 2001: see the Anti-terrorism, Crime and Security Act 2001, s 127(2)(h).

Definition "radioactive material" inserted by the Anti-terrorism, Crime and Security Act 2001, s 120(2)(b).

Date in force: 14 December 2001: see the Anti-terrorism, Crime and Security Act 2001, s 127(2)(h).

Definition "nuclear weapon" (omitted) repealed by the Anti-terrorism, Crime and Security Act 2001, ss 120(2)(c), 125, Sch 8, Pt 7.

Date in force: 14 December 2001: see the Anti-terrorism, Crime and Security Act 2001, s 127(2)(h).

56 Directing terrorist organisation

(1)   A person commits an offence if he directs, at any level, the activities of an organisation which is concerned in the commission of acts of terrorism.

(2)   A person guilty of an offence under this section is liable on conviction on indictment to imprisonment for life.

57 Possession for terrorist purposes

(1)   A person commits an offence if he possesses an article in circumstances which give rise to a reasonable suspicion that his possession is for a purpose connected with the commission, preparation or instigation of an act of terrorism.

(2)   It is a defence for a person charged with an offence under this section to prove that his possession of the article was not for a purpose connected with the commission, preparation or instigation of an act of terrorism.

(3)   In proceedings for an offence under this section, if it is proved that an article—
   (a)   was on any premises at the same time as the accused, or
   (b)   was on premises of which the accused was the occupier or which he habitually used otherwise than as a member of the public,

the court may assume that the accused possessed the article, unless he proves that he did not know of its presence on the premises or that he had no control over it.

(4)   A person guilty of an offence under this section shall be liable—
   (a)   on conviction on indictment, to imprisonment for a term not exceeding 10 years, to a fine or to both, or
   (b)   on summary conviction, to imprisonment for a term not exceeding six months, to a fine not exceeding the statutory maximum or to both.

58 Collection of information

(1)   A person commits an offence if—
   (a)   he collects or makes a record of information of a kind likely to be useful to a person committing or preparing an act of terrorism, or
   (b)   he possesses a document or record containing information of that kind.

(2)   In this section "record" includes a photographic or electronic record.

(3)   It is a defence for a person charged with an offence under this section to prove that he had a reasonable excuse for his action or possession.

(4)   A person guilty of an offence under this section shall be liable—
   (a)   on conviction on indictment, to imprisonment for a term not exceeding 10 years, to a fine or to both, or
   (b)   on summary conviction, to imprisonment for a term not exceeding six months, to a fine not exceeding the statutory maximum or to both.

(5)   A court by or before which a person is convicted of an offence under this section may order the forfeiture of any document or record containing information of the kind mentioned in subsection (1)(a).

(6)   Before making an order under subsection (5) a court must give an opportunity to be heard to any person, other than the convicted person, who claims to be the owner of or otherwise interested in anything which can be forfeited under that subsection.

(7)   An order under subsection (5) shall not come into force until there is no further possibility of it being varied, or set aside, on appeal (disregarding any power of a court to grant leave to appeal out of time).

Inciting terrorism overseas

59 England and Wales

(1)   A person commits an offence if—
   (a)   he incites another person to commit an act of terrorism wholly or partly outside the United Kingdom, and
   (b)   the act would, if committed in England and Wales, constitute one of the offences listed in subsection (2).

(2)   Those offences are—
   (a)   murder,
   (b)   an offence under section 18 of the Offences against the Person Act 1861 (wounding with intent),
   (c)   an offence under section 23 or 24 of that Act (poison),
   (d)   an offence under section 28 or 29 of that Act (explosions), and
   (e)   an offence under section 1(2) of the Criminal Damage Act 1971 (endangering life by damaging property).

(3)   A person guilty of an offence under this section shall be liable to any penalty to which he would be liable on conviction of the offence listed in subsection (2) which corresponds to the act which he incites.

(4)   For the purposes of subsection (1) it is immaterial whether or not the person incited is in the United Kingdom at the time of the incitement.

(5)   Nothing in this section imposes criminal liability on any person acting on behalf of, or holding office under, the Crown.

Terrorist bombing and finance offences

62 Terrorist bombing: jurisdiction

(1) If—
  (a) a person does anything outside the United Kingdom as an act of terrorism or for the purposes of terrorism, and
  (b) his action would have constituted the commission of one of the offences listed in subsection (2) if it had been done in the United Kingdom,

he shall be guilty of the offence.

(2) The offences referred to in subsection (1)(b) are—
  (a) an offence under section 2, 3 or 5 of the Explosive Substances Act 1883 (causing explosions, &c),
  (b) an offence under section 1 of the Biological Weapons Act 1974 (biological weapons), and
  (c) an offence under section 2 of the Chemical Weapons Act 1996 (chemical weapons).

PART VIII
GENERAL

118 Defences

(1) Subsection (2) applies where in accordance with a provision mentioned in subsection (5) it is a defence for a person charged with an offence to prove a particular matter.

(2) If the person adduces evidence which is sufficient to raise an issue with respect to the matter the court or jury shall assume that the defence is satisfied unless the prosecution proves beyond reasonable doubt that it is not.

(3) Subsection (4) applies where in accordance with a provision mentioned in subsection (5) a court—
  (a) may make an assumption in relation to a person charged with an offence unless a particular matter is proved, or
  (b) may accept a fact as sufficient evidence unless a particular matter is proved.

(4) If evidence is adduced which is sufficient to raise an issue with respect to the matter mentioned in subsection (3)(a) or (b) the court shall treat it as proved unless the prosecution disproves it beyond reasonable doubt.

(5) The provisions in respect of which subsections (2) and (4) apply are—
  (a) sections 12(4), 39(5)(a), 54, 57, 58, 77 and 103 of this Act, and
  (b) sections 13, 32 and 33 of the Northern Ireland (Emergency Provisions) Act 1996 (possession and information offences) as they have effect by virtue of Schedule 1 to this Act.

121 Interpretation

In this Act—

"act" and "action" include omission,

"article" includes substance and any other thing,

["British Transport Police Force" means the constables appointed under section 53 of the British Transport Commission Act 1949 (c xxix),]

"customs officer" means an officer commissioned by the Commissioners of Customs and Excise under section 6(3) of the Customs and Excise Management Act 1979,

"dwelling" means a building or part of a building used as a dwelling, and a vehicle which is habitually stationary and which is used as a dwelling,

"explosive" means—

    (a) an article or substance manufactured for the purpose of producing a practical effect by explosion,

    (b) materials for making an article or substance within paragraph (a),

    (c) anything used or intended to be used for causing or assisting in causing an explosion, and

    (d) a part of anything within paragraph (a) or (c),

"firearm" includes an air gun or air pistol,

"immigration officer" means a person appointed as an immigration officer under paragraph 1 of Schedule 2 to the Immigration Act 1971,

"the Islands" means the Channel Islands and the Isle of Man,

"organisation" includes any association or combination of persons,

["policed premises", in relation to England and Wales, has the meaning given by section 53(3) of the British Transport Commission Act 1949 and, in relation to Scotland, means those places where members of the British Transport Police Force have the powers, protection and privileges of a constable under section 53(4)(a) of that Act (as it relates to Scotland),]

"premises" includes any place and in particular includes—

    (a) a vehicle,

    (b) an offshore installation within the meaning given in section 44 of the Petroleum Act 1998, and

    (c) a tent or moveable structure,

"property" includes property wherever situated and whether real or personal, heritable or moveable, and things in action and other intangible or incorporeal property,

"public place" means a place to which members of the public have or are permitted to have access, whether or not for payment,

"road" has the same meaning as in the Road Traffic Act 1988 (in relation to England and Wales), the Roads (Scotland) Act 1984 (in relation to Scotland) and the Road Traffic Regulation (Northern Ireland) Order 1997 (in relation to Northern Ireland), and includes part of a road, and

"vehicle", except in sections 48 to 52 and Schedule 7, includes an aircraft, hovercraft, train or vessel.

NOTES

Definition "British Transport Police Force" inserted by the Anti-terrorism, Crime and Security Act 2001, s 101, Sch 7, paras 29, 32(a).

Date in force: 14 December 2001: see the Anti-terrorism, Crime and Security Act 2001, s 127(2)(f).

Definition "policed premises" inserted by the Anti-terrorism, Crime and Security Act 2001, s 101, Sch 7, paras 29, 32(b).

Date in force: 14 December 2001: see the Anti-terrorism, Crime and Security Act 2001, s 127(2)(f).

Postal Services Act 2000

2000 CHAPTER 26

An Act to establish the Postal Services Commission and the Consumer Council for Postal Services; to provide for the licensing of certain postal services and for a universal postal service; to provide for the vesting of the property, rights and liabilities of the Post Office in a company nominated by the Secretary of State and for the subsequent dissolution of the Post Office; to make further provision in relation to postal services; and for connected purposes.

[28th July 2000]

PART V
OFFENCES IN RELATION TO POSTAL SERVICES

Offences of interfering with the mail

83 Interfering with the mail: postal operators

(1)   A person who is engaged in the business of a postal operator commits an offence if, contrary to his duty and without reasonable excuse, he—

   (a)   intentionally delays or opens a postal packet in the course of its transmission by post, or

   (b)   intentionally opens a mail-bag.

(2)   Subsection (1) does not apply to the delaying or opening of a postal packet or the opening of a mail-bag under the authority of—

   (a)   this Act or any other enactment (including, in particular, in pursuance of a warrant issued under any other enactment), or

   (b)   any directly applicable Community provision.

(3)   Subsection (1) does not apply to the delaying or opening of a postal packet in accordance with any terms and conditions applicable to its transmission by post.

(4)   Subsection (1) does not apply to the delaying of a postal packet as a result of industrial action in contemplation or furtherance of a trade dispute.

(5)   In subsection (4) "trade dispute" has the meaning given by section 244 of the Trade Union and Labour Relations (Consolidation) Act 1992 or Article 127 of the Trade Union and Labour Relations (Northern Ireland) Order 1995; and the reference

to industrial action shall be construed in accordance with that Act or (as the case may be) that Order.

(6)   A person who commits an offence under subsection (1) shall be liable—

(a)   on summary conviction, to a fine not exceeding the statutory maximum or to imprisonment for a term not exceeding six months or to both,

(b)   on conviction on indictment, to a fine or to imprisonment for a term not exceeding two years or to both.

84 Interfering with the mail: general

(1)   A person commits an offence if, without reasonable excuse, he—

(a)   intentionally delays or opens a postal packet in the course of its transmission by post, or

(b)   intentionally opens a mail-bag.

(2)   Subsections (2) to (5) of section 83 apply to subsection (1) above as they apply to subsection (1) of that section.

(3)   A person commits an offence if, intending to act to a person's detriment and without reasonable excuse, he opens a postal packet which he knows or reasonably suspects has been incorrectly delivered to him.

(4)   Subsections (2) and (3) of section 83 (so far as they relate to the opening of postal packets) apply to subsection (3) above as they apply to subsection (1) of that section.

(5)   A person who commits an offence under subsection (1) or (3) shall be liable on summary conviction to a fine not exceeding level 5 on the standard scale or to imprisonment for a term not exceeding six months or to both.

Prohibition on sending certain articles by post

85 Prohibition on sending certain articles by post

(1)   A person commits an offence if he sends by post a postal packet which encloses any creature, article or thing of any kind which is likely to injure other postal packets in course of their transmission by post or any person engaged in the business of a postal operator.

(2)   Subsection (1) does not apply to postal packets which enclose anything permitted (whether generally or specifically) by the postal operator concerned.

(3)   A person commits an offence if he sends by post a postal packet which encloses—

(a)   any indecent or obscene print, painting, photograph, lithograph, engraving, cinematograph film or other record of a picture or pictures, book, card or written communication, or

(b)   any other indecent or obscene article (whether or not of a similar kind to those mentioned in paragraph (a)).

(4)   A person commits an offence if he sends by post a postal packet which has on the packet, or on the cover of the packet, any words, marks or designs which are of an indecent or obscene character.

(5)   A person who commits an offence under this section shall be liable—
   (a)   on summary conviction, to a fine not exceeding the statutory maximum,
   (b)   on conviction on indictment, to a fine or to imprisonment for a term not exceeding twelve months or to both.

Additional protection for universal postal service

88 Obstruction of business of universal service providers

(1)   A person commits an offence if, without reasonable excuse, he—
   (a)   obstructs a person engaged in the business of a universal service provider in the execution of his duty in connection with the provision of a universal postal service, or
   (b)   obstructs, while in any universal postal service post office or related premises, the course of business of a universal service provider.

(2)   A person who commits an offence under subsection (1) shall be liable on summary conviction to a fine not exceeding level 2 on the standard scale.

(3)   A person commits an offence if, without reasonable excuse, he fails to leave a universal postal service post office or related premises when required to do so by a person who—
   (a)   is engaged in the business of a universal service provider, and
   (b)   reasonably suspects him of committing an offence under subsection (1).

(4)   A person who commits an offence under subsection (3)—
   (a)   shall be liable on summary conviction to a fine not exceeding level 2 on the standard scale, and
   (b)   may be removed by any person engaged in the business of a universal service provider.

(5)   Any constable shall on demand remove, or assist in removing, any such person.

(6)   In this section "related premises" means any premises belonging to a universal postal service post office or used together with any such post office.

Sexual Offences (Amendment) Act 2000

2000 CHAPTER 44

An Act to reduce the age at which, and to make provision with respect to the circumstances in which, certain sexual acts are lawful; to make it an offence for a person aged 18 or over to engage in sexual activity with or directed towards a person under that age if he is in a position of trust in relation to that person; and for connected purposes.

[30th November 2000]

3 Abuse of position of trust

(1)   Subject to subsections (2) and (3) below, it shall be an offence for a person aged 18 or over—
   (a)   to have sexual intercourse (whether vaginal or anal) with a person under that age; or
   (b)   to engage in any other sexual activity with or directed towards such a person,

if (in either case) he is in a position of trust in relation to that person.

(2)   Where a person ("A") is charged with an offence under this section of having sexual intercourse with, or engaging in any other sexual activity with or directed towards, another person ("B"), it shall be a defence for A to prove that, at the time of the intercourse or activity—
   (a)   he did not know, and could not reasonably have been expected to know, that B was under 18;
   (b)   he did not know, and could not reasonably have been expected to know, that B was a person in relation to whom he was in a position of trust; or
   (c)   he was lawfully married to B.

(3)   It shall not be an offence under this section for a person ("A") to have sexual intercourse with, or engage in any other sexual activity with or directed towards, another person ("B") if immediately before the commencement of this Act—
   (a)   A was in a position of trust in relation to B; and
   (b)   a sexual relationship existed between them.

(4)   A person guilty of an offence under this section shall be liable—
   (a)   on summary conviction, to imprisonment for a term not exceeding six months, or to a fine not exceeding the statutory maximum, or to both;
   (b)   on conviction on indictment, to imprisonment for a term not exceeding five years, or to a fine, or to both.

(5)   In this section, "sexual activity"—
   (a)   does not include any activity which a reasonable person would regard as sexual only with knowledge of the intentions, motives or feelings of the parties; but

(b)   subject to that, means any activity which such a person would regard as sexual in all the circumstances.

4 Meaning of "position of trust"

(1)   For the purposes of section 3 above, a person aged 18 or over ("A") is in a position of trust in relation to a person under that age ("B") if any of the four conditions set out below, or any condition specified in an order made by the Secretary of State by statutory instrument, is fulfilled.

(2)   The first condition is that A looks after persons under 18 who are detained in an institution by virtue of an order of a court or under an enactment, and B is so detained in that institution.

(3)   The second condition is that A looks after persons under 18 who are resident in a home or other place in which—
  (a)   accommodation and maintenance are provided by an authority under section 23(2) of the Children Act 1989 or Article 27(2) of the Children (Northern Ireland) Order 1995;
  (b)   accommodation is provided by a voluntary organisation under section 59(1) of that Act or Article 75(1) of that Order; or
  (c)   accommodation is provided by an authority under section 26(1) of the Children (Scotland) Act 1995,

and B is resident, and is so provided with accommodation and maintenance or accommodation, in that place.

(4)   The third condition is that A looks after persons under 18 who are accommodated and cared for in an institution which is—
  (a)   a hospital;
  (b)   a *residential care home, nursing home, mental nursing home or* private hospital;
  [(bb) provided by a care home service;]
  (c)   a community home, voluntary home, children's home or residential establishment; or
  (d)   a home provided under section 82(5) of the Children Act 1989,

and B is accommodated and cared for in that institution.

(5)   The fourth condition is that A looks after persons under 18 who are receiving full-time education at an educational institution, and B is receiving such education at that institution.

(6)   No order shall be made under subsection (1) above unless a draft of the order has been laid before and approved by a resolution of each House of Parliament.

(7)   A person looks after persons under 18 for the purposes of this section if he is regularly involved in caring for, training, supervising or being in sole charge of such persons.

(8)   For the purposes of this section a person receives full-time education at an educational institution if—

(a) he is registered or otherwise enrolled as a full-time pupil or student at the institution; or

(b) he receives education at the institution under arrangements with another educational institution at which he is so registered or otherwise enrolled.

(9) In this section, except where the context otherwise requires—
"authority" means—

(a) in relation to Great Britain, a local authority; and

(b) in relation to Northern Ireland, an authority within the meaning given by Article 2(2) of the Children (Northern Ireland) Order 1995;

["care home service" has the meaning given by section 2(3) of the Regulation of Care (Scotland) Act 2001 (asp 8);]

"children's home" has—

(a) in relation to England and Wales, the meaning which would be given by subsection (3) of section 63 of the Children Act 1989 if the reference in paragraph (a) of that subsection to more than three children were a reference to one or more children; and

(b) in relation to Northern Ireland, the meaning which would be given by Article 90(1) of the Children (Northern Ireland) Order 1995 if, in Article 91(2) of that Order, paragraphs (f) and (g) and the words after paragraph (h) were omitted;

"community home" has the meaning given by section 53(1) of the Children Act 1989;

"hospital" has—

(a) in relation to England and Wales, the meaning given by section 128(1) of the National Health Service Act 1977;

(b) in relation to Scotland, the meaning given by section 108(1) of the National Health Service (Scotland) Act 1978; and

(c) in relation to Northern Ireland, the meaning given by Article 2(2) of the Health and Personal Social Services (Northern Ireland) Order 1972;

"mental nursing home" has, in relation to England and Wales, the meaning given by section 22(1) of the Registered Homes Act 1984;

"nursing home"—

    (a) in relation to England and Wales, has the meaning given by section 21(1) of the Registered Homes Act 1984;

    (b) . . .

    (c) in relation to Northern Ireland, has the meaning given by Article 16(1) of the Registered Homes (Northern Ireland) Order 1992;

"private hospital" has—

    (a) in relation to Scotland, the meaning given by section 12(2) of the Mental Health (Scotland) Act 1984; and

    (b) in relation to Northern Ireland, the meaning given by Article 90(2) of the Mental Health (Northern Ireland) Order 1986;

"residential care home"—

    (a) in relation to England and Wales, has the meaning given by section 1(2) of the Registered Homes Act 1984;

    (b) . . .

    (c) in relation to Northern Ireland, has the meaning given by Article 3(1) of the Registered Homes (Northern Ireland) Order 1992;

"residential establishment" has the meaning given by section 93(1) of the Children (Scotland) Act 1995 as the meaning of that expression in relation to a place in Scotland;

"voluntary home" has—

    (a) in relation to England and Wales, the meaning given by section 60(3) of the Children Act 1989; and

    (b) in relation to Northern Ireland, the meaning given by Article 74(1) of the Children (Northern Ireland) Order 1995.

NOTES

Sub-s (4): in para (b) words "residential care home, nursing home, mental nursing home or" in italics repealed, in relation to Scotland, by the Regulation of Care (Scotland) Act 2001, s 79, Sch 3, para 25(1), (2)(a).

Date in force: 1 April 2002: see the Regulation of Care (Scotland) Act 2001, s 81(2) and SSI 2002/162, arts 1(2), 2(f), (h); for transitional provisions see SSI 2002/162, arts 6, 7.

Sub-s (4): para (bb) inserted, in relation to Scotland, by the Regulation of Care (Scotland) Act 2001, s 79, Sch 3, para 25(1), (2)(b).

Date in force: 1 April 2002: see the Regulation of Care (Scotland) Act 2001, s 81(2) and SSI 2002/162, arts 1(2), 2(f), (h); for transitional provisions see SSI 2002/162, arts 6, 7.

Sub-s (9): definition "care home service" inserted, in relation to Scotland, by the Regulation of Care (Scotland) Act 2001, s 79, Sch 3, para 25(1), (3)(a).

Date in force: 1 April 2002: see the Regulation of Care (Scotland) Act 2001, s 81(2) and SSI 2002/162, arts 1(2), 2(f), (h); for transitional provisions see SSI 2002/162, arts 6, 7.

Sub-s (9): in definition "nursing home" para (b) repealed, in relation to Scotland, by the Regulation of Care (Scotland) Act 2001, s 79, Sch 3, para 25(1), (3)(b).

Date in force: 1 April 2002: see the Regulation of Care (Scotland) Act 2001, s 81(2) and SSI 2002/162, arts 1(2), 2(f), (h); for transitional provisions see SSI 2002/162, arts 6, 7.

Sub-s (9): in definition "residential care home" para (b) repealed, in relation to Scotland, by the Regulation of Care (Scotland) Act 2001, s 79, Sch 3, para 25(1), (3)(c).

Date in force: 1 April 2002: see the Regulation of Care (Scotland) Act 2001, s 81(2) and SSI 2002/162, arts 1(2), 2(f), (h); for transitional provisions see SSI 2002/162, arts 6, 7.

Criminal Justice and Police Act 2001

2001 CHAPTER 16

An Act to make provision for combatting crime and disorder; to make provision about the disclosure of information relating to criminal matters and about powers of search and seizure; to amend the Police and Criminal Evidence Act 1984, the Police and Criminal Evidence (Northern Ireland) Order 1989 and the Terrorism Act 2000; to make provision about the police, the National Criminal Intelligence Service and the National Crime Squad; to make provision about the powers of the courts in relation to criminal matters; and for connected purposes

[11th May 2001]

Chapter 2
Provisions for Combatting Alcohol-Related Disorder

Alcohol consumption in designated public places

12 Alcohol consumption in designated public places

(1)   Subsection (2) applies if a constable reasonably believes that a person is, or has been, consuming intoxicating liquor in a designated public place or intends to consume intoxicating liquor in such a place.

(2)   The constable may require the person concerned—
   (a)   not to consume in that place anything which is, or which the constable reasonably believes to be, intoxicating liquor;
   (b)   to surrender anything in his possession which is, or which the constable reasonably believes to be, intoxicating liquor or a container for such liquor (other than a sealed container).

(3)   A constable may dispose of anything surrendered to him under subsection (2) in such manner as he considers appropriate.

(4)   A person who fails without reasonable excuse to comply with a requirement imposed on him under subsection (2) commits an offence and is liable on summary conviction to a fine not exceeding level 2 on the standard scale.

(5)   A constable who imposes a requirement on a person under subsection (2) shall inform the person concerned that failing without reasonable excuse to comply with the requirement is an offence.

(6)   In section 24(2) of the 1984 Act (offences to which powers of arrest without warrant apply), after paragraph (q) there shall be inserted—
   "(qa) an offence under section 12(4) of the Criminal Justice and Police Act 2001."